Some of Us Just Fall

Also by Polly Atkin

NON-FICTION
Recovering Dorothy

POETRY
Basic Nest Architecture
Much With Body

SOME OF US JUST FALL

On Nature and Not Getting Better

Polly Atkin

sceptre

First published in Great Britain in 2023 by Sceptre
An imprint of Hodder & Stoughton
An Hachette UK company

3

A CIP catalogue record for this title is available from the British Library

Hardback ISBN 9781399717984
eBook ISBN 9781399717991

Typeset in Sabon by Manipal Technologies Limited

Printed and bound in Great Britain by Clays Ltd, Elcograf S.p.A.

Hodder & Stoughton policy is to use papers that are natural, renewable
and recyclable products and made from wood grown in sustainable forests.
The logging and manufacturing processes are expected to conform
to the environmental regulations of the country of origin.

Hodder & Stoughton Ltd
Carmelite House
50 Victoria Embankment
London EC4Y 0DZ

www.sceptrebooks.co.uk

For all who fall

The kingdom of the sick is not a democracy.
Sinéad Gleeson

To take up residence in my body again, I write.
Jacqueline Alnes

Contents

Prelude   1
Fracture   7
Dislocation   40
Diagnosis   83
Genetic   125
Chronic   165
Maintenance   202
Pacing   244

Acknowledgements   287
Notes   291

Disclaimer

This book reflects the personal medical experiences and opinions of the author about her own medical treatment and should not be read in any way as medical advice or endorsement of any treatment or procedure.

I stand thigh-deep in the lake, eyes closed, arms extended a little from my sides, my fingertips just touching the still surface of the water. I am trying to capture the sun in my body. I think if I can draw enough of it into me now, I can last through the winter. I am trying to charge myself up, to store light in my bones.

The lake is the last mouthful in the bottom of the bowl of the Vale of Grasmere. A blue eye – the wooded island a green iris at its centre. The fells form a kind of circle around it, like a super-sized henge, like a cupped palm. William Wordsworth described Grasmere as a 'huge concave', naming it a bower, a shelter, a nook, a recess, a temple, a harbour, a safe retreat, a hallowed spot.[1] He wrote of feeling the guardianship of the cloud-capped hills, asked them to embrace him, to close him in.[2]

Mid-October, and the first full day of sun this month. It has been an unusually mild month: unusually, aggressively wet, even for here. The Lake District is famous for its rain, for its unpredictable weather. Within its saturated bounds, the wettest inhabited valley in England lies only ten miles over the fells from my home in Grasmere. This summer, whilst most of England desiccated under drought conditions, we dissolved in rain. Daily the fells have been erased and reconstructed out of mist, as storms move over and through the vale. The persistent rain here feels as ominous as the drought elsewhere. This is weather pushed to the extremes of itself.

Today though, the sun is dazzling – ludicrous in its unforecast intensity – the sky exquisitely blue.

I am trying to make the best of it, to take comfort where I find it. I am trying to not think too much of the future, of the coming winter, of everything beyond.

Once my legs are numb, once I have sucked as much sun into my face and chest as I think I can carry, I launch softly into the water. I don't want to disturb the brilliant mirror of its surface more than I need to. I breathe out as I push my arms forward like an arrow pointing towards the light. I breathe in as I draw my arms back to my sides. It is a kind of meditation, a spell against the shock of the cold. I swim fast, count strokes until my body has settled into the movement, the chill medium.

I swim up the lake, parallel to the tree-lined shore, to keep the light as long as possible. At 4 p.m. the sun is already hanging low over Deerbolts Wood to the west, almost touching the tops of the trees. The wood is in shadow, casting the coming dark over the far side of the water, portentous.

By midwinter it will slide behind the screen of the fells before 11 a.m., peeking out briefly at noon as though the whole vale is a cosmic clock.

I count sixty strokes before my muscles begin to relax, my movements lengthen, and I can rest for a little while.

I spread my arms out on the surface and rotate my legs, spinning my body round like a whirligig. The village is smudged into fields and woods, the long stony beach at the south, the thin line of the weir. The trees blur into streaks of amber and rust. I love to see Grasmere like this, from in the water, from what Roger Deakin called the frog's-eye view. It is a different kind of knowing. I watch cars move up and down the wide U of Dunmail Raise, the route north out of the village, named for an ancient warrior king said to be buried beneath the pass. A buzzard circles over Helm Crag. In the bright low light all the fells are cut out in sharp relief.

Facing the raise I wiggle my feet under the shining surface, enjoying the patterns the light and water make on my skin. This may be the last swim of my year with bare legs, bare feet. I have to savour it whilst I can. Soon I will have to slither into a second skin of neoprene before I can swim comfortably, and swimming comfortably is my priority.

I am not one of those outdoor swimmers who relishes the cold. Quite the opposite. The cold hurts. I get no thrill or relief from it. If I get too cold, I can't warm up again. In the cold my body seizes up, muscle system by muscle system. It doesn't take much of a drop in temperature for me to lose all remaining feeling in my hands, my feet, my nose. I do not swim for the cold, but despite it. I dread the cold and the coming of the cold. All winter, I long for summer. I swim in the lake all year because, when forced to choose, I prefer to be in water and cold than to be on land and warm.

If I could, I would live in the water. To be a body in water, not a body on land. A body that can't fall over. Accepting the cold is a part of my negotiation with the lake. I grit my teeth and breathe into it, and the lake keeps its side of the bargain, releases me from the weight of my own body for as long as I can stay in it. It bears me, if I can bear it.

The lake is in my favourite mood today – the surface still as a scrying glass, reflecting the fells, the trees, the sky – the sun gleaming on and through it. I swim breaststroke, mostly, and when I push my arms out, palms together, through the water, I feel I am swimming through the sky. Swimming through the fells. I am splitting forests apart with my arms. I am opening mountains and folding the sky into them. As I turn my palms and bring my arms back to my sides I am opening mountains and folding them into my body. It is the closest to flying I can get.

I float, luxuriating in the touch of the sun even through the water. If I could only keep hold of this feeling.

I am a speck of dust in the blue eye of the vale. From here, the hill I live at the foot of looks as green as summer. But the sun is dipping behind the fells to the west, and shadow has crept from their feet to engulf the whole southern end of the lake.

I am so thankful for the sun on my face, for the water holding me, for everything that means I can be here. For the ways I have been able to reconstruct my life to prioritise care for my body – a swim on a fine day, a rest on a bad one – and everyone and everything that has helped me to do that. All the people from whom I have learnt how to prioritise that care, and the people who taught me what care could look like. The patience and support of my partner, who reads quietly under a tree on the shore as I turn about and about in the water like a happy seal. That he could be here today, waiting to carry my kit, heavy with lake, home, to save me pain in my neck and shoulders. The conspiracy of circumstances that brought me to this village in the first place, sixteen years ago. The conspiracy of circumstances that meant we moved back together, and stayed. The luck of timing that meant there was a cottage to rent near to the lake when we most needed it. The painkillers that make the ten-minute walk from the cottage to the small wooded beach I swim from endurable.

There is a scattered flotilla of leaves on the water, their reflections making doubles of themselves. In the bright sun their rich colours catch and flare. The insignia of autumn. I swim towards a great brown oak leaf, curled into a shape that reminds me of an ancient ship – a tall bow curving into its body – like a trireme. It mirrors its hulk back at itself so perfectly in the still blue – the polished red timbers of a high hull. The veins of the leaf look like the sections of a sail. It brings a D. H. Lawrence poem into my mind, lines I thought I had forgotten, that I pored over as a student twenty years ago. *Now it is autumn and the falling fruit / and the long journey towards oblivion.*[3] It is how I always feel at this time of year, that I can smell death on the air. I shudder to think *the grim frost is at hand.* Like the apples that fall in the poem and *bruise themselves an exit from themselves,* my body is always already *fallen, bruised, badly bruised.* In summer I can forget it for a little while, forget the fragility of my body. Every summer still I fool myself like a teenager – I am getting stronger in the sun, this winter will be easier. I swim most days, sometimes more than once, and sometimes I even have energy left to do other things. I walk home from the lake in the long gloaming, and the warmth melts the distance. I barely limp. I carry myself more lightly. It feels possible for a few weeks that I could be making energy as my limbs flash through the sparkling water, not sloughing it off. Autumn brings any lingering illusion crashing down like fruit from the trees.

Treading water before the tiny ship of the oak leaf I ask it, the lake, the turning trees and the small birds, the one cloud in the sky, the black-headed gull that keeps circling me, my self – *have you built your ship of death, O have you?* I turn onto my back, skull away, mutter, O *build your ship of death, for you will need it.*

The heron rises from trees on the west shore and swoops down the length of the wood. In the sunlit tops of the trees along the near shore a throng of long-tailed tits flits from branch to branch, rustling the gold-green leaves, their high-pitched trilling carrying across the water.

A grey wagtail flies over my head as I glide into land and perches on a half-submerged rock by the beach, strutting and bobbing. Once a grey wagtail watched over my friend E and me as we swam in a waterfall in a tree-lined gorge. No soul about but the wagtail, pacing the perimeter of the deep red pool, and us, within it. Above us the river travelled under a bright blue sky before it tumbled down into the shade, carrying the sun within it. It felt as though when we'd stepped off the path we'd slipped out of our world and into hers, that she'd let us in. We named her the spirit of the swim, guardian of the foss. Small, ever-moving goddess of radiant water. Every time I see a grey wagtail I think of that afternoon, of how suddenly seams of magic can unfurl from a quite ordinary stand of trees, a well-trodden path. Their yellow bellies under thundercloud wings sing to me of light in winter, their

5

presence of protection and companionship. Every wag of their tail says *joy*. Joy is still possible.

In Lawrence's poem the body has to go down into darkness, *completely under*, to come back out again. You have to go into oblivion, and through it, so the whole thing can start again.

A tawny owl calls somewhere in the wood, as though to confirm that night is coming. I swim towards it, into the growing shadow.

When I step out of the water, steadying myself as I learn to move upright again, it is into a kind of mountain twilight. The sun gone from the beach and the trees, a few final rays split over the lake. Mist rises off the surface like breath on a cold day. In the shallows, fat brown acorns and red and green leaves cover the grey stones. The leaves that still cling to the trees glow fluorescent in the dusk. I shiver as I change.

On the way home we will turn off the main road and climb up through the woods to chase the last slivers of sun, but we will be losing a race with the earth's rotation. We will walk the last quarter-mile with bats swooping over us down the gully of the old road, colour draining from the sky. The owls will follow us to our door, calling to each other, *I am here, are you here too?* All night it will seem they are sitting on our window ledge, inviting us into the dark.

Fracture

Long before I knew I was sick, I knew I was breakable. My first break predates my first reliable memory by the amount of time it takes a toddler's bones to knit back together, to form a callous around a fracture, to heal.

There is a story we tell in our family, one of many we tell and have retold so many times that it has become what my mum, if someone else told it, would call a cheap laugh. It goes like this:

> When I was eighteen months old, my brother ran me over.

Or:

> When I was a toddler my brother ran me over and broke my leg.

Or:

> My brother broke my leg when I was a toddler.

When I tell it, it is met by gasps. By disbelief or horror. Awkward laughter.

In my medical records it says *closed fracture of tibia and fibula, distal*. The long bones of the leg. This is another way to tell the story.

*

I spent the weeks following the break with a full-length plaster cast on my leg. I learnt to move myself, awkwardly but effectively; I kept running. When I ran the bottom of the cast ragged for the nth time, and the hospital got tired of replastering it, my dad made me a plaster-protecting shoe from an old Velcro trainer.

There are many photos of me at this time, comic, smiling, unbothered by the new physical status of my cumbersome, solid leg. Unremarkable family pictures of two boys with bowl cuts and a curly-haired toddler. Only, the toddler has one leg in plaster.

I wear the same in-between expression in each photograph – half-smile, half-glazed – as though I have just been interrupted in the course of some intense thought or activity, and have looked up, only half-present, as my name was called.

In one, I am standing in front of a fitted wardrobe and drawers, wearing a pale blue babygro with clouds or sheep appliquéd onto the chest. The left leg of the babygro is missing. My thigh pokes out of the babygro and down into the plaster, both of which look oddly architectural, hovering aloof from my skin for that inch or two. The foot of the plaster is fuzzy, unravelling. I am facing the camera and half-smiling, one arm raised, with a look of movement interrupted. To my left and slightly in front of me stands my brother, the accused, his body half-turned towards me, looking over his left shoulder to face directly into the camera. He is dressed all in cricket whites – white shorts, white shirt and jumper, and white knee-high socks. He is standing closer to the camera than me, turned towards me, his arms reaching towards me, gesturing in display. There is something archetypal in our relative positions, like a scene in a Blake painting. In this version, he is the angel. The carpet is a thick pink-brown sludge.

Another shows me sitting in the red chubby car that was passed down from one sibling to another. Good leg tucked in, pedalling, bad leg stretched out, resting on the side of the car, on a small red cushion, to save the plaster. I loved that cushion. It was small and round and made of soft red velvet. All through my childhood it was a favourite thing. When I mention it to my mum she tells me that her mum made it for me to help with the plaster. Something soft and lovely and especially mine that came out of the trouble. Something that brought me joy for many years.

I remember almost nothing of this time. I don't know how it felt to be in my body. To be that toddler in the photographs with her knee fixed ridged in a strange, half-bent position, for weeks and weeks and weeks. Such a large proportion of my life that far. I know nothing of what she felt, what she wanted. It is not my own story I remember, but other people's.

*

When my leg healed and the plaster was removed, I was no worse off than anyone should be. I grew up with this story as fact, but not as memory. I remember nothing of it, and nothing before it.

The story worked on my brother, too. He had a lifetime of being told he ran over me. Being introduced to other people as *my brother who ran over me*.

The story was a secondary accident which did its own violence. The stories we tell about each other, and how we tell them, form us. Change what we can be.

My family have big hearts, but they also have quick tongues. They enjoy their own cleverness and humour. They are what they would call *pass-remarkable*, though they don't often apply this to themselves. They like to tell a story, and they like a reaction.

But no story is neutral.

Recently, I have started using the story of my first fracture as an example in writing workshops. I tell it as I have told it a million times, *when I was eighteen months old, my brother ran me over and broke my leg*. Then I ask, 'What do you imagine when I tell you that?' The workshop participants might mention a car. They will mention intention, agency. The running over of my small body as a positive action.

Then I might tell them some details that change the story, their understanding of it. My brother was not quite seven. He didn't 'run me down' like it sounds. I was toddling across the garden and he was cycling across the garden, and we collided, that was all. What none of us knew, back then, was that my bones are less dense than most people's. So, when we collided, my leg broke.

I might tell them that we told this story, in my family, in this way, so many times that I didn't realise until I was in my twenties the position it placed my brother in. How it was not a story but an accusation. How it was not the event itself but the telling of it in this way that conferred guilt on him.

I use this story now to show how we dramatise for effect, how we adjust a story for maximum impact, subconsciously, every time we repeat it, not realising with each tiny change – in word choice, in syntax, each time we leave out another detail that would place the event in context – that we alter the story's fundamental meaning. The key detail missing from the story – the fragility of my bones – was something none of us knew for decades. We did not know at the time of the accident, we did not know in the years the story settled into its solid state, became history.

*

I knew I was breakable before I knew how to spell my own name.

I may remember nothing of being that toddler with the broken leg, but she lives inside me all the same. I carry her

10

with me everywhere I go. My sense of self is defined by falling, by breaking.

The world is dangerous and full of obstacles that will launch themselves at you from nowhere. The body is dangerous and full of tricks. It will throw itself down without warning. Neither the body nor the world are to be trusted. I have known this from as far back as my memories will take me.

I went through a long phase, from the age of nine or ten through my teens, of not tripping but collapsing forward onto my knees. Almost as though pushed. As though someone cut my wires, and I just dropped. Forward, with force. Smacking onto my knees. Thinking about the pain even now makes me feel a little sick. In those pre-teen years, there were permanent stains on my knee pads from antiseptic. Soon there were permanent scars, so overlaid I thought for a long time that everyone's knees had a kind of stucco gravel pattern embossed on them.

Falling was just what we did in our family. We would joke that certain of us could trip over nothing. It's not our fault: the ground does it to us. That you mustn't leave a bag on the floor, because we'd fall over it. That some of us have injured ourselves by trapping one foot in an empty plastic bag and falling into it. That some of us *just fall*. Once, years back, in a London life that seems like someone else's, I was walking down the street with friends. We were walking fast, together, to the Princess Louise to meet more friends, to go dancing. It was cold, and I had shorts, sparkly tights, and little silver shoes on. J was telling a story about another, absent friend, about her great capacity to fall: 'You know M, she falls down all the time, she just falls down!' J kept walking, and I was no longer by her side. I had fallen down a drain. The fall is all about the timing.

It is this capacity to fall that made all my childhood accidents seem inevitable rather than pathological. We did not know then we were all pathological.

I have carried that toddler with a broken leg around for over forty years now, but I am still only beginning to understand a little more about her, about us, how we came to be us. I am trying to carry her more lightly, to bear less of her pain, and more of her casual, blithe resilience. I am trying to listen.

*

There is a walk I take from the cottage I live in with my partner W and the cat who chose us, up the old road that leads to the south, up away from the straggly fringes of the village and into the woods.

Our cottage was once home to agricultural labourers. It belonged to a farm, and the dead-end lane that leads to our front door is all that remains of an ancient droving road. Sometimes we look out of our living room window and see sheep trotting past, following a course they have handed down generation to generation.

The cottage squats below the old road, tired but stalwart. Its slate walls are two foot thick, and speak of its antiquity. We have seen a map that shows it standing as long ago as 1646. It may be much older. I find it hard to picture how different the village would have looked when it was just farms and cottages skirting the slopes, and the church in the valley centre, like an island in the floodplain.

The old road is lined by moss-topped drystone walls, so it feels like a ravine, but a field gate gives a glimmer of lake, to show its weather.

Depending on my mood, the mood of the skies, my pain and fatigue, I walk clockwise or anticlockwise on a circuit of the high craggy common that bridges the vales of Grasmere and Rydal.

The common leads to nowhere but itself, but will never lead you quite the same way twice. I love it because it is always surprising, but I also love it because I trust it. I know which paths are safe in which weather. I know how to go there and not hurt myself. I know if I trust it, it will always show me something: a view I haven't seen before, a red stag backlit by low winter sun, an ocean of bluebells moving in waves, a bird that is said not to live here any more.

I can lose whole afternoons there amongst the oaks and rowans, the rustling silver birches, hovering above the village like a kestrel.

The lime-washed tower of St Oswald's church shines through the trees, distinct amidst the slate grey. Once it stood alone on the banks of the Rothay, built on a site where Oswald preached.

Oswald had an incorruptible right hand, because Aidan blessed it. I picture him waving his perfect right hand as he talks, whilst his left hand aged and withered, and wonder what that blessing is standing in for, explaining over. Was Oswald sick, disabled? Oswald was a warrior king, ruler of the vast kingdom of Northumbria. He died in battle, and his head and limbs were cut off. A raven carried off one of his severed arms, and touched it to an ash tree that thereafter healed the sick with its leaves and even with its shade. The raven dropped the arm, and a healing well sprung up from the ground. Oswald's head, gathered a year after his death, is said to have thrown up a pillar of light into the sky from its wild grave to mark its place.

Years later, travellers would stumble onto the place of his death and find healing. It became a site of cures. People came to the site of his death and took pieces of it away with them. So much earth was removed over time that there was a hole as deep as a human, standing.

Any part of his body was supposed to have healing powers, but so was anything he had touched when he lived, including

the ground of Grasmere, the water of Grasmere. The river,
the lake and the rock.

*

The first winter I lived in Grasmere I got lost on the common
in the snow. I followed a route I have followed hundreds of
times since, up the old road towards the coffin path, along
the last strip of tarmac to the end of the tarn, then turning
off by the bridleway, following a thin indentation round the
back of the crag and up onto the common. In the snow the
path was as clear as a river, but when it turned the corner
and reached a plateau it vanished into untrodden ambiguity,
as so many paths do. It went everywhere, or nowhere. I was
less than a mile from home. But I knew my limits: my apti-
tude for falling and for breaking. The tiny, flickering store of
energy I had to carry me back. I thought of Lucy Gray, the
girl who dissolves into snow in William Wordsworth's poem.
I thought of the people I knew on call for mountain rescue.
I turned back, retraced my steps. I hated to retrace my steps.
Back then I thought to return the same way I went out was a
kind of failure. I had so much to learn. The common helped
teach me.

The second time I took that path it was late spring. The
foxgloves were out. It was raining, heavily. I didn't want to
go far from home. I thought the path would become clear
to me, that the way through would be easy, but I had not
accounted for how growth changes everything. Paths that
seemed confusingly various in the snow had vanished completely into waist-high bracken. I got turned around again.
I turned around again. I gave up.

Both times I only took that path because of bad weather.
I didn't know the name of the place then, or its history.
I would not know for many years the range of the common,

the vastness of it, how many small and various worlds it encompasses. I had only wanted to walk out but stay close to home. The path sent me home, but not the way I planned.

In 2015 W and I move into this cottage, tucked in next to the house I lived in when I got lost on the common eight years before. I am returning to old ground. Our living room faces its kitchen. The attic that was my first home in Grasmere looks down, with its raised eyebrow, on our bedroom window. I used to sit in its little open eye and gaze out on a square of fell top. My bed was tucked under the eaves – it felt like sleeping in an upturned ship, sailing in the sky. Our new house sits so low tucked beneath the old road it feels half underground. I call it the cave house. I call it our burrow. We are so much lower here. We live part of the year in shadow.

The first autumn in the cottage I watch day by day as light leaves the little garden I was so grateful for in the summer. I go uphill, seeking light. In the time between the attic and the cave house I have got iller, the distance I can walk shorter. I remember the little path that confounded me all those years before, in the snow and rain. In the sharp autumn air I find a wonderland of moss and amber treelight, with views so spectacular but achievable I feel ridiculous for missing them before.

For a long time after I begin to walk there I only go so far, and turn back. Years pass in which I only know this one small corner of the common, the first one I found in the snow. I don't dare go further, not knowing where the paths lead, not knowing how much energy I might lose on a trail that trickles out into nothingness again. When the ground feels uncertain, I retrace the path I know. I keep safe. I am no longer ashamed to go back on myself. I am not afraid of returning the same way any more, but of running out of fuel to return at all. It is the common who taught me this. I have to respect the lesson.

Little by little I gain ground, turn corners, find new views, new safe routes.

Though I'm sure there is a way to cross the common from the tarn back down to the old road, I can't find it. One winter day I think I have it, following a wall which I know meets the road, but I lose the way in the undergrowth, the overgrowth spilling out from the garden of the big house over the wall. The big house is empty most of the year – its garden belongs to the birds and the animals – roe and red deer, red squirrels, tawny owls. The ground is saturated, slipping out from under my boots. I am afraid of falling, and turn back. So many times I turn back.

It is a deer who shows me the way. A roe deer, whom I meet on the old road one late November afternoon in 2018, the light already fading. I watch where she goes, how she turns to look back at me before disappearing behind a wall. I wait until I can't see her any more, and I follow her hoof-prints in the wet earth.

This is how I learn the circle, how to go through. This is how I learn how long it takes to learn.

*

There is another story about the first break. Mum knew I had broken a bone, but when the X-rays came back, the young doctor on duty couldn't see a fracture, wanted to send me home. I have heard this story so many times I have furnished the scene with props from rooms I came to know later: the beige windowless walls; the X-ray film pinned up on the light box on the wall. There are four actors: the doctor, the mother, the ward sister and the crying baby.

My mum, who used to work as a radiographer, could see the break. She also knew her baby. She knew her baby was broken. The sister – with decades of experience behind her

– could see the break. Neither woman could admit to seeing the break when the doctor didn't. The agreement between them was tacit. The way my mum tells it, the sister just turned to the doctor and said, 'I'll be ringing the plaster room for you, then.'

This story is about how patients, particularly women, can't be seen to know more than the doctor in charge. Subordinate staff, particularly women, can't be seen to know more than the doctor in charge. To share your knowledge, you must make it look like the superior thought of it. That this is the only way it will be accepted, understood. What I learnt from this story is that doctors can be wrong, but also that you mustn't tell them that, not outright.

*

If I could send myself back in time and watch the accident as it unfolded, I'd position myself somewhere with a good overview – the upstairs window next door, or behind a tree, or somewhere else entirely watching through a hidden camera. I know my time-travel narratives well enough to know two things: I must not try to stop what happens and I must not let my younger self see myself now.

I would not want to undo anything, anyway. I'd just want to understand. To know exactly what happened. As though this is the beginning of everything and if I understand this I would understand my entire life. But there is no knowing. I could go back a million times and I would only know what I know now: it happened, no one was to blame, it was the first in a long chain of things that happened for which no one was to blame, but which changed me, inside and out.

Because I cannot time travel, I ask my parents what they remember. Even after I've realised the only way to know more about it is to ask them, the adults who were there, it takes me months to slip it into conversation. I call them from Grasmere, sitting at the drop-leaf table by the window where I work, and tell them I need to ask them some questions about that day, about what followed. They know I have been writing about my life, my illness, *our* illness. Over the last few years I've asked them other questions about my childhood, about their families, as I try to understand my own history better. It is September 2019. I'm almost the age now that my mum would have been when it happened, and I try to imagine how I would feel if our roles were reversed. I don't know why I keep putting off talking about it. I don't know why it is frightening, to ask about something that happened long ago, has always been only a fact in your life. What is it you don't want to know? What is it you think might change everything?

'The first time, we were in the garden, at Davies Road,' my mum starts.

I interrupt her to ask who was there, were we all there?

'Dad wa—,' Mum starts, and he interrupts her, 'I wasn't,' but she carries on. 'I thought you were there, you were there, you were at the far side of the garden. A was on his bike, I was out there, and we were on the lawn, I don't know where T was but you started off to run' – she means me now, not Dad, I started off to run – 'and A set off on his bike at the same time, and it was inevitable, none of us could stop it.'

They put me down to sleep. When I woke, I couldn't stand up in my cot. 'You couldn't weight-bear,' Mum says, using the words she used at the hospital to show them she knew a bit of what she was talking about. 'Your leg went down from under you.'

So they took me to the hospital, not the big one I remember from so many later visits, but the old Children's Hospital, off Mapperley Road. My parents interrupt themselves to argue a bit about where exactly the Children's Hospital was. This is like all our memories, not quite mappable onto each other.

18

'Anyway, that doesn't matter,' Mum says in the end, but by then Dad has started asking about where he was born, if that was the same place, and if my mum remembers what his mum would have told her, because he doesn't, and we get lost for a moment in things none of us really knows any more.

Dad asks how old I was then, and we try to work it out, calculating that I was younger than my littlest niece is when we are having this conversation. It was summer, we all repeat, yes, it was summer, though later I check my records and it wasn't, it was April, just a nice day in April when we were all in the garden together.

They are telling me this, taking turns, and I am listening like it is a story about someone else entirely, making sympathetic noises in the right places, as though it is not my leg they are talking about.

When Mum continues, she is working through events carefully not to miss anything out. Meanwhile Dad has started looking on his computer for the old home movies he digitised a few years ago, and he finds the right year. He turns the screen around to show me. There I am, in the back garden at Davies Road, with my stiff white leg, pushing a plastic walker shaped like a truck across the patio until I meet A in his go-cart and I have to turn around. There we are, sitting on a blanket on the patio – Mum, T and me. I am propped up on a beanbag but like a beetle I keep getting stuck on my back. I watch myself repeatedly tumbling over, and using my upper body to swing myself back upright. In another clip we are all in a field. I am in a pushchair, waving my stiff white leg in the air with my arms to point towards the boys, who are driving mini-motorbikes around a track made of hay bales. T is going so slowly they take him off the bike in the end because he is making the brakes smoke. A goes so quickly he crashes into the one same corner every time he tries to turn it. And then we are all in the paddling pool, and the plaster is off.

'So I took you up there, and the guy insisted on X-raying your knee, and I felt it wasn't your knee, it was your ankle. So we got the X-rays done, and he said, there's nothing wrong with her, it's alright, just give her some Calpol and put her to bed. And the sister took me to one side – she was a wise old bird, the sister – and she took me to one side and said, if you have any trouble, Mrs Atkin, you come right back.'

We all make a little noise then that says that we all know what that meant, that the sister knew what the doctor didn't: that Calpol wouldn't make it right, that he had missed the problem.

They took me home. They gave me Calpol. I slept. In the morning I tried to stand up in my cot, and my leg went down from under me.

Mum drove me back up to the hospital, and they did another X-ray, a bigger one this time. 'I said, I don't think you X-rayed the right part,' Mum says. I'm surprised at her forthrightness, knowing the next bit, and the next bit is as I remember.

'The films came back, and I could see the break, and the sister could see the break, and this young man was saying, there's no break there, and I looked at the sister, and I was going to say something, but before, the sister said, "Oh look, doctor, I'll just ring the plaster room shall I?"'

I remembered the punchline – the part where the two women work around the doctor who won't see what's in front of him – but I forgot, or never knew, that it happened twice. That I was sent away with a broken leg. That a doctor looked at me, and looked at clear evidence of brokenness, and refused to see it. My life with hospitals begins like this, and this is how it carries on.

*

At the time of the first break everyone assumed it was just a normal accident. It wasn't thought to be a sign of anything. To collide with a bicycle is a fair reason to break a bone. There was no reason to suspect anything more.

Back then, in 1982, I was just an ordinary enough toddler, who had had an ordinary enough accident in the course of ordinary play.

Meaning is accumulative. One event cannot be understood as anything but itself, but a series of events clusters meaning together into pattern, into a narrative from which conclusions can be drawn.

There is a version of my life story that can be told entirely through breaks, or breaks and not-quite-breaks, through sprains and dislocations.

All through my childhood we kept a folder of X-rays in the cupboard where all the important papers lived. Big wobbly charcoal-coloured sheets in brown or grey card envelopes. The file in our cupboard grew and grew. It wasn't just limbs, but teeth. Teeth growing wrong, teeth doubled up, the gaps where teeth had been removed. You could take the X-rays out and look at them, hold them up to the light and see your own insides, fixed in a moment in time. Your insides broken, or sometimes not broken after all.

*

The second break happened when I was four.

I fell parking my tricycle. It was early May. I know this because Patient Access tells me so. It says 9 May 1984, though I remember it only as summerish. It is always summerish in the childhood where you break your leg.

I had been pedalling around the L-shaped drive of the house we were soon to move into. I was reversing my tricycle into a space under the kitchen window, by the open front door.

I could hear grown-ups talking: my mum and some friends. The dining room was being replastered, and I remember the Germolene look of the damp, salmony walls when I was carried in screaming.

I am not sure how I fell. In my mind, in my memory, I am always parking lamby bike. Lamby bike had a powder blue seat with a lamb face on it, white handles, and white wheels with splashes of red around the spokes. I was really too big for it by then but refused to give it up. I felt safe with it. It was a kind of comfort. Stable and reliable. But really I had been parking the large red Raleigh tricycle I had recently inherited from another family, whose boy had outgrown it. It was big, and timeless looking, with wide handlebars and – its best feature – a huge square boot attached to the back, a big metal box you could store anything in. Later, once we'd moved into the house and discovered the garden filled up with frogs, my brothers would goad me into loading the boot with them and cycling around with them in there, then tricking Mum into opening it so they all leapt out.

Mum remembers being on the drive when I fell, and hearing me cry out that I'd hurt my foot, though in my version they are always already inside, and rush out when they hear me.

This time the break was low, just above my ankle, and the cast on my leg only came halfway up, like a chunky knee-high sock. This time Dad was prepared with his cut-up trainer, and the plaster lasted the full term, without amendment. Perhaps it had already begun, by then, to seem inevitable that we would soon be back at A&E, back at X-ray, back at the plaster room.

Still, it was an accident. Normal enough. The following year I spent a week off school with the mumps at the same time as my dad was off work with a broken foot. He had dropped a crate of bricks on it. It was late in the school year and, although I missed a longed-for trip to the zoo, I got to spend long light days drawing and playing outside in the company of my dad. None of this was unexpected. We were an accident-prone family.

Accidents were normal in our home, in our lives. We fell a lot. We tripped over things. We fell out of trees. We fell down holes. We stepped the wrong way and fell into streams or over cliffs. We dropped things on our feet. We dropped ourselves. There was no reason to think of it as pathological. There was no reason to think of it as the meaningful basis of a narrative for any one of us.

*

The second time I broke my leg, I remembered the first time. Not the break itself, not the accident, which was fable already, but a snippet of a moment: being rolled down a subterranean corridor with a vaulted ceiling to the plaster room. I remembered a rotary saw that split the plaster open. I remembered it whirring towards me.

I remembered this the second time – not in the pain of the break or the direct aftermath, not in the long weeks of discomfort and awkwardness – but at the end. The memory came through repetition. As I was being delivered to the room where the plaster that encased my leg would be removed, I remembered: this had happened before. I remembered being rolled down a basement corridor, looking up at the ceiling, the vague sense of dull green light. I remembered the rotary saw whirring towards me, remembered that this was not something to fear, because it would not cut my skin, although it looked like it wanted to. This was the first time I felt sure I knew that time was layered, that it stacked moments on top of one another, so that the present could also be the past, and the past be the present, that they were

23

not separate things. They were all one thing together. Time was a long strip wrapped around itself and stuck on top of itself, hardened in particular spots, becoming solid only where it re-met itself and bonded with itself, like the plaster on my leg.

Only later could I make sense of it, the layers of corridor, the layers of memory. When I could stand back and unpeel the present, like bandages released from their binding by soaking for a long time. But I was old enough then to understand how memories will project themselves onto the uneven surface of a present moment. At one point I had thought it was a dream I was remembering, and maybe it had been a dream as well, an unconscious echo of the event itself.

*

For a long time, I thought bicycles were to blame for my breakages. One ran me over; one threw me off. Aged eight I fell off another and hurt my thumb badly, badly enough for a trip to A&E, but didn't break it. I thought this was progress.

In the final year of junior school a rope on the swing in our garden snapped and flung me through the air and to the ground, and though I screamed and couldn't stand, I did not break my leg. I only ripped all the ligaments down one side of it. I had a backcast put on: a plaster that covered three-quarters of my leg and was held at the front by bandages to give space for the swelling to grow and subside. It took the same time to heal as a break would have, but drew astonishing colours on my skin as the bruising evolved from purple-black through greens and blues and yellows.

Children have accidents. It was an acceptable consequence of play and action. There was always someone in my class with their arm in a cast. Sometimes I managed whole years with just bruises and mild sprains. We kept Tubigrips of various sizes in the bathroom drawer, became adept at wrapping bandages. I thought this was something everyone did.

*

The third break was secondary, a side effect of a different kind of falling apart, that began to mean everything.

It was early November 1997. I was revising for exams. My parents had gone out for the day. They wanted to make a commitment to being healthier. They had signed up at a new gym that had opened down the road and had gone for induction. This was out of character. I was alone in the house and I did not know when they would be back.

I was sitting at the kitchen table with the TV on low, copying out my own notes. I remember things by writing. I was bored of myself. I leafed through the pile of CDs next to the stereo, clicked Ella Fitzgerald in and the lid down. I sang and danced across the kitchen to the fridge, looking for something to occupy my restless body. I remember this moment very clearly now, though I could not have told you about it a week ago, a day ago, if you had asked specifically. I remember it mostly for the guilt I felt at making something to eat when I was bored and not hungry. Anxious and not hungry.

I was dancing across the kitchen with – I'm sure – a plate in my hand – although I don't remember it falling – singing along with Ella – when somehow I was no longer dancing. I was on the floor and the pain was articulate, and my leg was all wrong, and I knew what my boredom had cost me.

The kitchen tiles were cold, which helped soothe the sweat I'd broken into. I knew my kneecap was out, and I knew it was bad.

Over the previous five years, I had slipped one or other of my kneecaps out of their sockets many times. Sometimes one would just slip out mid-movement and then slip itself back in before I had a chance to act or falter, or I would catch it in my hand as though it was a mouse on the run, and ease it back to where I wanted it to be. They always ran to the outside of my leg, away from me, as though they wanted to escape completely. Later I found out this was because they sit off-centre even when they are in place, as do my mother's. But we didn't know this then. We didn't know anything then.

I was stuck on the cold tiles of the kitchen floor. My right arm was starting to feel strange, tingly. From where I sat, between two rows of kitchen units, I could see the phone. It was impossibly far away, hooked on its base unit halfway up a full-height cabinet. I don't know how long I sat there. I don't remember if I cried. When I did pull myself up – clawing at the cut-out patterns on the underside of the units – hauling section by section – using my good leg as a kind of wedge – my kneecap grated back into dock. A kind of soundless clunk, felt not heard. Sickening. I balanced myself there, leaning on the kitchen surface. There was no point now in calling an ambulance, which I had thought I was planning to do. I reached a shaky hand for the phone, and pressed the speed dial button for my dad's mobile. It went straight to answerphone. I left a message, voice shaky. I called my mum's mobile. The same. I thought I ought to get myself ready for the hospital. I tested movement, using the parallel surfaces as a kind of crutch. I got almost to the back door this way, making it the last bit to the coat rack by rolling myself against the wall and bracing through the door frame. I put on my coat, and scarf, and shoes. I manoeuvred myself back around the kitchen, and managed to reach a chair. I stared out the window. I rang the neighbours. No answer. I rang my boyfriend. No answer. I rang my best friend. No answer. Neither of my parents had called back. Half an hour passed, then an hour. No one called. I spent a good amount of time shuffling myself down the growing corridor to the downstairs loo. I was finding it hard to move my right arm by this time, and struggled to do up the button fly on my favourite jeans. The effort made my eyes leak a bit at the corners. I shunted back up to the kitchen, and waited.

*

At the hospital everyone was so focused on my knee it took a while before anyone thought to check my arm. Because I had replaced my own kneecap by standing, I arrived at A&E non-urgent. Hours ticked by whilst I waited to be seen, in pain but not in danger. It was past midnight by the time they X-rayed my arm and found a fracture where the bones of my forearm met the elbow. It was a simple crack of the radial head, a break typical from falling with an arm outstretched. It only showed because there was blood in the joint.

It wasn't until this third break that we would begin to understand my breakability as part of a longer narrative, that all these breaks added up to make a narrative of their own. It would be another half-life again before we would understand why. But it was the point we began to understand me as sick, as unwell in some way that was more than transitory, although we still all believed it would go away, that I would get better.

I had been ill for over a year. Not seriously ill, but ailing mysteriously. I felt exhausted all the time – so far beyond tired the word had become meaningless – as though someone were siphoning my energy out of me like petrol from a car. I was listless and increasingly weak. I was so cold, all the time, I felt like my bones had been extracted and replaced with ice. I had taken to wearing two coats outdoors and one coat indoors. I felt sick constantly, whether I ate or didn't eat. I got thinner and thinner. I had, wherefore I know not, lost all mirth. I kept getting tonsillitis, over and over.

After the accident, it got worse. My body forgot how to sleep. Sleep was an instruction I had lost. I was given pills to help me remember, which made me feel so distanced from my own body that I could stare for hours at my own sleepless hand. I had trouble moving my limbs. I would stand up and fall back down. So cold all the time. I felt mostly dead. Sometimes I wished I was.

It was a frightening time. There were so many tests, so many weeks of waiting for terrible words to be written in or out of my story, possible causes being eliminated, slowly, one at a time.

During these worst, terrifying years I kept a journal as though my future depended on it. I wrote to make sense of what was happening: to weigh up what I was feeling against what I was told about what I was feeling. I would read back over it as months of confusion passed by, trying to find meaning or confirmation in its pages, trying to find proof that I wasn't creating my own illness.

Now those journals are the only record I have. The tests and consultations have not been digitised. My journals – their rambling introspection, dream diaries, dissection of friendships and teenage love affairs, pain diary, insomnia diary, diary of fear and frustration – are the best medical history I can access.

*

Sometimes I think about the strange versions of your own story you will find repeated back at you in a doctor's letter.

All the bad clones of myself that exist in letters that begin, 'Thank you for sending this young lady to see me . . .' which garble my symptoms, my medical history and personal history. That make a lazy fiction of me. That show how much the doctor has not listened, or has forgotten or misunderstood. That make me wonder how they could possibly comprehend the complexity of my life in my body, if they cannot understand what I do for work, or how old I am, or what my name or title is. I wonder if I would recognise them as versions of myself if we were to meet.

Illness makes storytellers of us all, but patients know that our version of the story is mistrusted, instinctively and as a matter of course. We go to the doctor, to the emergency department, to a consultant, to a physiotherapist. The first thing we are asked is why we are there. We are made to explain ourselves, to justify our presence, even if the reason we are there makes it impossible to do so clearly. We are made to explain ourselves over and over again, as though each separate account will be checked against the others for inconsistencies. We are unreliable witnesses to our own bodily histories. We misinterpret. We falsify. Our testimonies cannot be trusted.

When we repeat one simplified story, over and over again, all other possible versions of events are forgotten, undone, erased. It becomes the truth, not just one version of it. It bears no relationship to events as experienced, to the body in the moment of an event.

*

I carried on, because I had no choice. I got a bit better, better enough to consider university after a year of recuperating from school. I chose a course that I thought I could manage, and where no one knew me as sick. I moved to London, worked on appearing to be well. In the second semester of my first year, I slipped in the over-bath shower in halls and smashed the elbow I had broken two years previously on the enamel. My flatmate and her boyfriend drove me to A&E in his vintage Beetle and waited patiently whilst the young doctor dismissed my pain as bruising. I told him about the previous break, how it barely showed on the X-ray. I told him about my history of fracture, but even as I did so I realised I just sounded whiny and paranoid. I went back to halls shamed by my conviction and by my fear, by my certainty of my own truth in the face of professional disavowal. But I treated it like a break, and it hurt and healed like a break.

When I was twenty-two I broke my left elbow, not unlike the way I broke my right four and a half years earlier, falling from standing, jarring my arm as I fell, breaking myself on myself. I was on the way to work in central London, working out the last month of a short-term contract that had been my first full-time job after university. I was walking to Mile End station, preparing to cross the road as I had done hundreds of times before. Only this particular morning there were flyers scattered all over the pavement by the crossing. I described them later as leaflets, but I think in my pain I confused the word. When I picture it, they are flyers, the kind printed on slightly glossy paper.

My foot touched a flyer, and the flyer slipped over another flyer, and I flew backwards towards the pavement. Instinctively I stuck out my left arm to break my fall, stuck it out in the direction of the fall, angled diagonally backwards. When my hand hit the pavement I heard a crack, and felt the pain, and knew right away, by this age, that I'd broken a bone.

I have described it time and again as though I was in a cartoon and slipped on a banana skin, and that is just what happened. This is the story I tell against myself, my own clumsiness.

Perhaps for that reason, when a woman stopped to help me up, and check if I was alright, I thanked her and told her

I would just carry on and get on the Tube. The hospital was only two stops away. I knew if I could keep going it was by far the quickest way to get myself there.

But every movement of the Tube jolted me. Every jolt made me involuntarily tense the muscles in my hurt arm. Every reflex brought up tears, which I kept trying to swallow down.

I made it to the hospital. I took myself to A&E. I had graduated from childhood to adulthood. This was what adulthood meant: managing your own injuries. Taking your own broken limb to X-ray.

I took myself to work, afterwards, showed them the sling, asked what I should do. It was the first time I had had to explain an injury to an employer. I was working at the Royal Society of Arts, administrating the Student Design Awards. At this point in the award cycle, my job consisted mostly of carrying large boxes of student artwork from storage by my basement office to the lobby. They were then collected by couriers and taken back to the university that had submitted them. The sight of me buckling under piles of outsized boxes caused some amusement to the porters in the building. On more than one occasion I joked that I would break my wrist and then they'd be sorry; they'd have to carry them instead. So that morning when I rang the office from outside the hospital, reporting that I had slipped on a leaflet like a banana skin and broken my elbow, they thought I was joking. It does sound like a joke. It was only when I turned up, grey-faced and shaky, with my arm in a sling, that they realised it was for real.

To end my first real job incapacitated by injury made me sick with frustration. I'd managed four and a half years without a break, but it seemed timed to remind me: this is who you are, what you are. You fall, you hurt yourself. You fail. Some of us just fall, and you are one of them. Falling is just what you do.

*

For years after I broke my elbows, either one of them would click and get stuck, would stick until I could shake it out. Like rusty joints on a folding chair they would jam at a slight angle, so I couldn't straighten an arm or bend it. I am rusty joint on rusty joint. It would happen at the least convenient times – the one time I went with L to the climbing wall, when I was halfway up, without ropes – or carrying something, holding a door, trying to take a fragile object from someone else. All the times you can't stop, release your arm, shake it out.

It changes the sense of how you move through the world when you're constantly getting stuck against it, like you've got tangled in netting, or flown into a window, except there is literally nothing there, not even something you can't see, or can't imagine. It is just your own body, unable to cope with the gravity of real space. Unable to negotiate continuity in this world.

So you slip piece after piece from yourself, fracturing bit by bit, and you tumble down, and you fall, and fall, and fall.

*

When I was thirty-two I broke a rib, and it was this break that led – slowly, and with many false turns – to my diagnoses.

A few months beforehand I had been away for a weekend with a group of old friends. At some point one evening, as we sat around the long kitchen table in the haunted priory we'd rented, the conversation fell to scars. I mentioned how I'd realised you can feel one of my leg breaks through the skin, you can feel the callous, all these decades later. Everyone in turn felt my shin bone, the strange dip and lump in it, whilst one guest, a doctor, leant back in his seat. He was the sceptic in a room of believers. He suggested it was cellulite or something else, some soft tissue, but certainly not what I said, it couldn't be that. So I made him feel it too, and watched his face change to something between surprise and approval. I didn't know then that I'd spend the next two years trying to get doctors to notice where I was broken, and believe in what was really there, not what they expected to find.

*

My latest break happened in October 2017.

It's a familiar story. I was walking across a room. Rooms are so treacherous; negotiating them so fraught. You make one wrong move and a room you have moved through a million times becomes your enemy.

This time it was our living room. It's a small room, so small that, after my brother A and his sons had visited that summer, my nephews could not stop talking about Aunty Polly's Tiny House. *So Tiny!* We are continually rearranging furniture to try to fit everything we need in. All objects are in constant rotation, like the ever growing and shifting piles of books we both bring in like the cat brings in mice.

I was rushing to pack a bag with my swimming kit, so that I could get to a hotel pool in the village before it closed for the night. I'd just bought a pass for the month, now it was colder, and I wanted to make the most of it. But I kept getting my timings all wrong. I told W to remind me I'd feel better if I went, even if I could only swim for ten minutes. It had been dark and wet all week, and I'd barely been out of the house. Ten minutes in the sauna and ten minutes in the warm pool would make everything better.

The culprit was a tall stool I had bought from a charity shop to use in the kitchen at our previous house. Here, there was no way to sit at a counter in the poky galley kitchen. For a while it loitered in hibernation in the cupboard under the stairs, but it had re-entered the lounge that week for a reason I cannot remember. Maybe, as it has since, to rest a laptop or a lamp on. Whatever the logic, it had ended up tucked into the doorway, next to the upright piano I had bought as a promise for myself when I moved away from London. The stool's legs were sticking out slightly into the doorway and, in my rush as I turned to leave the room and swing my swimming bag onto my back, I missed the doorway and swung my left leg into it.

I fell back into the sofa, instinctively covering the injury with my hands whilst the first vast wave of pain crashed through me. When I recovered enough to take my hand away, I could see the scale of the miscalculation I'd made. My second-to-littlest toe was drifting away from my foot at a new jaunty angle, as though it had other, more important places to be. I turned to W. *We're going to have to go to the hospital.*

*

Getting to the car is an effort. At one end of the remnant of the droving lane, closest to the house, there are slippery slate steps up to the old road. At the other, uneven cobbles lead out to a narrow tarmacked lane connecting the old road with the A road. It looks passable, but people are always getting their cars stuck in its awkward angles. To walk, I have to put as much weight as I can on my heel, to keep it away from my toes. We plump for the shortest route rather than the easier ground, and W brings the car round to the top of the steps whilst I talk myself up them, one by one. I think of the other times I've had to do something like this. I think of how I picked myself off the kitchen floor and got myself ready to go to hospital. I think of how I got up off the pavement and took myself to the hospital on the Tube. I can get myself up ten steps in the dark, when there is someone to catch me. I don't have to do this alone.

Fracture

Twenty years had passed between this break and the first time I broke my elbow, when I thought my life had been ruined by my falling. So much of my life in between had been spent going to and from hospitals, and in hospital waiting rooms, that I knew exactly where I was going and what would greet me.

Our nearest emergency department is a minor injuries unit in Kendal, twenty miles away. This is not the first time W has had to drive me there whilst I've been half insensible with pain. I am furious with myself, and terrified, and furious that I am terrified. The pain is disproportionate to the injury, and that too makes me angry, and scared. The angle of my toe makes me scared. I know it will not ruin my life. That six to eight weeks to heal in the scheme of things is nothing. I live far outside school term times now. I have different measures. Still, I cry hot, panicky tears on the long, jolting drive to the hospital. It is evening, and the roads are quiet, so it only takes forty minutes. My muscles tense with every bump and the pain blazes.

I have broken my toe, cracked it through at the base, where it meets the foot. At the hospital they strap it up, send me away with tape and dressing, book me into the fracture clinic in a few weeks' time.

By the next day the top of my foot is a spectacular teal colour. I dye my hair to match, with dye I bought in a pain-induced daze in the supermarket next to the hospital late at night. I realise if I get in the bath, and rest my bad foot on the side, I can fill the bath whilst I'm in it, and keep the dressing dry. For the first couple of weeks it is very difficult to walk at all. The timing of the break means I am immobilised at the precise time the sun stops entering our garden for the winter. By week four I can limp around without too much trouble. I limp up the old road to the duck pond, sit on a rock in the November sun. It still hurts a lot, and the toe feels odd. I ask about this at the fracture clinic. The sensation in my entire foot is peculiar.

Something important doesn't feel right. But it's only a toe. I am making a fuss about nothing, again.

The next summer my foot is still troubling me. I feel I can feel the break, every time I move my toes, every time I put my foot on the ground. As months pass, the pain gets worse, not better. Every time I put my weight on my foot I can feel a searing through it, at the site of the break.

Imaging shows a nerve overgrowth called a neuroma at the base of my toe, most common – ironically – in runners. The size of a pea, the width of my toe itself, an excruciating bead – the neuroma will alter the way I walk forever. My foot will never be the same. There will be more trips to the hospital. More pain. More tears shed. The breaking of this tiny bone has changed my life, changed the way I meet the world. It will not let itself be forgotten.

People with little experience of breaking bones think it is simple to mend bones. They think that it is simple to identify a break, and that once it is identified, it is simple to stabilise it. They think that once you stabilise it, it is simple to heal it. They think that once it heals, it is as though there never was a break. The bone, the body, the movement of the body, is restored to a pre-break state. But nothing is without consequence. The smallest break in the smallest bone can be the butterfly whose wingbeat stirs the storm of the future.

Not all breaks are equal. I try not to think too much about what might come next. I try not to fall.

*

I've written this book because I think the stories we tell, and how we tell them, are important. I want to change the stories we tell about living with pain, about disability. I know I can't change other people's ways of telling. What I can do is offer a different narrative.

In recent years, health services have championed the patient story as a way to encourage better care, and better understanding between doctors and patients. It is seen as giving the patient agency, giving them the narrative control.

But a patient story is a redacted document, impossible to make sense of without the key words. If you don't know why something is happening, you don't know how to understand it or describe it to someone else either. You use the language you have been given to describe the problem. You repeat one version of the story, even if it doesn't quite reflect how you feel, until it becomes the story.

How do you know when something is a sign or symptom when it is your life? How do you know what is part of your patient story and what is just your story, your history? Where the pathological and narrative meet, or diverge?

How do you tell a story to someone else when you can't understand it yourself as something with a beginning and a middle and an end, but only as an assembly of interwoven episodes? Of fracture after fracture.

This is the chronic life, lived as repetition and variance, as sedimentation of broken moments, not as a linear progression. I don't know what a linear progression might look or feel like: all I know is fracture and moments building up around it like a callus, trying to knit it back together. So that is how I've written this book. It's the only way I know how to tell this story with any honesty.

You might expect a patient story to start with a break, and end with diagnosis, and with cure, but that's not how my patient story goes. It starts with a break, and then keeps splitting apart, again and again. I've told this story how it is: in pieces, and looped back on itself. It's how I understand it myself. If I tried to unroll it and smooth it out for you, it wouldn't be true to any of us. I can't pretend that when we get sick, we get help, and we get better. This is the chronic life. This is the story of how it is to not get better.

The way we talk about illness and disability dictates what is possible for all people who are affected by it. The narrative odds are too often stacked against disabled people. There are two options that seem to be available: triumphal recovery or inspirational death. There are too few stories of continuation. Too few stories of joy. Too few stories of the millions of ordinary ways a disabled life may fold and unfold, like any life.

In trying to tell my story, I've also turned to the stories that have been important to me along the way – the other narratives of illness and disability that have changed the way I could think about my own, about my life in my body. Stories help us to communicate with others who have different experiences to our own, but they also give us a chance to find ourselves reflected back through other lives. Throughout this book I include the writing of others – of my extended chronic writing family – from books I have read that gave me that vital sense of recognition, of shared humanity, to books that helped me think through what it means to live well with disability. I couldn't tell my story if they hadn't told theirs.

I've written this book because I can tell my story. I hope it will help other people who can't, or who haven't been able to, and help other people tell their own stories too. Maybe if enough of us tell our own stories we can change the narrative. We can write ourselves back in, in all our variousness, with our pain, our joy, our mundane everydayness, our truths.

This book is for everyone who has been told they are not broken, when they are holding up their body full of cracks as evidence. For everyone who has been told there is nothing wrong with them, when they know there is something very wrong with them, everyone who has been told that they are just *too sensitive*. That they need to do more exercise, or less.

That they just need to get outside, reconnect with nature. That they need to take up yoga or prayer. That they only appear to be ill because they are too fat, or too thin. That they are making themselves ill, consciously or unconsciously, with their wrong behaviour. That they need to eat more or less or differently. That they have the wrong attitude. That they just don't want to be well.

I am writing this to remember. To record. To testify that my body is real, that my story is real, that this happened and keeps happening, that people like me happen. The world is full of us. But mostly I am writing it for you. Because you might be like me, or know someone like me.

This is for everyone who has been dismissed from further examination because of how they looked, acted, spoke, because of their gender, their sexuality, their nationality, their race or religion or ethnicity, their ability, their background. I am not writing this because I think my experiences are in any way exceptional, but because I know they are common. Far too common. There are many of you. Of us. I believe you. I know you know your body. I know you will find your answer. This book is for you.

Dislocation

In midwinter the common holds the afternoon light long after it has slunk away from our house, from the valley floor. I walk after lunch to catch the last of it, chasing it upwards until it evaporates into starlight.

On the way up the road the low sun catches in the bare branches of Henry's Wives, the six great oaks on the ridge of the field between the old road and the lake. The branches split it into rays.

I crunch through frost-rimed leaves and snow-crusted bracken, winding back and forth till I reach the highest point on the common. It is low enough and high enough that you can see both Grasmere and Rydal – both lakes, down both valleys – the angles implausible. Its sides fall into terraces that feel both man-made and geologic. The top is flat, a natural or unnatural stage – a boggy centre enclosed by a walkway of stone. It feels purposeful. An ancient fort or settlement. It has an air – both peaceful and watchful – of being occupied a very long time ago, and occupied still. The bog is teeming with undisturbed life. There is a ruined sheepfold, one bright white birch growing out of a dais of stone, which holds the afternoon moon in its branches against an ice-blue sky. Both lakes are swirled with dark spirals and mandalas where the water moves under thin ice.

For a long time I thought it was too hard for me to climb, that there was too much risk of falling, seeing only its harshest face, and I avoided it. Slowly I found the easiest ways up, and down, the ones I could trust myself on in any weather.

Dislocation

Every time I sit up here, on one of the perfect seats formed from the rock, I think I might never be able to turn my eyes away and leave.

On a snowy afternoon you can sit here and watch the white fells turn pink as the sun falls, the moon ascends. Outside of time, and immersed in all of it at once.

The air feels charged here, the space never empty. Maybe it is only the deer watching from some hiding spot on another crag, but I always feel the friction of other minds working, a faint buzz like electricity.

Dorothy Wordsworth recognised something strange here, an uncanny perspective and quality of light. She wrote in her journal:

> There was a strange mountain lightness . . . between the two valleys. There is more of the sky there than any other place. It has a strange effect sometimes along with the obscurity of evening or night. It seems almost like a peculiar *sort* of light.[4]

One March evening in 1802 Dorothy climbs the summit of the common at twilight, on the way back to Grasmere from fetching the post in Ambleside. The peculiar sort of light here makes her feel 'more than half a poet' –

> night was come on & the moon was overcast. But as I climbed the Moss the moon came out from behind a Mountain Mass of Black Clouds – O the unutterable darkness of the sky & the Earth below the Moon! & the glorious brightness of the moon itself! There was a vivid sparkling streak of light at this end of Rydale water but the rest was very dark & Loughrigg Fell & Silver How were white & bright as if they were covered with hoar frost.[5]

So often Dorothy's descriptions of Grasmere and Rydal are like this – a revelation of a different landscape under the mundane one, 'unearthly & brilliant', as she writes half a lifetime later in 1830.

For so many years I read about that time she called herself 'more than half a poet' and did not connect it with the site of the vision. Once I know the place, I understand. There is more of the sky here than any other place. Anyone who eats the moonlight here could never be the same again.

I sit for as long as I can bear the cold, as long as I dare in the darkening day, before I inch back down the hill to the house.

*

I was eleven the first time I dislocated one of my kneecaps. It was early evening. My dad and my brothers were all away, and Mum and I were alone in the house. She had sent me to my room to try some new pyjamas on, and check whether they itched or hurt me at all. If I itched my skin broke and scabbed and wouldn't heal again. The pyjamas were made of silky cream fabric with a faint swirly pattern on them, and the seams didn't scratch or dig in. I came dancing from the landing, down the three steps into my parents' room, singing along to an advert on the TV, showing off my silky costume, flinging my limbs around and pulling faces. *More reasons to shop at Morr-eeeeee-sons*. And then I was not dancing. I was on the floor facing the mirrored wardrobe doors. I was going off like a siren. I was watching my own face pulling itself apart. My leg was all wrong. I don't know when I felt it, when I saw it, but in my memory the knowledge of it is there right away when I picture myself on the floor, in front of the wardrobe. Where my knee should have been there was a hollow, with the skin sucking down into it, a crater where there should have been a mound. My kneecap was on the wrong side of my leg, on the back, underneath where it should be, as though it had dropped right through that crater and stuck to the underside. Of course, I couldn't see it like that. I had long pyjama trousers on and all I knew was that my leg was wrong. I can remember the silky fabric sucked into the crater but I don't know whether I'm remembering a nightmare or my own reconstruction or the actual event. They say you don't remember pain, which seems to be true – I can't repeat the feeling in myself that I felt that night – but I do remember my terror, the emotion of *being in pain*, feeling a new pain, a pain I did not understand. I had broken bones, and torn ligaments, but this was different. Mum rang for an ambulance. I had never been in an ambulance before.

I spent the next decade knocking my kneecaps out of joint, never as badly as that first time though, never again the bumpy ride in the ambulance to A&E, and the slicing open of the trousers, and the twisting of the leg to manipulate it back into a useful thing.

*

People say *pull yourself together* as though you have the power to winch the disparate parts of yourself in on command. I can't imagine what that would be like.

In trying to piece together my story, the history of my body, I started looking at photographs from my childhood. There are so many in which most of my body is facing in one direction, and my feet another entirely. I can't imagine what it's like to point in the right direction all the time, the one you mean to be going in. To not be pulling yourself apart. In some photos, the line of my arm, shoulder to hand, shows three distinct, improbable angles, as though I have been photoshopped together.

As a small child I saw myself as a push puppet – one of those little figurines made of wooden lozenges that collapse on their strings when you press under their podium. I was made of distinct parts that tumbled away from each other under the slightest pressure. Funny to watch, from the outside. I had a push puppet that I would collapse repeatedly, trying to understand what it meant. What it meant to be collapsible.

Now I know that dislocation of joints is one of the most common symptoms of Hypermobile Ehlers-Danlos syndrome, that this is why I can't keep myself together. The tissues – the ligaments and muscles – around the joint are too elastic, and simply can't hold it in place under pressure. The pressure could be great – a push, a fall – or something tiny. I dislocate the little finger on my left hand on a conveyor belt in Carlisle Tesco. I pull two out picking up an awkward bag. I knock the middle joint of my left index finger out of place doing nothing, sitting still, in a room. Standing, filling time waiting for the kettle to boil, not even shifting weight from foot to foot, my ankle slips out of joint. Some people with EDS dislocate small or large joints dozens of times a day. Some can't walk because their tissues are so pliant their hips and ankles dislocate with every step.

Most of the time these days I only subluxate joints rather than fully dislocate them. To subluxate is to slip out only slightly from the correct placement. Like that shiver of uncanny disjuncture you get when you say someone just walked over your grave. I know a joint is subluxed when it just *feels wrong*. This happens a lot. If you see me pulling on my wrists or rotating my hands or feet, or clacking my knuckles, it's not because of stiffness, it's because my ankles or wrists or fingers have subluxed and I'm trying to coax the joint back into its rightful home. I wake up and crack my shoulder and clavicle back into joint. I stand up and click my ankles back into place. This is how I begin the day, how every action starts.

Dislocation

That night in 1991 when I first dislocated my knee, I was pulled apart in another way, too. From a spot just below the ceiling, I watched myself being carried along the corridor and down the stairs and out of the house on a red folding chair, a paramedic on either side. They turned the siren on and gave me gas and air as we jolted to the hospital over potholes and speed bumps. There they slit my new pyjama trousers and, later, laid hands on my leg, and twisted it hard to shoot the kneecap back up and round to where it belonged. I was dislocated from my whole body. I remember watching myself, and not being myself. I saw myself from outside – an omniscient narrator to my own pain. I was me, completely out of joint.

This is another story of my life. I am always being displaced, separated from myself, always trying to get myself home.

*

When I first learnt to walk, I walked with my feet turned in so far they would flap against each other and trip me up. They call this 'in-toeing'. I learnt this word through Patient Access, a website that shows you your medical record, and allows you to order prescriptions and book appointments online.

My Patient Access record is partial – huge chunks of my life, my body's story, are missing, as though they might never have happened. The site shows me an alternative reality in which key events never occurred, or happened at another time. There is a gap between 1998 and 2010 where nothing is registered at all. A life I lived in London is erased entirely.

The first entry in this partial record of my body's history, under the heading *Problems*, under the sub-heading *Past (Minor)* is 'in-toeing'. When you search instead under *Consultations* it is listed under the date 5 October 1986 as 'Problem – O/E intoeing', with the addition 'Examination:

Hypermobility Syndrome'. A word I wouldn't hear for another eleven years. A word I wouldn't know could help me place myself for almost thirty.

I know this wasn't the first time I'd seen the doctor about my feet. By 1986 I knew Paediatric Outpatients so well I had favourite toys in the waiting room play area. I looked forward to getting to play with them.

The doctor told my mum that I'd have some problems, but she could try to get me into gymnastics or dance. I was double-jointed, he said, and needed to strengthen up.

I learnt, through years of retraining, to walk with my feet almost straight, but even now when I get tired they creep inwards, as though the toes of each foot are magnetised to each other. To try and make them fall straight, I have to imagine I am placing them pointing outward, duck-toed, instead. I go back to Miss Lisa's ballet lessons in Wilford Village Hall – a leafy graveyard away from the river Trent – and visualise my feet in fifth position. But even when it feels to me like they are turned out at forty-five degrees, they are not quite parallel.

I can still find myself standing with my feet pointing directly in towards each other, at right angles to my legs, a straight line below my hips. It is quite comfortable. I can do the opposite too, although never by default. Either way, it is hard to balance. It has worsened again, these last few years. Every photograph I see of myself I am knock-kneed, my toes drawing towards each other like compass points to an invisible magnetic north.

*

The summer I turned sixteen I felt something change. I clicked into myself. I felt really myself, for the first time. It was as though I had been somehow walking round for years with my whole body subluxed, with my self dislocated from my body. Sometimes I overlapped with it, like a shadow. Sometimes I was tethered to it but floating at a distance like a balloon, or a dinghy. My body was sailing ahead through the material world, and I was bobbing behind it, without direction or agency, slapped by waves. I had been travelling in my body's wake, and it decided everything.

It didn't seem to help my body though, to feel myself in it. We had a hard time adjusting to moving forward together.

The year I was sixteen was also the year I would stop sleeping. I just forgot how. During the worst of many bouts of tonsillitis that year, I took painkillers with caffeine added to them before bed without thinking and cancelled sleep. I was staying in London for a night with my parents to go to the theatre, and I lay awake all night in the B&B, staring at the ceiling. I did not know that would be the first of so many nights unsleeping.

I had whole weeks of it: finally slipping away from myself sometime around six, jolted sickeningly awake by the alarm at seven.

It never leaves you, the fear of not being able to sleep.

The horror of insomnia is the horror of repetition. You are meant to sleep every night, and every night comes, and your body still refuses to lie down and stop. To do what it is meant to. You are stuck in a loop, and the loop kicks you out of your proper place and time. You are dislocated from everyone and everything else. You walk through the day like a ghost, haunting your own life, trying to tell it something, but you have got out of time, and you don't know what the message is yet.

That year I dislocated my knee, I broke my elbow. At school, we studied *Hamlet*. My marginal notes skew halfway through as I switch to my left hand. When Hamlet said 'the time is out of joint' I felt it in my body. I felt it non-metaphorically. I knew what time being out of joint really meant; how dire were its consequences.

*

On my medical record, my patella dislocations are listed as *dislocation of knee NOS*. I google *NOS*. Does it mean No Other Symptoms? Not Offered Sympathy? No Ordinary Suspect?

No. It means *Not Otherwise Specified*.

It is a way of placing you on a code, of making your injury legible, of making it fit into a prescribed narrative.

Not Otherwise Specified means you have no place in prescribed narrative.

It reminds me of the first time a doctor listened to me when I told him about the devastating dizziness and nausea I was experiencing, and he wrote me a doctor's note which said 'dizziness of unknown aetiology'. Dizziness of unknown biological cause.

There are symptoms, but they are disconnected from meaning. They cannot be rearranged into sense.

After my first *dislocation of knee NOS*, I began to dream about dislocations. As in my waking life, they would interrupt the normal process of the dream. One moment I would be walking, or flying, or having a sword fight, the next I would be cradling my useless kneecap in my palm like a cracked egg or a fallen fledgling. Sleep replaced my kneecaps with landslide debris, with stones tumbling from the ridge of decaying drystone walls: repositioning myself as old stone, as a geological feature. I would wake up petrified.

Over the years, I realised I had The Knee Dream most frequently when my joints were at their loosest, and learnt to treat it as an early warning sign: a reminder to do my exercises, to pay attention to the way I was moving. This gave me an illusion of control, at least, and kept down the terror of that crater of skin. I reconstructed myself, stone by crumbling stone.

*

In 2006 I moved from London to Lancaster, a town I knew nothing of. I had been in London for seven years: all my adult life away from home. All my friends were there. All my sense of myself as an independent person was there. I moved to begin doctoral research on Dove Cottage in Grasmere, the house where Dorothy Wordsworth lived with her brother William and his family from 1800 to 1808. The move was dislocating, but not in the way I was used to.

For the first nine months, before my field research rehomed me in Grasmere, I lived alone in an old silk mill worker's cottage a few miles from Lancaster, in a place I had no ties to and no previous knowledge of. It was the first time I had ever lived by myself. Living alone, on the out-skirts of a town I didn't know, forced me to think about my relationship with place and with myself and my body in a new way. The cottage was a twenty-minute amble downhill from the university, which is one of the reasons I chose it. When I recall living there, I find myself midway on the walk to or from campus. I walked past a small industrial estate in the old silk mill, past cows in a low field, past cottages and Victorian villas, and a small, towerless church and its graves. After years in London, where there is always a shop or take-away open, always a bus running if not a Tube, this new place with its handful of buses a day and shops that shut up before dark in winter was like moving to a different time, as much as place. It worked on different time, or time worked differently there.

When I moved to Grasmere the following spring, for the first time in my life I felt – suddenly and irrevocably – *in* place. Just like a joint clicking back into its socket. Only this time the socket was the landscape, the world. My body the joint. Seamus Heaney once described Dove Cottage as 'socketed into the hillside like an elemental power point' and that's how I felt in Grasmere.[6] I'd been plugged in. I felt a sense of locatedness I had never previously imagined, and a sense of connection with where I was physically that I did not know was possible.

I also felt physically stronger, more coherent, than I could remember feeling. I didn't feel *normal*, but I felt *possible*.

The research I had to do in Grasmere was about Grasmere. My research was on how meaning is created around place through different activities, including writing, but also walking, gardening, tourism, and just being in a place.

The core of my project was to trace how the 'little unsuspected paradise' the poet Thomas Gray described when he visited Grasmere in 1769 became the cultural centre and hub of tourist activity it is today, the kind of place doctoral students might go to study. My hypothesis was all about William Wordsworth, and the adoration of William Wordsworth, but it was Thomas De Quincey who helped me understand my place here.

Like me, De Quincey had left London for Grasmere because of William Wordsworth. De Quincey wrote *Confessions of an English Opium-Eater* whilst living in Dove Cottage, just a few doors down from my first home here, and my current one. *Confessions of an English Opium-Eater* is considered the first memoir of addiction, recording and describing De Quincey's opium use, and its effects on his body and mind over time. He had come to live here to follow in the footsteps of William, whom he thought not only a brilliant writer, but a person who had somehow unlocked the key to living a good, happy and healthy life. Imagined through his poetry, De Quincey sees William's as 'a life of unclouded happiness'. He thinks that by moving to Grasmere, he might become happy too.

In the *Confessions*, De Quincey recalls his 'first mournful abode in London', and how he would dream of escaping to the North:

> my consolation was (if such it could be thought) to gaze from Oxford Street up every avenue in succession which pierces through the heart of Marylebone to the fields and the woods; for *that*, said I, travelling with my eyes up the long vistas which lay part in light and part in shade, '*that* is the road to the North and therefore to -----, and if I had the wings of a dove, *that* way I would fly for comfort.[7]

The blank could be Grasmere, or William, or both. In the 1856 edition 'Grasmere' is filled in, but he admits it did not bring the happiness he imagined: 'in that very northern region it was, even in that very valley, nay, that very house to which my erroneous wishes pointed, that this second birth of my sufferings began'.[8]

I didn't share De Quincey's misery or his hope. I had a vague idea that I wanted to move to Scotland, not the Lake District, but like De Quincey, when I saw Grasmere I fell in love.

My first night in Grasmere I slept at the Glenthorne Guest House, part way up Easedale Road, connected to the village centre by a footpath through fields. I had driven up from London via Nottingham for an interview. I had in my mind the words of one of my MA tutors when I had asked for feedback on a failed application to continue studying there, that I needed to take time outside academia. That I wasn't ready. I was sure he was wrong. I was also sure he'd forgotten I'd already taken time out, but I couldn't get rid of the echo of him. How he'd said I was stuck in the grey places in my mind.

It was mid-July, and it was hot. I stopped at a motorway service station halfway for lunch and, looking for somewhere to perch to eat away from the stuffy buildings, I found a white horse, shaking its mane in a field in the sun. It seemed to promise something to me, something about room to move.

That night I sat on the hotel lawn, shivering in the clear cool air, dazed by the stars. The next morning I woke up to the bleating of sheep at my window, and the whole valley shimmering in heat. I was already in love before I had chosen which shirt to wear.

The humanist geographer Yi-Fu Tuan coined the term *topophilia* – love of place – to describe just this kind of feeling.[9] He recognised how 'we can have a strong feeling for a place, not just a visual appreciation or abstract understanding of it, even though no complex experiencing is possible', that we can fall in love with places at first sight.[10] I knew nothing about Grasmere, about what it would mean to live there, but I knew I wanted it more than anything. I knew it would change my life. Like De Quincey, I swear I could feel it already changing, changed.

When you spend four years studying something – reading it over and over again, picking it apart – it inevitably becomes part of your thinking. Part of the way you see things and understand them. I understood Grasmere and the Lake District differently through De Quincey, through his eyes and words and his own experiences. I understood my love for them differently. But I also understood other things about myself.

*

In his 1856 revisions to *Confessions* De Quincey traces his preoccupation with the Lake District back to his early childhood, describing how

> That little mountainous district, lying stretched like a pavilion between four well-known points . . . had for me a secret fascination, subtle, sweet, fantastic, and even from my seventh or eighth year, spiritually strong.

He describes a sense of 'mystic privilege' in knowing, as a child, that part of this region lay in 'the upper chamber of Furness', which at that time was still part of Lancashire, his home county. This lets him think of this 'fairy little domain of the English Lakes' as a kind of magical garden outpost of Greater Manchester.

De Quincey's Grasmere is a place imagined in childhood, then re-imagined and re-seen as a teenager through reading Wordsworth's poetry. His fascination with the poet and his life becomes impossible to disentangle from his thoughts and feelings about the lakes. So when De Quincey writes in 1856 that it was the 'deep deep magnet [. . .] of Wordsworth' that made him want to escape his school in Manchester for the Lakes as a teenager, he is writing not so much of wanting to escape to a real place, but into a realm of imaginative possibility – that fairy dominion – the only place one could achieve a life of unclouded happiness.

It didn't surprise me when I began to realise the place I'd made my home, that I'd fallen in love with on first sight like something from a fairytale, had an uncanny history not only of enchantments, but of hauntings. Even in William Wordsworth's poetry, read so often as clunkingly realist in its preoccupation with real flowers in real earth, there is another Grasmere, one far stranger and wilder, buzzing with magic and fairies and places folded into other places. It was this Grasmere I unintentionally fell in love with – one where the normal laws of space and time don't apply, one where distant places are folded into woods and lakes, where the veil between worlds is thin.

*

I have two other recurring nightmares which have endured through my adult life: The Tooth Dream, in which, with various degrees of bloodiness, my teeth are falling out, and The Worm Dream, in which I realise my body is infested with parasites which must be drawn out. The Tooth Dream, I once read, is a common anxiety dream, and is meant to be to do with a fear of change, as we lose teeth at pivotal moments in our lives.

For me, it was more literal. Between the ages of ten and fourteen I had a significant number of teeth extracted. When my adult teeth started to come through, there was not enough room for them in my mouth. I have large teeth and a small jaw. Or this is what I was always told. There was a time I had two rows of teeth, like The Alien. I had so many teeth pulled that the wait at the dentists, the horror of the injections into the thin gum tissue, browsing the video shop down the road oozing blood into the cotton lozenges, and the long wait through a couple of films for the bleeding to stop, seems like something I was doing every week. Even now, my teeth are continually regrouping, piling in on themselves, becoming more and more crooked. They want to be parallel to my jaw, not at right angles to it. They want to spoon each other, not stand side-by-side in a neat line.

Now I know my tooth overcrowding is a product of the marfanoid body habitus, a particular body shape associated with Marfan syndrome, a connective tissue disorder related to EDS. Many people with EDS have features of the distinctive Marfan body shape, and it is part of the diagnostic criteria. To test for the marfanoid body habitus, parts of your body are measured against each other, and if the ratio between them is out of the normal range, it means you are marfanoid. In other words, being disproportionate to yourself is the sign.

Dislocation

Picture Leonardo da Vinci's sketch of 'Vitruvian Man': his spread limbs encompassed in a circle showing how every part of the body relates to another part in size. Da Vinci's drawing, fully called, 'The proportions of the human body according to Vitruvius', illustrates the Roman architect Vitruvius' theories of the geometry of the human body. Da Vinci's notes from Vitruvius surround the figure of the man. Together, the drawing and notes are known as the canon of proportions: they tell us what it is to be human, and how the proportions of the human body are reflected in the construction of everything in the known universe.

You would not think of Marfans to look at me. I am short and curvy. Marfans people are long and thin. Their bones shine through. They have *arachnodactyly* which translates as *spider fingers*. As a child, I knew someone who was diagnosed with Marfans late in life, and it is him I still think of when I think of Marfans. It is his figure – so tall and thin it seemed insupportable – that I think of.

When I was measured against the canon of proportions I was found distinctly disproportionate, but only in part. My arms, as I already knew, are much longer than they should be. So much so, the doctor measured them twice. The span of your arms should equal your height, or thereabouts. My arm span is 10 cm greater than my height. In my diagnosis letter this becomes 'a markedly elevated span-height ratio'. No wonder I have never been able to find sleeves to cover my wrists. I have elongated palms, but no spider fingers. I have the differently shaped mouth – the high narrow palate – and its dental overcrowding, and a 'mild just significant' curvature of the spine. The letter reads 'interpret these features as indicative of an incomplete marfanoid habitus'. I am part-Marfan, incomplete in my ascension, like a cartoon of a teenager mid-growth-spurt, or a shapeshifter part-transformed, completely out of sync with myself. No wonder I feel so awkward.

In deviating from this canon of proportions, do we deviate from what is human? Do we redefine the symmetry? The test for the marfanoid body habitus is a way of checking how far outside the normal bounds of humanity you are – not just how far you fall from the Golden Mean, and all its notions of perfection and beauty. It is a way of being dislocated, not just from yourself, but from your species.

Not long after I was asked to stand against the wall for my arms to be measured against a notion of humanity, I was sitting in my living room in Grasmere, reading the opening of Ben Lerner's novel *10:04*, and was shocked to find the same process described there. I had never heard of such a diagnostic procedure before it had been done to me, I had never known that the canon of proportions could be used this way, and here it was, in a novel. Lerner's protagonist has to go to the hospital to be measured, to have Marfan syndrome confirmed or denied, because an issue with his heart has been detected. In the book's blurb, Marfans is not mentioned, only a heart condition, a strange elision of the novel's commitment to specificity. Throughout the chapter, images of an octopus reoccur, a creature we're told 'decorates its lair, has been observed at complex play'. In the opening paragraph the narrator admits to having just eaten an octopus at a celebratory lunch with his agent, despite knowing it is capable of creativity, despite knowing 'the first intact head [he] had ever consumed' may have been capable of theory of mind. After the lunch, he finds his perception altered, or half believes it is:

> I am kidding and I am not kidding when I say that I in-
> tuited an alien intelligence, felt subject to a succession of
> images, sensations, memories, and affects that did not,
> properly speaking, belong to me: the ability to perceive
> polarised light; a conflation of taste and touch as salt was
> rubbed into the suction cups; a terror located in my ex-
> tremities, bypassing the brain completely.[11]

Through eating the octopus, he has become and not become the octopus. His sense of self and location within himself are completely disrupted. In this disruption, the ways he can know the world are altered too: his nervous system is no longer centralised.

It is a joke. It is not a joke. It sticks. The room where he goes to be measured has an octopus painted on the wall, part of a children's ward mural; he sees himself sitting 'underwater' throughout the consultation. The process of being measured leaves him feeling as though his limbs 'had multiplied'. He supposes that his altered connective tissues create an altered sense of the self not only in space but in time. He hypothesises that his body, with its non-normative dimensions, cannot understand the world around him properly. The subject switches between 'me' and 'it', and, as octopus–narrator, he finds he cannot integrate sensory information, he 'cannot read the realistic fiction the world appears to be'.[12] He can make narrative sense neither of the world, nor his place in it.

When I first read this the buzz of recognition overwhelmed me to the point I had to stop reading. The marfanoid body was also me, the reader. I was the octopus. I was the narrator. It was possible to be both or neither.

The realistic fiction the world appears to be. One of those phrases that made me make some kind of strange sound aloud. That is it, yes. To feel oneself unable to feel oneself in space is to be sure of one thing: the solidity of the shared world is a lie. There is no consensus reality. When we enter a place, we each enter a different place, overlayered. The space your body inhabits is not the same space mine is dislocated from.

Under the diagnostic gaze, Lerner's protagonist becomes fragmented, split into parts that are not tied to the central self. He sees that 'those parts were coming to possess a terrible neurological autonomy not only spatial but temporal, my future collapsing in upon myself as each contraction expanded, however infinitesimally, the overly flexible tubing of my heart'. Is this just a way of saying that in that moment of uncertain diagnosis, his heart held the answer to his fate? His body is Schrödinger's cat, simultaneously canonically perfect and marfanoid. His heart is simultaneously fatally affected, and adequately proportioned. Almost dead, and safely alive. Or is it more, that a non-centralised sense of self is a dislocated self, unable to be fixed in place, since place is a lie – a realistic fiction – and so unable to exist in time?

This 'terrible neurological autonomy not only spatial but temporal' creates a kind of enfolding of his own timeline. He is able to reflect: 'including myself, I was older and younger than everyone in the room'. For Lerner's narrator, this dissociation from time both collapses the future, and creates endless possibility. He is reminded of Marty McFly in *Back to the Future*, seeing his hand fade after he changes his past, leaving him dislocated from his own future present, and, ultimately, undone.

Within Lerner's novel we never find out if the protagonist actually has Marfan syndrome or not. In some ways Marfans is forgotten in the later chapters, except the narrator takes a writing residency in a town called Marfa, which seems to be a sign in itself. Lerner is known for blending biography with fiction in his writing, and the notes and acknowledgements give us some clues. They confirm that the residency in Marfa is a real residency that the real person, Ben Lerner, held, and the poem he writes there in the book is a real poem he wrote and had published. But what is realistic fiction and what is real? With my own diagnostic gaze on red alert and that octopodal recognition, I convinced myself that the hidden narrative of the novel was Ehlers-Danlos – not Marfan – syndrome, so desperate was I to see myself represented somewhere.

I was so used to being outside the narrative: the octopus, not the human. Dawn Rothe has argued that 'illness, and perhaps particularly chronic illness, can be analysed in terms of its (dis)locations/locatedness' where 'locatedness' comes to represent both 'a material dis-location from society and also a metaphorical capturing of how people with chronic illness, particularly those with mental illness, are placed outside the category of legitimate social beings'.[13] Physically, bodily dislocated, socially dislocated, dehumanised. This is living outside the canon of proportions.

*

My childhood tooth extractions were compounded by other symptoms of my undiagnosed condition: slow blood clotting; poor healing; resistance to anaesthetic. They became a normalised horror for me: something terrible, but which I accepted as part of my routine. In The Tooth Dream there was rarely anything routine. It differed in detail in each incidence. As with The Knee Dream, it often interrupted a perfectly routine dream narrative. It was rarely the primary plot. I would be going about my dream business, as myself or someone else quite different, and suddenly my teeth would be dropping out of my mouth like hail, or pouring out in a fountain of blood, or quietly slipping one by one from their sockets like spiders from the ceiling. One time, as they hit my palm, they turned into sugar glass. The last one to come out was shaped like a star. This is the only time I have realised I was in a dream whilst dreaming, and pulled myself out of it, like a bad tooth.

Sometimes The Tooth Dream transforms my mouth into a feature of the landscape. My gums become a henge; my teeth standing stones that have fallen long since or are crumbling away or turfed over. My mouth is an ancient monument. My teeth are megaliths etched with spirals whose meaning has been lost for millennia. They have been dragged into the field of my jaw from somewhere so far away their unlikely appearance will baffle generations to come.

The worst variations of The Tooth Dream I remember so vividly I might have just woken out of them this second. Their horror is still fresh, as with so many of my dreams. The harbour town I visited year by year as centuries came and went there; the time my head was severed in a warehouse and I crossed over to play the piano on the other side, whatever I understood by that; the time I was a swashbuckling buccaneer and the credits rolled over the final sword fight, on a sea-girt rock; the time my brother died midway through my chemistry exams. I still remember conversations I had in dreams decades ago.

I have written about these dreams often, because I find them hard to shake off. Making them into poems helps. It puts some of the power of the images outwith myself. Often, I find myself about to mention something to someone that happened recently then realise, as I begin to say it aloud, that it happened in a dream. It is difficult to tell. My dreams seem very real. My life can feel very surreal.

When I was a teenager and first really ill, I began to get what I described as 'feelings of unreality'. Feelings that the world was not quite solid, which made my vivid dreams even harder to separate from waking life. I would look at the sky, and see specks like atoms. They moved in waves or murmurations. I felt I was seeing a different level of reality, deeper into the stuff of things than everyone around me. Since my diagnoses I've wondered if these feelings of unreality were a warning sign of the damage being done to my body and my processing systems, the dissociative effects of changes to my nervous system, a kind of migraine aura or simply the effects of extreme fatigue and pain. Damage to my brain, or my ocular nerves. What I do know is how it made me feel: out of joint with reality.

This is central to my sense of self. Being, feeling, completely out of joint.

*

Dislocation

De Quincey understood about dreams, about dreaming, about how very real they were, and how hard to climb out of. He also understood how untrustworthy the world is, and all its fake certainty about place, and most of all, that we cannot take for granted the realistic fiction the world seems to be.

In De Quincey's dreams, distant places are juxtaposed and distant times are made co-present. They look outward to actual and imagined geographies near and far, and inward into the landscapes of the mind. The scenes they offer seem both real, and impossible. To dream is to go down into another place. He records, 'I seemed to descend into chasms and sunless abysses, depths below depths, from which it seemed hopeless that I could ever reascend. Nor did I, by waking, feel that I *had* reascended.'

In the *Confessions*, De Quincey classifies the dream as including 'waking or sleeping, day-dreams or night-dreams'; 'apparitions' of 'all sorts of phantoms' he sees whilst lying 'awake in bed'; 'nightly spectacles' within sleep; and even a 'mysterious sense of pre-existence' he describes at one point, imagining his future life. In describing his dreams De Quincey makes note of their distortion of time and space, which overflowed into his waking life:

> The sense of space, and in the end, the sense of time, were both powerfully affected. Buildings, landscapes &c, were exhibited in proportions so vast as the bodily eye is not fitted to receive. Space swelled, and was amplified to an extent of inutterable infinity.

He describes the 'vast expansion of time' his dreams create so that he 'seemed to have lived for 70 or 100 years in one night', or that a millennium might pass in one dream.

Doesn't this sound like what Lerner is trying to say about the marfanoid body? That, like a dream, it collapses space and time? Later in that first chapter Lerner describes 'an increasingly frequent vertiginous sensation' when he looks at a familiar object in his hand, when it becomes suddenly alien, and the hand with it. He calls this 'a condition brought on by the intuition of spatial and temporal collapse' or rather 'an overwhelming sense of its sudden integration'.[14]

Not only is it impossible now to tell the difference between the waking dream and the real, or the sleeping dream and the waking dream, it is impossible to tell the effect of spatial and temporal collapse – the undoing of space and time – from their integration – all spaces and times overlayed at once.

*

From our earliest days we are taught to recognise five senses – sight, taste, smell, touch and hearing. We learn to navigate the world by them, by using our perception. Perception is the ability to become aware of something through a sense or senses. It comes into English in the late fourteenth century from the latin *perceptio*; a receiving or collection. In the seventeenth century *perception* starts to be used more to mean, as we most often do, an 'understanding'. Perception is understanding; it is receiving information and collecting it. We build our worlds from it.

There are many more than five recognised senses – excluding the mysterious sixth one – the more mundane ones, like *thermo ception*, the sense of temperature, or *equilibrioception*, the sense of balance, or *nociception*, the sense of pain. These senses are known as the *exteroceptive* senses – extero because they are exterior to ourselves – they are activated by something outside our bodies and our control. We understand the external world, and our place in that world, through these externally activated senses. *Intero- ceptive* senses are the opposite – senses activated by stimuli within the body. Interoception is our sense of our internal weather.

Proprioception is the sense that tells us about our body in relation to other bodies – to other objects in the external world. It tells us how our limbs are moving in the spaces of the world; it tells us how they are moving in relation to the spaces of our bodies. It tells us how far one part of our body is from another part of our own body, and how far that is from a door frame, or chair, or rock, or cliff-edge. Proprioception is what enables us to steer our bodies through the sensory world. *Proprio* comes from the latin *proprius* meaning 'one's own', or 'particular to itself'. *Proprioception* is an interface between the external and internal. It is self-perception. It is self-reception.

When a doctor asks you to close your eyes and touch the tip of your nose with your index finger, they are checking your proprioception. When they ask you to run your heel down your shin, they are testing your proprioception. You may have never heard of it, but it is what enables you to function in our complex, ever-changing habitats. It is what allows you to negotiate the realistic fiction of the world.

Proprioception is about knowing the self through the relationship between the self and the non-self. Self and Other. The relationships between different parts of ourselves in a world that is not ourselves. Proprioception depends on knowing the difference between self and non-self, on recognising boundaries and barriers, on recognising the distance between them, on working out like and not-like.

I have never been very good at telling where I end and other things begin. When I was fifteen and learnt about nanomolecules I thought the world made sense finally. Or my experience of the world, my body in it, made sense. On a nanomolecular level, we aren't solid, discrete objects at all, but fuzzy at the edges, permanently blurring into and exchanging nanoparticles with everything around us. The formulation I remember learning is this: when you lean on a table it might look as though the hand and table are solid and separate, that one is resting on top of the other, but the nanoparticles of each are in a haze of inbetweenness. Of indeterminacy. Your hand is really partly in the table and the table is really partly in you. This is how I feel about everything that is meant to be external. The grass under my bare feet, the deer at the edge of the woods. Where do I stop and they begin? How do I separate enough to move safely alongside them?

Often, I lose proprioception walking down stairs. I have the sense of myself as footless, suddenly, or the stairs as a viscous liquid, or a treacherous cakewalk in an old-fashioned fairground. I find myself clinging onto the banister, inching one step, one leg at a time, and not just because of the pain of bending each joint. It is worse in low light, or if my senses are otherwise disrupted. It is linked to a feeling I sometimes get that I am walking not on the ground, but a few feet above it, like a ghost, or else a few feet below it, as though the ground is the ghost, and I am dragging through its shallow sludge. Neither of these is as bad as the times the ground seems to be swaying or rocking as I stumble over it. At those times, nothing is reliably solid, or stays where you think it should be. Nothing is at all reliable about the world when your proprioception is altered.

All three of these terms – extero-, intero- and proprioception – were developed by Charles Scott Sherrington at the turn of the twentieth century. Sherrington gave us the language we use to describe the nervous system, from neurons to synapses. He recognised the complex nature of the nervous system, proving its 'integrated action'. To do so, he experimented on animals: on cats, dogs, monkeys and apes.

This was not unusual. He was better at it than his peers. He found that, despite the removal of portions of their brains, they were able to remain upright against gravity. He recognised that this was because of responses in their muscles and nerve cells – in the proprioceptors in their tissues. He perceived this. Even when the nerves that would help them place themselves were severed, he found that they could still stand, even when they couldn't feel the ground. They didn't need to *feel* where they were; proprioception allowed them to sense it through means other than touch.

The same happens in reverse of course. When proprioception fails, you don't know which way is up, even if you can feel the ground beneath your paws.

In *The Worst of Evils: The Fight Against Pain*, Thomas Dormandy footnotes his biography of Sherrington with the declaration:

> Such a paragon should be beyond criticism; but the present writer would be untrue to himself if he failed to mention that Sherrington's 'decerebrate cat' and other classical 'preparations' (reproduced for decades in every textbook of physiology), showing cats in different attitudes of spastic and flaccid paralysis after having different parts of their central nervous system sectioned or extirpated, has always filled him with horror.[15]

Dormandy means Sherrington paralysed and semi-paralysed cats to open his doors of perception. He cut out essential parts of their nervous systems to study the effect. The perception of pain comes out of pain. Dormandy means that this causes him pain. Emotional pain, of course, not like that of the cats.

My altered proprioception is compounded by altered sensation in my hands and feet. I know they're there, but I can't really feel them, not properly, not like they belong to me. It is like in chemistry class, when you put your hands in the safety gloves in the cabinet to do an experiment. The double hands seem to move at a slight delay, awkwardly, with less finesse than your own hands would, even though it is your own hands moving them, directing them, inside them. That is how I feel about my own body. I don't really feel it properly: I am moving it, but it is not me. It is a clumsy puppet, and I am a bad puppeteer.

Some days it is worse than others. Sometimes I feel like I'm moving through a misaligned copy of the world, where everything appears to be a few inches over from where it really is, which is why I keep bumping into the real object. My copy is a bad copy. Other times it is clear it is me who is out of place, misaligned.

When I am feeling particularly bad, and people ask, 'How are you?' I have long since stopped lying and saying, 'Fine.' Often, I say, 'Still standing.' Since reading about Sherrington's experiments, I can't help picturing myself as a decerebrate cat. I might not know where the walls are, or be able to feel my extremities or where they are in space, but if I'm lucky I can still stand up through it.

*

When I was a child and couldn't sleep I would read my mum's books of Scottish folktales in bed. I learnt about the Faery Queen, and true speech as a poison gift. I learnt about how time works differently in different places. I learnt about selkies, how they would put off their seal skins to become like humans, and how some would fall in love and some would have children with humans. How sometimes the human would try to keep them on land by hiding their skin, and how it made the selkie man or woman so sad. They were stuck, neither one thing nor another. They had given up their world, their family and culture, or it had been taken from them. Sometimes they were tricked. Love became a prison forbidding them from returning to their first life. On land they were always pretending to be like the other people around them, but they weren't. They longed for the sea, to be at ease in the water, to be quick and agile and beautiful in their protective skins. I knew exactly how they felt. The land was always trying to hurt you and trick you, to pull you down or push you over. Water held you up, let you glide.

I learnt the signs. How to recognise a selkie, beyond their pining for the sea. Some had calloused fingertips where their seal skin was once attached, some had webs between their fingers and toes. These could be passed on generation to generation, so you could tell if your ancestor was a selkie if you carried the sign, even watered down. I lay with my folktales under the covers, shining a torch through the low webs between my fingers, turning the light on and off to watch my hand go from human to something else. The glow through the extra curves of skin orange as the street lamp glow on the other side of the house. The blood suddenly unhidden.

I might be a disaster on land, but in the water I was a wonder. I felt like a different creature in the water. I began to think I might not be a failed human but something else – I might belong to something magical, something ancient and beautiful.

When I read Susan Cooper's novel *Seaward* I began to think the legacy might not be lost. I could still, perhaps, go back to the water. In the story, Cally is trying to make sense of her place in the world after her mother's death. In the second chapter Cooper describes Cally's 'strangely marked' palms, shared by her mother, how her mother had described it as 'an obscure inherited disease'.[16] I knew what this meant right away. The marks on the hands were the sign of a selkie, and it could be passed on, mother to daughter. You did not have to be born in the sea to belong to the sea. Cally had to make a choice, in the end, to join her mother's people and become a seal, which would mean stepping outside time for ever, or to return to the human world, and human time. I found it unbearably sad that she didn't swim away with them, that she gave up her seal life and became just a girl. When she chooses, her palms change – the 'thick horny skin of the selkie' is magicked away as though it was never part of her.[17] She is told 'there is no right or wrong, here. There are only different ways of living', but it felt like such a loss to me. The cost of being normal too high. Why did they make her choose?

My best friend and I knew what it meant to be water creatures. In between watching *Watership Down* and *The Land Before Time* to make ourselves weep, pausing the tape over and over to sketch our favourite scenes, we lived in another element. When we weren't rabbits or being chased by wolves or held captive by giants in the house which had a different hazard in every room – the collapsing stairs, the lava carpet – we were our best selves. We were mermaids all summer every summer. We developed our own stroke, based on our extensive research in *Splash* and *The Little Mermaid*. We called it Mermaid Stroke and practised it for long hours: pushing off from the side underwater, with our arms elegantly pointed ahead of us, until it was time to draw them down to our sides, and waft our hands gently like fins, as our legs and bodies undulated in a form of underwater butterfly. Soon we could do whole lengths of it. We felt our tails, our scales as we soared through the depths. But I knew in my heart what no one quite said out loud. She, with her long fair hair and her natural grace, was the mermaid. When she stepped out of the water and her legs grew, her legs were lithe and obedient. They went where she wanted them to. I was what I always had been: plump, unwieldy, loud and quiet in the wrong ways at the wrong times entirely. Human in the eyes only, and only almost. Uncannily not quite a girl. Not in control. A seal. A selkie. Something from another place and time.

*

I am swooping through water the clouded turquoise of sea-glass when a dark shape glides alongside me for a moment. I recoil instantly, kick to the surface, panicked like someone in a shark attack film.

I turn around and around looking for a sign of my companion. When they surface, they are already metres away, just a head like a rock rising out of the still water, only notable because there was no rock there earlier. We watch each other for a minute, then they dive, and are gone.

I am the only human swimmer in this island bay on this overcast autumn afternoon. It is unspeakably beautiful – green turf edged by smooth grey rocks like sleeping animals around a small curved bay of silver sand. The water is calm. A couple of small white yachts are anchored at the edge of the bay, their reflections in the sea unbroken.

W sits on rocks at the side of the bay, reading and drinking tea from a flask, wrapped up in a jumper. The water is cold, but not freezing. I paced up and down in the shallows, looking at all the shells and scuttling crabs on the sea floor, until my legs and feet acclimatised, and I dove in. I slip under water and back to the surface, over and again, enjoying the novelty of salt water. It doesn't take long until I am comfortable enough that I don't want to get out. But I know we only have an hour and a half before the last ferry back to the mainland, and there is no option to miss it.

I am swimming in a long-sleeved, leg-less wetsuit I call Fat Seal Suit – named because when I first bought it I thought the black glideskin on my belly made me look like a glossy, well-fed seal. It was my first experiment in wetsuits, and is still in many ways my favourite. It is meant to be a spring suit for surfers, but it helped me expand my swimming season from fine days from May to October to all weathers, all year. It is easy to slip into, not too heavy to carry when wet. I got it for a good price in a sale so I don't worry too much about ruining it. It is battered and patched up, but still gives me just enough extra fortitude to be able to put my shoulders under on a day like today.

I always thought – in a childish, unexamined way – that if a seal approached me in the water I would feel its kinship. Haven't I always been waiting for them to claim me? When it happens, I shrink back in fear. Before I realise it is a seal it is nothing but shadow and unnamed fierceness, potential harm. My fear in turn repels it. I am disappointed in my fear, but I understand something from it. I am much more human than I think. I do not want to let go of my humanness. I cannot let it go.

*

In her 1926 essay *On Being Ill*, Virginia Woolf shows us a whirring world of healthy activity, progressing towards a definite goal. Life as endurance test. Unable to compete, the ill fall by the sidelines. When we are ill 'we cease to be soldiers in the army of the upright; we become deserters'.[18] Fifty-three years later, in *Illness as Metaphor* Susan Sontag writes of 'the kingdom of the well and [. . .] the kingdom of the sick' and the movement between them: 'although we all prefer to use only the good passport' we are all 'obliged' at some point to cross the border.[19] She calls illness 'the night-side of life, a more onerous citizenship'. Illness is not a state of *being*, it is an actual State – an alternative realm of existence which runs parallel to that of the well. A night-side, shadow world.

Woolf calls these the 'undiscovered countries' of illness, land-scapes modelled not on solid, phenomenal geography, but on the impossible and improbable worlds of dreams and hallucinations: 'what wastes and deserts of the soul a slight attack of influenza brings to view, what precipices and lawns sprinkled with bright flowers a little rise of temperature reveals'.[20]

When Woolf writes 'what ancient and obdurate oaks are uprooted *in us* by the act of sickness' she has hit upon the secret of this otherworld's operation.[21] The unwell body is not simply 'the transmitter of all experience' but also the undiscovered country itself – the place where experience happens.[22] Like a dreamscape, these strange countries are not merely observed, but felt. We do not just become aware of our own mortality in illness, we 'go down into the pit of death and feel the waters of annihilation close above our heads'.[23] The features of this landscape are simultaneously external to us, and internal. They are not the seemingly inert things of the well and waking world.

The journey into the kingdom of the sick is a *katabasis* – a going down – a term used to refer in ancient literature to those trips to the underworld that heroes would take to learn what they needed to know, to fetch what they needed to fetch. Back then, the underworld was a geographically locatable place. Embodied, physical. Somewhere you could follow instructions or a map to, somewhere you could sail your ship to, and then climb down into through a cave, or follow a path to.

From my mum's books, I knew my Tam Lin and my Thomas the Rhymer before I read the *Odyssey*, or the *Aeneid*, long before I read *Gilgamesh*. When I did read them, I recognised their journeys to the underworld, the entrance being somewhere in the Scottish Borders, in my mother's family's country.

It has many names, many doorways. Faery. The Upside Down.

You go to a particular place, you cross a river. The river may be of blood, all the blood that's shed on earth.

For true *katabasis*, you must come back up, you must perform anabasis, otherwise you belong to that other realm forever, and that is called death.

All I know is that in every iteration it takes something from you, and if you take something from it – food, drink – you belong to it forever.

*

In 2004, after a failed quest for help for my body's struggles which ended with misdirections and misdiagnoses, I read Susanna Clarke's novel *Jonathan Strange & Mr Norrell*. I had come away from a medical odyssey with a prescription for low-dose amitriptyline and no further help. I took my pills, I slept, I felt a little better. I tried different diets. I adjusted to different pain. I tried to skip lightly over the despair bubbling up under me. But there was something strange about the sleep.

I began to understand myself as having a problem like the characters in the book, under the sway of the gentleman with the thistle-down hair. Not myself, not my own.

The gentleman with the thistle-down hair is a fairy but the characters in the book who see him do not recognise him at first as belonging to a different place, a different order. Why would they? Like a well person unable to imagine the illness place, the reality of his existence is inconceivable to them.

Stephen Black tells the gentleman with the thistle-down hair 'ever since I first visited your house I have been stupid and heavy. I am tired morning, noon and night and my life is a burden to me.'[24]

I read this and understood my problem. I too am tired morning, noon and night. My life is a burden to me.

Under his Faery enchantment, Stephen Black 'felt he was a person sleepwalking. He did not live anymore, he only dreamed'. He feels like he is dreaming in the day, and in the night, his waking can only be understood as dreams. He finds himself plagued by dreams, dreams in which real places from his daily life transform into uncanny versions of themselves, with extra staircases, and hallways, a spatial uncanny to equal De Quincey's:

> It was as if the house in Harley-street had accidentally got lodged inside a much larger and more ancient edifice. The passageways would be stone-vaulted and full of dust and shadows. The stairs and floors would be so worn and uneven that they would more resemble stones found in nature than architecture.[25]

The reader knows that these aren't dreams, but no one in the narrative understands why they seem to see ancient woodland creeping around buildings where it shouldn't be, or hear a bell tolling where there is no bell. Places are not what, where or when they seem.

Lady Pole has the same strange feeling, and ailment, but no one thinks to connect her bodily experiences to Stephen's. He himself reports 'she complains of aches in all her limbs, odd dreams and feeling cold. But mostly she is silent and out of spirits. Her skin is icy to the touch.'[26] But when he starts to feel the same, he is too dazed, too deep into the waking sleep to piece it together.

It is a long time before they are able to recognise each other, to know each other as sharing the same nightly dislodging, displacing, the same haunted half-present days.

I knew those days, I knew that feeling. It came as no surprise when I read that Susanna Clarke had been ill with a mystery bug when she began to work on *Jonathan Strange & Mr Norrell*, and that after publication she developed chronic fatigue. Only someone who knew what it felt like to live half in the underneath could have written like this, could have written 'the dreary landscape was suddenly very close, just beneath the skin of England'.[27]

I'd grown up on stories like these. The Twelve Dancing Princesses, Katie Crackernuts. Those stories had always rung a haunted bell with me because I knew exactly how the enchanted sleepers felt. I would wake exhausted, worn out from sleep. The puzzle was that my slippers were not worn down, no one followed me to the underneath, there was no sign I had been dancing all night, except the ill ease of my body. Except the bruises and the deep, deep fatigue.

I had written about Tam Lin and Thomas the Rhymer in my undergraduate dissertation, along with retellings I'd read as a child: Alan Garner's *Red Shift* and Diana Wynne Jones's *Fire and Hemlock,* which I had read so many times its Polly had become part of me. The way she was made to agree to forget her own story, the way she lived two lives: the real one, and the one she was tricked into accepting. The vases in the garden of Laurel, the Queen's house, how you could turn them to read Now/Here or Where/Now or No/Where or Here/Now.

I came to accept my dreams, my nightly excursion into the underworld – the daily remaking – as part of life in my particular body. After all, hadn't it always been like this, or at least, somewhat like this? Hadn't my sleeping life always interjected into my waking day? Hadn't I always been stuck sometimes, gazing into the memory of a scene I had dreamt, overlaid on the quotidian world? Hadn't I often found it hard to tell which was which, felt a shudder like subluxation when I realised something I thought was real had only been real in a dream?

It seemed to make sense that it would get worse with the years, that the longer you spend down there, the more they take of you – Hades, The Faery Queen, the gentleman – whichever iteration you are met with, whatever you call them. I didn't question it, as the nights became more and more real to me, and the days were veiled and distant.

Years passed like this. One, two, then five, then ten.

I am always either not sleeping at all, jolted awake continually by inappropriate bursts of adrenalin from a body too alert, or I am sleeping for ever, sleeping for Britain, sleeping as though it is the only competitive sport I have any chance at winning at, sleeping the sleep of the very almost dead, or at the least, the more than lightly enchanted.

Ten years of this strange, medicated sleep dream by. So much changes – where I live, how I live – so much has passed. Finally I have diagnoses that explain why I feel like I do, why I experience the world as I do. But still every day I take these small blue pills as though my continuation depends on them. Then my mum and one of my closest friends are both prescribed amitriptyline for back pain. Both report sensations of being unable to shift out of sleep. Diagnosis has given me a new sense I can take control. I consult my doctor, reduce my dose. My pain does not increase; my sleep does not lessen in quality. If anything, it feels less haunted. Over months, I reduce my dose to nothing.

I had given the other place ten years of my nights, my heavy mornings, and it didn't seem to be protecting me at all.

For a while I feel released from its hold, as much as I know it might claim rights over me. I tell myself it does not own me. But all I had done was close off one door of many. The other place is a world inside me, I carry with me wherever I go.

*

De Quincey haunts his own future, viewing himself as 'a phantom self – a second identity projected from my own consciousness', already living in Grasmere, years before he moves there. He claims presentiment not only of place, but of his life there, and its twists and turns, asking

> how was it, and by what prophetic instinct, that already I said to myself oftentimes, when chasing day-dreams along the pictures of these wild mountainous labyrinths, which as yet I had not traversed – Here, in some distant year, I shall be shaken with love, and there, with stormiest grief – whence was it that sudden revelations came upon me [of] scenes that made the future heaven of my life.[28]

In a kind of imaginative time travel, he claims to have 'rehearsed and lived over' this future life. In this account there are two young De Quinceys, one certain 'London would be the central region of [his] hopes and fears', and one already sure of 'Grasmere and its dependencies as knit up [. . .] with [his] future destinies'.[29] He both 'thought [he] *was* and yet in reality was *not* a denizen, already, in 1804–5, of lakes and forest lawns which [he] never saw till 1807'.[30] Just around the time that in the world of Jonathan Strange, Lady Pole lost her finger and began dancing her nights away in the Faery Kingdom at Lost Hope.

*

On Epiphany 2019 I am walking back down to the house from the woods, and I sense something moving in front of me on the road. It is dark. I stayed out too long and lost the light, talking to neighbours on the path through the trees as the grey day slipped away. The dark between the walls of our house and the wall on the far side of the road shifts, splitting into different textures of dark. I can sense it more than I can see it: a huge stag, waiting outside the house, separating me from it.

Dislocation

Before I have time to think, a car comes up the road behind him, just two glaring headlights in the dark. I try to wave at them to slow but they can't see me. They push up the road, impatient, forcing the stag to run right past me and over the wall, into the field between the old road and the lake.

The evening before, a red stag had been standing outside the bookshop in the village when W closed up for the night. Just standing in the street, watching the shop. A twelfth night vision. I know at once it must be the same deer.

A few days later he is seen at Faeryland, the tea garden by the lake.

I do not see him again until the following autumn, but when I do it is on the old turf path, the way up onto the common the roe deer showed me. The next day I see him with a hind, and young. He has brought his family to the common.

From then on I see them every now and again, when they let me, their faces proud and indignant every time I spot them. Sometimes I don't see them until they run from me. They are so huge compared to the roe deer – when they run it is like wild horses running. I feel the vibrations through our shared ground.

For two years I hold a kind of waking vision of the red deer under a particular oak tree in my head, like a dream I am remembering. In the vision it is snowing lightly. The tree is the most perfect dome, growing from a mossy pier of stone at the edge of a bog. I am quite in love with it, though I try not to let the other trees know. In my dream, I see the deer lying below the tree like greyhounds in a medieval tapestry, or like a tame unicorn.

On a bright afternoon in February 2021, W and I step down from the height of the common and there he is – the red stag under the oak. It is snowing, but so lightly it barely touches the ground. The winter sun is shining palely but brightly on the bare branches and the red bracken. And there he is, like a stone lion, a lion couchant, just where my vision placed him.

As we watch, he stands, hiding his antlers in the tree. His family stand too, unfolding themselves from the bracken, separating their red winter coats from its.

*

Illness, pain, fatigue – they are dislocating. You can be kneeling in bracken, watching a stag recline under a tree like a monument of itself, when your kneecap shifts slightly under your weight, and you are ten again, in an ambulance. You are floating over yourself in the stairwell of your childhood home. You are crying in your classroom. You are crying on the pavement. You are in a bay in an emergency department, too exhausted to cry.

Illness, pain and fatigue remove you from the place you know, and take you somewhere else, that other state, where the laws of space and time are altered. You are five minutes' walk from home or a thousand miles of pain away. Distances you knew to be small become vast. It takes you an hour to move from the bed to the bathroom, from the sofa to the kitchen. Except the other state is where you have been all the time. The place you are in is folded into or on top somehow of the place you were in. You have moved nowhere, but everything is different. Everything is the same. The kingdom of the sick and the kingdom of the well are an optical illusion. The old crone and the young beauty. We only elect to not see the sick one when we are well: no one wants to see the sick one unless they have to. You can see all the same things, all the same people. Except they seem to be very far away, like everything else, and everything has a kind of grey film over it, like dust sheets, but very, very fine. You think you must be dreaming it, but you aren't. This is reality. This is your place now. Only time knows if you will move between them, and we haven't got there yet.

*

De Quincey writes of his first experience of taking opium: 'what an apocalypse of the world within me!'[31]

He doesn't mean an undoing or an ending but the literal meaning of apocalypse – an unveiling of what was always there, but hidden.

Two hundred years later, Kathleen Jamie undergoes the same unveiling in a pathology lab, looking at slides of human tissue and seeing geological space, made suddenly aware of 'the unseen landscapes within' – a new frontier – 'strange new shores' enfolded within us all.[32]

In 1838, in her ninth year of ongoing illness, Dorothy Wordsworth writes to her niece Dora: 'My own thoughts are a wilderness.'[33] Does she mean that her thoughts are wild, unapproachable, untameable, unknowable?

There are those who think of wilderness as empty, untouched, other. Out of time. But there is no place on earth empty, no place undisturbed, no place which does not mean something to some breathing thing.

Wilderness was once the place of wild deer, uncultivated, uncivilised, undomesticated. But wilderness is not the opposite of civilisation. Wilderness has its own life, its own laws, its own society and social contract. Wilderness is the state of being wild in the way wild deer are wild. It is not uncivil to be wild, if to be wild is your gracious and affable nature.

The onerous citizenship is so often portrayed as a terrible fate – *onerous*, burdensome, heavy – but what if it is your life? What if those undiscovered countries are your brave new world? Is it so terrible? Is there a way to belong to both states at once, to carry dual citizenship, to live in both or move between? Is there a way that under kingdom can be good?

In her essay 'Welcome to the Kingdom of the Sick' Sonya Huber writes of the company of the sick, of taking solace in the onerous citizenship, in that strange other place. When 'that bright country of the well' is barred to her, 'only the kingdom of the ill is of comfort', the kingdom and its inhabitants: 'only the legion in the land of the ill offers comfort'.[34]

She repeats, three times, like a spell or a curse: 'When you have arrived, you have arrived. Welcome and blessings.'

To her neither the land nor its inhabitants are imaginary, or other: they are all of us, and 'the land is the most reliable and most vast of the human experience'. We all go there sooner or later: 'it is the borderland all bodies must pass through'.

Except it is not a borderland, it is a centre, or it is everything. It is both 'unfamiliar territory' in which we are suddenly aware of the body, suddenly at 'dis-ease', but also a 'vast bedrock' running under the familiar country of the well, the upright.

To get there, 'we have dropped down the well'. The language is of Faery, where the sick 'reel in a slow-motion dance, treading where others fear to tread, continuing to breathe in the postnormal existence'. Except it is not a captivity, nor 'a departure from the itinerary, not a battle, not a failure'. In Huber's vision the sick are active citizens of their other country, secure in the knowledge 'we cannot be invaded or defeated'.

Where are we going down into when we go into the kingdom of the sick? The underside of the earth, the deep cave systems of illness, a place so outside and beyond our experience we cannot even imagine it when we are well – or do we simply go deeper into ourselves, our own undiscovered countries? Illness not as exile, but as a ray of sudden sun, cutting through ancient trees, to light a landscape enveloped within us all along.

Welcome, and blessings.

I am not a deserter any more than I could be a soldier. My body has not made a choice to be my body. We simply are.

Letty McHugh writes in her *Book of Hours* about the potential held within the kingdom of the sick – what she calls 'the illness place' – 'the farthest edge of a universe that is always expanding'.[35] It is the place you go to 'when your body is such a terrible place to be that you need to send your mind as far away from it as you can'. To her, the illness place is not a location, but a portal dimension, buzzing with endless possibility. There is a multiverse of the illness place waiting to be explored:

> I'm telling myself the illness place is just one universe in a vast multiverse I can visit. Some of them are dark and scary, but some of them are bluebell filled woods on May afternoons, some are polluted waters, some are light-soaked and made of love.[36]

The illness place can be transportative, not restrictive. It is not a cave, but a corridor, a passage through. The wood between worlds. The doorway to everything else.

When I go to the other place that is the place of the sick, I am going into my own body, into its unseen landscapes and undiscovered countries. My own body is a wilderness. It has been a wilderness to me. But this is not a punishment or a curse. I can see the paths and I am not alone. I go down into my body and through it, into the expanding universe.

Oh what an apocalypse of the world within.

*

My problems with telling dreaming and waking apart meant that for several years of my childhood I thought I really did once know how to fly, and had simply forgotten as I became domesticated by the world of school, and rules about things like staying on the ground, and not floating away. I remember being eight and jumping off a low wall in the school playground, on a day when we had been making dancing ladies out of pairs of cherry blossoms. As my feet hit the ground and my ankles clunked out of and back into place, I remembered suddenly and vividly how I had once stepped up into the air off just such a wall, and kept climbing, kept climbing until I was swimming through the air. I still remember the memory, and the conviction I had in that moment that I was ground-bound because I had willingly forgotten. I had made a decision to unlearn. I had given flying up for a reason I couldn't understand. I must have given up the reason too.

Later, of course, I realised I was remembering a dream, not a real event. I knew, logically, I could never have flown up from that earlier wall and up over the houses of Nottingham, but even now what I remember most is the feeling of being sure it was true.

When I think of Grasmere I think of the place I know, of course – I think of my home, the lake, the woods and everything that lives in them – but I also think of the night I flew through it, a creature of the air not the land or water, soaring over the vale alongside a benign lion. I remember looking at the lion and his mane rustled in the wind, looking down at my hooves and realising I was the unicorn, and we were flying north together.

Diagnosis

On the first day of December 2021, I see a deer in the garden at the corner of the road up to the common. The garden belongs to a huge Victorian house divided up into holiday flats. The deer linger in the dense upper reaches of its rhododendron sprawl. At quiet times they repossess the lawn, grazing on daffodils and sticky buds in spring.

It takes me a moment in the low winter light to realise he is a buck and not a doe. His head is almost bare, two dark shiny coins where his antlers were and will be. His gaze back at me seems tired and curious more than scared. I feel like I'm looking at myself looking back at me.

Over the coming weeks I see him often, so often I begin to expect him when I walk out in the afternoon. I see him several times in the same spot on the common, his head poking up from where he rests in a sheltered nook on a mossy crag when I walk below him in the boggy gully. I watch his antlers grow from tiny stubs like cartoon bumps to fuzzed columns the height of his ears. They look like they've been dipped in cinnamon sugar. They look like your fingers would sink into them.

I begin to measure time by antler. In this bleakest part of the year their progress seems a kind of promise. Something is moving forward, something is growing.

As January turns to February his antlers fork into branches. I call him Two-Prongs. I am unreasonably proud of his antlers. I take photographs of him and share them online in the way people do of their grandchildren, their pets. Someone comments his two prongs look like furry mittens, and they do.

Sometimes he is alone, sometimes with a doe. I think of him as Bucky, her as Lady Swivel Ears, for the way she turns her ears like radar dishes to register my movement. By mid-February I have begun to think of them as my friends, though in truth they only tolerate me. At the very least, I think of us as neighbours. I have learnt their favourite places, where they like to eat, where they like to take a nap. I like to know they are there, and okay. I can walk right past them as they're eating and they barely even look up. I see them glance at me, glance at each other and agree oh, it's only that one, she's no threat, and carry on about their business. I am just another animal passing by. There is a reassurance in this, in this co-tenancy of the land, in this recognition.

I have built a whole narrative around these deer in my head. I see them every day. I think I know them. I think we have some kind of understanding.

Then on 22 February I see Bucky and Lady Swivel Ears three times on the same walk, in three separate, impossible places. I have been seeing three sets of deer and assuming they were one.

As soon as I know, it is obvious. They look completely different. They keep to their own territories, have their own habits. One has a much darker coat and is shyer than the others, one has a little bare triangle on his rump. One has distinctive plush coronets where his antlers meet his head and the pile of their velvet is particularly luxurious. Each has his own unmistakable personality. How could I have ever thought they were the same deer? How could I have been so fooled by my own presumption of knowledge?

All these weeks of mistaken identity, because I thought I knew what I was looking at. I saw what I already expected to see. I thought I was observing so carefully, but my observations only confirmed what I already believed.

*

Diagnosis

Diagnosis is like a wedding: not an end point, but a beginning. Diagnosis is a door opening on the rest of your life, and if the diagnosis is correct, when the door opens, behind it there will be the tools you need to make life manageable, or the chart that tells you where to go next to find what you need, or a whole new world to walk into.

When I was thirty-four, I was given a diagnosis that changed my entire life, before it, and after it. It made everything after it possible. It made everything before it comprehensible, in a way that had never seemed possible. I could understand my own life, my own body. My own story.

To diagnose is to distinguish one thing from another, to discern, to know thoroughly. You have to ask the right question to get the right answer. This is as true of the human body as it is of the earth. It is as true of a human as a plant that won't thrive, of a sick person or a poisoned lake. Sometimes it is the whole system at fault, sometimes it is one element out of balance you have not even considered. The rhododendron that chokes the forest floor, the blackout blind of algal bloom that throws the water into darkness.

You can only diagnose a condition if you are aware it exists in the first place, and if you have an idea of what its presentation might be. You have to believe there is a right question to ask. You have to believe there is an answer.

*

On 14 October 2014 I took a train down to London from my home in Cumbria. I was excited, and terrified. I was going to meet the man who might be able to explain me to myself. But I knew better than that, didn't I? I knew not to be too hopeful.

I was staying the night with one of my dearest friends, who I had lived with before I left London to come north eight years before. Then I would go to the appointment, before taking the train up to Glasgow, where I would be teaching the next day.

I was less than a month into my first full-time academic job. It was a proper lectureship, though only for a fixed-term of three years, replacing a more senior member of staff whilst they held a research grant. It was the first time I would be earning over the graduate wage, and I was thirty-four now. I had worked so hard to get to this point, and I should have been delighted to be there, after years of squeezing multiple part-time jobs into too-few hours, odd days of housekeeping in hotels to fill the gaps, applying for every lectureship or research role that came up. It would be four years that December since I'd submitted my doctoral thesis and I'd started to worry I would never get a salaried position. But I'd forgotten how exhausting it was to start a new job, to wander round a new campus in continual confusion, drained by bafflement. That month had been like being trapped in a continual anxiety dream where everyone was following a rule you didn't know, but was cross with you for not following. One of my new colleagues told me, 'The thing you need to know about this place is no one tells you what you need to know.' I laughed, but at home I cried. I hadn't been so unhappy in a job since I worked in a shop under a bad manager when I was the same age as my students.

At the time I'd interviewed for the job that summer, I'd been discharged by all the clinics I'd been sent to in search of diagnosis. I'd been told categorically *there is nothing wrong with you*. I'd made a complaint, by letter, and one of the consultants I'd complained about wrote back that I seemed to want to have cancer, and he couldn't make me have cancer if I didn't. How to respond to someone who so vastly misunderstood my intentions? Of course I didn't want to have cancer, I just wanted him to help me find out what was causing my pain.

I knew they weren't right, but what could I do in the face of so much qualified opposition? I tried to believe their diagnosis – nothing – and carry on. I wanted my life to move forward. The job was offered to me, and I took it. There was nothing wrong. I could carry on. But the workload was far greater than I expected – the contact hours double those of a full-time member of staff in my previous department, the classes twice the size – and everything new and bewildering. I was panicking, exhausted already. My pain was spiralling.

Then on 15 October I stepped into a large, airy consulting room where an elderly man greeted me kindly, shaking my hand gently between both of his. In the room he asked for my medical history and my family history. He listened carefully and made careful notes. He watched me. He assessed me. He moved my joints and measured my limbs and the extension of my limbs. He felt my skin and looked at my scars. He lay me down on a bench and took my blood pressure and heart rate lying, and standing.

I left the room an hour later, diagnosed with Hypermobile Ehlers-Danlos syndrome.

Hypermobile Ehlers-Danlos syndrome is characterised by hypermobile joints that shift in and out of place and by velvety, fragile skin. It is the most common yet least understood of the Ehlers-Danlos syndromes, known collectively as EDS. The symptoms of the various kinds of Ehlers-Danlos syndromes are caused by mutations in a gene or genes that make collagen, and are hereditary, passed from one family member to another. Presentation varies so much that some family members may be largely unaffected, whilst others may be severely ill.

Collagen is often described as the glue that holds the body together. My glue is not sticky, but stretchy. Everything in my body is stretchier than it should be. I am poorly strung together. My bones do not stay where they should be because the ligaments and tendons holding them in place are floppy. My stomach overextends every time I eat and my bowel is too floppy to squeeze food along it properly. Sometimes my throat flops closed. When I stand, the blood sinks down my body, pooling in my overly stretchy blood vessels so they can't get it back up again. It gathers in my hands and lower limbs until a grey film appears over my eyes, and I feel increasingly sick and unsteady. If I don't sit down, or put my feet up, my speech starts to slur, the light dims right down to dried-blood brown, and eventually I faint. The time in between, when I can't speak and cry at the light, can last for aeons. There are names for all of these things, and reasons for them. Things that might help them. They are not just *how I am*. They are not just *something I have to live with*. That is what diagnosis gave me.

All these years, these ridiculous years of not knowing, and it took one hour with the right person. Someone who could ask the right questions, and understand the answers. I left the shiny room, and the glass-walled reception area and went down in a lift to the entrance hall, and found a toilet, and locked myself in, and cried. Not because I knew now that what I had would not go away, and could not be taken away – was genetic, incurable – but because I finally knew what it was. That was all I had wanted, to know what it was. What I was.

*

There are many barriers to diagnosis: some of them are cultural, and revolve around biases and prejudices about patients, and ignorance about certain conditions. Some are more practical, and revolve around access to resources, and to up-to-date information. These practical barriers are also cultural: they reflect a culture that doesn't care enough about diagnosing chronic conditions, that ignores and prejudges whole categories of people, that doesn't prioritise getting the right answers for people, and making sure all people have equal access to healthcare, and to the information they need to manage their conditions.

I only got my diagnosis because my family could pay for me to travel to London to pay for a consultation with an expert in the field, and I only got to that stage because I kept asking and asking and asking and asking. Because I was a difficult patient. Because I was non-compliant. Because I would not accept unexplained as an explanation. Because I had support to keep faith in that belief.

*

The symbol used for EDS is a zebra. It refers to an oft-repeated aphorism coined by twentieth-century American physician Theodore Woodward: *when you hear hoofbeats, expect horses not zebras*. It has become so ubiquitous in medical teaching, few people seem to realise it has an author and origin story. It is treated like a parable. I see the point, and why it has become so widespread. It is, of course, statistically more likely that a patient presenting symptoms that could suggest a very rare disease has actually got a much more common one: that they are a horse, not a zebra. Zebras do exist though. There are certain circumstances under which they may in fact be common. If, for example, you are in grassland or savanna in southern or eastern Africa, you might be more likely to find a group of *Equus quagga*, or plains zebra, than a single horse. Equally well, if you are at a zoo. Sometimes hoofbeats will belong to a zebra, or a donkey, or a marwari, or a tapir, or an ox or hippopotamus, or a camel, or a pig, or a llama, or a giraffe, all of which, and many more, are hoofed creatures – ungulates – a much broader category than you might think. Whales and dolphins and orcas are ungulates, long since evolved out of their hooves. Sometimes hoofbeats will belong to a deer who looks back at you from the treeline, sometimes three deer standing behind you, hidden.

There is cartoon shared in EDS groups in which a zebra is sitting in a doctor's office, and the doctor is saying, 'You're a perfectly healthy horse, except for those stripes. But I wouldn't worry about the stripes too much. We see this sometimes . . . You just need to diet and exercise. If that doesn't work, try these antidepressants.' It's hilarious, because it's also horrifying. It's all of our experiences. EDS support groups have reclaimed the symbol of the zebra. Some people with EDS refer to themselves and each other as 'zebras', collecting zebra paraphernalia, and have adopted the collective noun for a group of zebras – a *dazzle*.

*

May, 2017. I am sitting in a very entertaining talk by a doctor who has written a best-selling book about the human body. He is funny, erudite, thoughtful. I think for a moment *this is the right kind of doctor*. And then the zebra line comes trotting out of his mouth, and my heart, I'm pretty sure, actually falls through my chest, melts a hole in the floor, and exits the building. He had been talking about patients who come into his office, have looked things up online, and think they have some kind of rare syndrome. Ha ha ha. Everyone laughed at the ridiculous Google patients. I shake through the rest of the talk. In the question and answer session afterwards, I raise my trembling arm and ask him whether he thinks that phrase has any place in medicine today, considering how it becomes a barrier to diagnosis for many people. May happens to be EDS Awareness Month, and I think, I can't let this pass, not here, not today, not whilst I have a voice to use. There is an awkward hush in the room as I try to say this; He admits that whilst zebras are rare, they do exist, but that unicorns don't.

The kind of people he was referring to are unicorns, really, not zebras at all. The audience laughs, the awkwardness is smoothed over. Except for me. He made it funny again; he made my question seem silly.

I couldn't stop coming back to this afterwards. Why did it upset me so much? I tried to unpack it to W. Is it because it perpetuates the notion that horses are normal and natural? Is it because all it does is shift the boundaries of what is implausible (zebra) to what is impossible (unicorn)? Is it because he was so sure that he would know how to recognise one from the other? Is it because I had still been willing to believe so readily in the Good Doctor, after all I'd seen? I came away quite sure that, for all his cleverness and wit, he would not have managed to help me find the right door. He seemed too sure he knew an antelope from a pronghorn. Unicorn is dangerously close in my mind to narwhal, another of the ungulates, the hoofed mammals, although it's strange to think of it so. A narwhal tusk was presented to Elizabeth I by Sir Humphrey Gilbert as the horn from a 'sea-unicorne'. Changing one unlikely animal for another does nothing to collapse the problem the aphorism poses. We need doctors to distinguish between different hoofbeats, to look at the evidence in front of them, and to consider all options, rather than assume all animals are horses.

*

A few months before my EDS diagnosis, I was sent to a pain consultant to try and manage my intractable, inexplicable symptoms. In one breath he said I was too young to be on the kind of painkillers I was on, but also that there was no point in seeking the source of my pain. I just had to accept it. He told me he never tells patients with what he called 'hyperflexile joints' that joint hypermobility can be part of a wider condition because *they would just worry about it*. He told me to stop searching for a reason.

Needless to say, he did not help me at all.

The problem was I just couldn't accept my pain.

The problem was I had to keep asking why.

*

On the way back north, on the train, after Professor G conferred upon me the diagnosis of EDS, I wrote about it in my notebook. It was an *unveiling of what has always been there*.

I was thinking of Thomas De Quincey, as I often found myself doing in those years of undiagnosis.

I felt like I was trapped in one of his dreams, walking back and back through an ever-extending labyrinth.

Oh what an apocalypse of the world(s) within.

It was the first of something like a journal entry I'd written for a long time. I'd been so defeated by unknowing I hadn't wanted to put pen to paper.

I wrote:

> I am on my way to Glasgow and I am so very tired. There are hours to go yet – we've stopped now at Lancaster – hours to go & the rain & the dark at the windows, and the train cold, and my coat still wet from the rainstorm L walked me to Euston in, we had gone for a celebratory cocktail in the womby comfort of the Midland Hotel. I had a Bee Keeper. She a Peach Gimlet.
>
> They had pansies floating on the surface; little dark purple pansy faces as beloved of my beloved gran. Did it come through her, I wonder, or the Muirs?
>
> What it will mean for the future remains to be seen. What it means for the past is everything.
>
> Would I, if I could, undo all those years of unknowing, frustrated, suffering?[37]

I didn't answer myself. There was no point.

Instead, I leave a note for myself to send my GP, his secretary, and my physiotherapist thanks. They have done between them what no one in my life up until this point has managed: they have kept asking questions until they asked the right one.

*

What I felt most of all after my diagnosis, immediately, was relief. I was exhausted by trying not to be hopeful for answers. I had long ago learnt not to expect to be taken seriously.

I had been searching for a diagnosis for years by the time Professor G took my hand in his. Though how many, exactly, it's hard to unpick. Throughout my life I have oscillated between actively seeking medical help, and pretending to be healthy to try and avoid medical help, whilst recovering from the last round of trying to seek it. Even now, armed with knowledge, I lie to myself when I look back at certain times about how well I was coping, how healthy I was. These phases never last for long. I managed to keep one going, for the most part, through my undergraduate degree, only floundering when I broke my left elbow at the end of that six-month job contract after graduation. *For the most part* glosses over the terrible headaches I had started to have, and the strange heart rhythms that sometimes came with them, and made for a fun few hours hooked up to an ECG machine in UCLH when I should have been working in a shop in Covent Garden. It covers the time in first year I slipped in the shower and re-cracked my right elbow. It covers a lot of stomach problems I chose to mostly ignore, because I'd found no help with them before, and had become afraid to mention them.

Pretending to be healthy when you're not is especially exhausting. It takes up energy you could be using keeping yourself as well as you can. But nothing is more exhausting than seeking help and not getting it, year after year after year.

*

In 1995, when I was fourteen, after repeated tests showed no obvious cause for the recurrent urinary tract infections that had plagued my year, the male, middle-aged consultant turned to my mother and me, preparing to give his verdict.

It was five years since I had been told to stop my three weekly dance classes, to stop school sports, to stop swimming, to stop really moving at all in order to save me from more pain in my knees. It was the only option, we were told. I had put on weight within months. I grew more and more unhappy in my body, which manifested its mutual unhappiness in accident after accident. It threw itself on the floor, it split itself into pieces, it separated itself from itself. Here I was, on a slow, tedious crawl into puberty, and everything hurt. Even pissing hurt.

The room was huge. It seemed so ridiculous: this huge, mostly empty room with one institutional laminate desk at one end, and a family of chairs huddled on the other side of it. The consultant, behind his desk, looked at us. Looked me up and down. Looked at me over the upper rim of his glasses, and told us that the problem was that I was too fat.

*

In 1997 repeated tests showed no obvious cause for my increasing fatigue and weakness, for the pain, for the nausea, the feelings of unreality. There was only a low B12 level, and some anomalies in my blood results: a low count of neutrophils – a particular type of white blood cells – and oversized red blood cells, overstuffed, abnormally shaped. My GP couldn't work out where to send me, but as blood seemed to hold my only traceable problems, she sent me to haematology.

The haematologist treated me with respect even when he couldn't find a reason for these abnormalities. He ruled out leukaemias. He ruled out pernicious anaemia. I lived with their potential months at a time, then saw them slip away, ghost diagnoses. Both relieved, and sorry not to have found my answers.

The last time I saw him, the haematologist told me *don't let anyone tell you there's nothing wrong with you.*

I was there, as always back then, with Mum. *Don't let anyone tell you there's nothing wrong with you* he said to me. *Don't let them tell you there's nothing wrong* he said to Mum.

We repeated this for years. In the darkest times Mum would repeat it back to me like a prayer or a charm. She'd say *remember what our lovely haematologist said* – just because they don't know what it is, it doesn't mean there's nothing there – don't let anyone tell you there's nothing wrong with you. We would say, *ah, he was one of the good ones.*

The lovely haematologist, having run out of options, referred me for CBT within the same hospital. I never received CBT, because someone else in the department had a different theory.

This is how we were told it: he saw my file when it came into the Psychology Department, and saw my details. He told us this. He told us *I've treated XX girls from your school with anorexia in the last two years.*

I may be getting some details wrong – was it ten girls, or twelve, or more? Was it two years, or less?

He told me that I wasn't ill at all, but that he understood, I was very worried about my father's business and that's why I was starving myself. He would help me. I just had to admit that I was starving myself. That it was about my father. That it was about my weight. My control issues.

After that appointment, I had my first experience of active suicidal thoughts. Not because of what he said in itself, but because I had reached the end of the diagnostic tunnel, and found a concrete wall and water rising. I had had one small bead of hope left, and he had crushed it. I was told I would be getting treatment that might help me, but there was nothing there but a man who wanted me to confess I was creating it all myself.

I wrote all the details in a letter to my boyfriend and I was so worn down by it all, the experience and the relating of it, that I couldn't bear to repeat it for myself. It is a lacuna in my journal. Too painful to walk myself back through, but I remember enough. I remember too well. This was the first week of 1998. Not an auspicious start to a year. It spread before me, a maze I had no guide through, and no light left to see by.

After my third appointment with him, he prescribed me Prozac, which just made me feel sick and headachey and even worse. He discharged me, writing in his letter to my GP that I seemed to be improving. All my improvement was determination to get away from him.

For me, the problem was his confirmation bias, the packet of gingernuts balanced precariously on the top of his filing cabinet as he encouraged girl after girl to confess she was causing all her own problems by refusing to eat them. His belief in his own brilliance.

For him, the problem was that I was too thin. I went to the wrong school. I was a teenage girl, and not to be trusted.

*

Even then, I could understand why he thought what he thought.

I had lost so much weight. At my thinnest, weakest, I weighed a little over seven stone. I was starving.

Part of my despair came from wondering if he was right. I felt in my body, all over my body, that he was wrong, but I also knew that when I was bullied for being fat I had wanted to be thin. I had associated thinness with health. I had written a mantra of lines in my notebook to manifest my strong, healthy future self:

> *I will get fitter and thinner and better*
> *I will get fitter and thinner and better*
> *I will get fitter and thinner and better*

Hadn't I, after all, begun to eat less and less? I could say it was sickness, that it felt wrong when I ate, that certain foods hurt me, that my gut complained against it, but isn't that just what someone would say if they were starving themselves?

And yes, I wanted to achieve things. I wanted to be good at what I did. Was that, as he said, pathological?

I trusted my body, my sick gut, but was I wrong? Was I the problem?

*

If enough people tell you you are creating your symptoms, you have to consider it. Maybe you even start to believe it, against the silent screams of your body.

In *Sick*, Porochista Khakpour writes about how she came to terms with the idea, that it made a kind of sense to her, being, as she was, a storyteller, a writer, an inventor: 'I was, after all, someone who created in the mind.'[38]

Years pass as you try to convincingly be sick only in the way they want you to be. As so much of your limited energy is lost on ignoring what you know to be real.

*

97

After the poor end of my first post-graduation job with that breaking of an elbow, I worked from home in East London for a while. I wrote content for a website and went to poetry readings all around London in the evenings. I thought I was doing pretty well, so when I needed more work, I didn't think too much about my physical capacity. I'd forgotten how much effort it took to leave the house every morning, to move about in a world designed for healthy people, to pass as one of them. I joined a temp agency and, after a week in a nursery, was placed in a primary school as a special educational needs teaching assistant. At the same time, my undergraduate supervisor encouraged me to think about starting a master's degree, and gave me some teaching on a contemporary writing course at my old university. On the days I was teaching, I finished school in Hoxton and hot-footed it back to Mile End, arriving for my 4 p.m. class with wooden bricks and bits of string in my pockets. I loved both jobs, but I was struggling with stamina and energy.

In school, the work was very physical. I worked in nursery for half the day, and in year five or six the other half. The school was one of those solid Victorian edifices – a blocky, beautifully bleak rectangle with stairwells at either end. All day was stairs and more stairs, and between stairs, crawling on hard floors and running. Even without the stairs and running around, the amount of sitting on the floor and getting up again in a hurry, the amount of one-on-one work, moving a child's hand with my own as we worked together through activities, the school in itself was exhausting. I pushed myself and pushed myself.

It's not that I hadn't been trying to get help, but who has the energy to keep pushing and pushing at such firm barriers? I'd been to the GP, again and again. A lot of promising doors leading to brick walls and trapdoors. I gave up in London, and went home, thinking *they know me here, they won't dismiss me.* I was referred to a rheumatologist, but this is where I stalled. He looked at my history of dislocations and other complaints. He manipulated my joints. I now realise he was scoring me on the Beighton score, a measure of the flexibility of key joints used to diagnose EDS. He asked about my symptoms, my pain levels, how I slept. He didn't look at my skin or scars, or ask me about family history, not that I would have known the right information to pass on then. He took everything I had to show and came to the conclusion I had benign joint hypermobility, asthma, IBS, non-restorative sleep, and Fibromyalgia Syndrome.

If you know EDS, this reads like a bad joke. The answer is so obvious when you know how to put it together.

'Thank you for referring this Lady,' this rheumatologist wrote back to my GP, 'on physical examination Polly is generally very well indeed.' He wrote, 'it sounds as though there has already been some recovery and improvement'.

I did not feel very well indeed.

I felt very unwell indeed.

I wonder what I or my GP could have said to make him think there had been recovery and improvement. Was it that I walked into the room? Was it that I didn't cry, or didn't cry enough?

At the time, his 'impression [. . .] that the symptoms are due to a limited form of Fibromyalgia Syndrome' seemed like progress from my teenage coding with Chronic Fatigue Syndrome, Anorexia and Depression with Anxiety. ME and Chronic Fatigue were, and still are, treated by most doctors as entirely psychogenic. It seemed to me then that Fibromyalgia was more widely understood to have a physiological basis, even if it wasn't know what that basis was.

Ten years later, in 2014, Professor G writes that I score 7/9 on the Beighton score, though he also notes 'outside the scale her shoulders, cervical spine (rotation), hips and fingers are all hypermobile, as are her feet which flatten on weight-bearing'.

Back in 2004 I scored full marks. The rheumatologist wrote 'she has a full house on the Beighton score for hypermobility', as though I should get a prize for it. BINGO! He said my joints had 'an excellent range of movement', as though their hypermobility were a thing to be applauded, yet could not connect that excellent score with the pain in the same joints, and with all my other symptoms.

In the ten years of inappropriate treatment and diagnostic delay my symptoms worsened to the extent that I lost hyper-mobility in two joints. I suppose the rheumatologist would probably consider that excellent too.

Now looking back at his letter I notice not only what he did notice – lymph gland swelling in my neck, pain in my abdomen – but what he didn't even check for. He didn't see my scoliosis because he didn't look for it. He didn't see my flat feet or my digestive failure. He didn't see the breakdown of my autonomic nervous system. He didn't see my pain.

The following year I started my master's, and gave up one day a week at school to travel into central London for classes. I was tireder and tireder, in pain, developing new symptoms: breathlessness and dizziness, a pain in my foot so intense I could hardly bear to put it on the ground for several months. I would lose my voice for weeks, start to recover, lose it again. The school and university holidays brought some relief: I didn't get paid, but I could at least rest. I knew I couldn't keep on like that, but what else could I do? I had got my diagnosis, and there was nothing to do with it.

What was the problem here? I had the same body that another consultant could clearly recognise as having hEDS ten years later, but I was younger, bendier, had suffered less by then to get there.

Diagnosis

It's almost as though the problem was that I hadn't been damaged enough.

*

Diagnosis entered the English language in the way we still use it today in the 1680s. Misdiagnosis was added in 1880. Misdiagnosis goes hand in hand with diagnosis, the flip side of the coin. The difference between one and the other depends on the kind of data you're working with, and your method of interpretation. Misdiagnosis is always hovering under diagnosis: the demonic twin. How can you be sure which is standing in front of you, taking you by the hand, asking you to follow it?

*

Going into a doctor's office is not a neutral act when you have been seeking diagnosis for a long time. It comes with the old panic, the old anxieties around not being believed, dragging a clanging tin can train of insult and abuse.

In 2009 I lost my voice, and began the long quest for diagnosis again. It hurt to speak and to swallow. Blood tests had shown nothing, which I was used to by now, but the problem was getting worse, not better. I was in the final year of my PhD. I'd managed another few years of being well enough, not well, but not exactly sick either. Exhaustible, but not excessively fatigued. But I'd run out of resources – financial and bodily. When my parents suggested moving home for a while, I knew it was the sensible thing to do.

Healthcare is not easily transferable between regions. I had begun the process of an ENT referral months before I decided to leave Lancaster, but by the time the appointment came through I had already moved back home to Nottingham.

I travelled up to stay with a friend for the night, and the next morning set off for the small hospital that I had never been to before in the next town along, with hope as well as trepidation.

When I got there, I found that the doctor I had meant to be seeing was stuck in traffic, and a replacement had been found.

The substitute examined me, looked down my throat with a camera threaded through my nose, asked questions. He said I had vocal chord nodules, though no one ever found them again. But that wasn't my real problem.

He asked me if I had a boyfriend. He told me how young people nowadays are always putting things in holes they weren't designed for. The nurse, sitting on a chair behind me, shifted uncomfortably. His voice was jovial, confiding. He said things about god and what god meant a man and a woman to do together. He said I had lost my voice because I was doing things god hadn't meant a man and a woman to do together.

The problem was that I was too sexually active. Also, that god disapproved.

*

In Nottingham, silent months passed before an ENT appointment came through. They dismissed the previous diagnosis, and repositioned my problem as muscle spasms in my throat.

After each time a doctor threaded a tube through my nose to look into my throat, I would ask them if my worsening voice symptoms could be related to my other worsening symptoms – the dizziness and pain that were becoming more and more overwhelming – and each time my inquiry was met with a shrug. I don't see why it would, they said. I wouldn't think so.

Diagnosis

I was sent to a therapist to learn how to speak more easily, to take speech easily on my throat.

She listened to me croak and told me I had my pitch all wrong. She taught me exercises. She taught me to massage my larynx. She told me to sip water constantly. She taught me to mmmmm to release the muscles in my throat.

I take a part-time job in a school, just two classes, enough and not too much. In the mornings I do my voice exercises in the shower. MMMmmmmmmmonday. Mmmmmmmmmmmonday. I sip water through class.

Other things are going wrong in my body, but everyone says they can't find a reason why. Some days my stomach hurts so much I lie on the floor and cry. At a gig I take W to for his birthday I start to feel so sick and peculiar I have to go and sit in the back. Every time the strobe comes on I burst into tears. No one can tell me why.

I begin to blame the city for it, the mould in W's flat, the disappointment of turning thirty with no job, no home of my own. I miss the mountains and lakes. When I'm offered a few hours of teaching a week that autumn at Lancaster University, we move together to the Lakes.

I'm only teaching part-time, paid hourly. Enough, but not too much. The rest of the time I work on finishing my thesis. I struggle to breathe lying down, and it feels like there is a lump in my throat all the time, but they all say it is nothing. I dream I am dying. I do my voice exercises. MMMmmmmmmonday. Mmmmmmmmmmonday. I learn to sip water all the time. Not to speak unless I need to.

The problem was I had been speaking wrong all these years. I thought I had a voice, and could use it, but I had wasted it. The problem was I misspoke, and it all meant nothing much at all.

*

It is November 2012. I am in a bed on a hospital ward, some-where in Lancaster Royal Infirmary. I have been brought up to a ward after taking myself to A&E because the pain in my abdomen that has been dominating my life for a month has become excruciating. I haven't slept. It is this bad because the day before I had an ultrasound to investigate the pain. The ultrasound did not find a reason for the pain, but during investigation the wand did press hard, for some time, on the area where the pain lived, and the pain, like an angry beast, woke up. This is how I come to think of it: a creature that lives in me, sleeps under my ribs, is made angry by contact. I learn to keep everything away from it. Do not disturb.

I went to A&E after teaching a class, translucent with pain, at the university, thinking that since the hospital and univer-sity are in the same town, I might as well do both. I taught my class because I couldn't afford not to, and because I had learnt to handle pain. Keep going unless you literally can't. In the hospital they pressed again on the places where the pain lived, and I was too exhausted by it to cry, but leaked at the eyes. My blood sugar dropped so they gave me a drip, and after some hours of confusion, admitted me to gynaecology, suspecting a problem with an ovary. Women have problems with their ovaries.

This is how I come to find myself in a ward bed, waiting to find out if I am to be admitted or sent home. When the young male gynaecologist does his ward rounds, he tells me it is hard to work out what might be causing abdominal pain in women, because there is *just so much in there.*

I imagine radiologists poring over CT scans of women's abdomens stuffed with space junk, tin cans, old bicycles, the Loch Ness monster, an actual kitchen sink.

He sends me home.

W only really understands, really, and not intellectually, the night later that winter he drives me to the minor injuries unit and a young male doctor explains to him that it is hard to tell when women are having *abnormal* bleeding, because *women bleed*. I am in the room with them at the time. I am in the room because I am having abnormal bleeding. All my insides seem to be coming out at once. I am grey and shaking, in shock with it, barely lucid. W knew this too, but what could I say, what could he say? What was my opinion of what was normal or not worth against this undeniable logic?

The problem was I was a woman.

The problem was that women bleed.

It is impossible to know what is normal and abnormal faced with such a baffling insistence on porosity. Such a refusal of boundaries, such as inside the body and outside the body.

*

In 2013 a 24-hour ECG test picked up abnormal heart rhythms and responses. The consultant endocrinologist who ordered the test had done so because he didn't know what to do with me. When the results came in he was surprised. He had expected them to come up with nothing. That they would confirm his assumption that I was perfectly well, and over-thinking.

The consultant told me the results didn't warrant further investigation. There was nothing more to find. Some women, he told me, are just very sensitive.

I cried all the way home, went straight into my GP, and told them, told them I would never see him again. That this was too much. It had all been too much, but this was the last time I would accept it.

Later when I made a formal complaint about the consultant, amongst others, he referred to me throughout his fauxpology as 'Mrs Atkin'.

The diagnosis was clear: the problem was that I was a woman, and women are too sensitive.

*

Later that year, I find myself in a smart white consulting room, being told by a young, smiling doctor that it was great news, I didn't have the rare kind of tumour they had been testing me for, I could go home happy in the knowledge I was perfectly healthy. It was so nice to be able to give someone good news. When I reach a safe distance from the antiseptic room, I cry and cry. It is a specialist centre and there is a beautiful bed of roses outside the front door. I weep into them. Not because I wanted to have a tumour, but because I knew I had reached diagnostic deadlock. I still have the symptoms that made them investigate me for a tumour, but because I don't have one, no one can help me with my symptoms. It's not good news to be told you're perfectly healthy when you feel like you're dying. I was seventeen again, hopeless, helpless. The kind, smiling doctor might as well have given me a card that read 'congratulations, it's all in your head'.

That, of course, was what happened next. I bounced back to a neurologist who tested me for Wilson's syndrome, a rare copper-loading disorder that can produce symptoms like those I had. When the results came back negative, he referred me to Neuropsychology, for the treatment of Functional Neurological Disorder.

Functional Neurological Disorder is a term used to describe neurological symptoms with no discernible organic cause. The focus for treatment is on physiotherapy and/or CBT. Some theories link FND to past trauma that the body presents as physical symptoms – this is also known as conversion theory. Some people embrace their

FND diagnosis, and feel it explains their situation aptly. But I felt I was being blamed again for my body's rebellion, as though I could control it. *Medically unexplained, soma-significant, psychosomatic, psychogenic* and *hysterical* are some of the other terms that have been used to describe the same theory. These are all ways of saying *it's all in your head.* Of saying you are creating your illness, whether you know it or not. Or worse, that something terrible happened to you in your past, and this illness is just a physical way of your body working out that trauma, that you haven't worked that trauma out properly, and so it has to come out like this. That you are not listening to your mind's pain, so it is speaking through your body, ventriloquising. As one term has become recognised as too obviously victim-blaming, another has superseded it. You might know something of the social and political history of some of these terms, and how they are applied unequally across genders, races, classes. I do, I know what they mean, how they are leveraged against the most vulnerable, but at this point, I began to wonder if I really was *somatising*. Could, after all, I be creating my own debilitating symptoms? Am I clever enough to trick myself so completely? Am I clever enough to incapacitate myself so effectively? Am I such a cunning saboteur?

I liked my neuropsychologist. He forgave me easily when I forgot an appointment, which I took as a sign of humane feeling. I chose to trust him, despite my wariness. I asked him whether, all things being considered, he thought I could have sublimated some particular trauma I wasn't aware of, and that could be causing my symptoms. I was so desperate by this point, I was willing to disbelieve my own convictions. After several meetings, he was as sure as he could be that my symptoms weren't somatic, and passed me on. This could have been the end of the diagnostic journey for me, but he had given me the tiniest seed of hope that there was something to find, we just hadn't found it yet. It was enough to keep me questing.

*

It was not that long after I was dismissed from Neuropsychology that I realised there was something palpable at the epicentre of the abdominal pain. A lump right where the pain was, that clicked and moved when I touched it. I showed my GP. He referred me to surgery, but when I drove down to Lancaster to present it to the consultant surgeon he couldn't feel anything. I cried in the outpatient toilets, hunting for the lump, its familiar, sickening clunking movement. If my GP had felt it, I couldn't be imagining it. Surgery's dismissal accidentally led me onto the right path. The surgeon supposed I might just have costochondritis, an inflammation of the cartilage of the ribcage. This was no great surprise: it had been suggested back in 2011, when I first started having chest pain so bad it would stop me in my tracks. It's the kind of condition normal people get after the flu or suchlike, and then it goes away. Later, I found out people with EDS are one of the lucky groups who can find once they have costochondritis, it never really goes away. At its least offensive, it is a dull ache spread throughout the chest or back, depending on which bit of cartilage is affected. At its worst, it feels like a vice is crushing your chest, or a large hand is squeezing your trunk, squashing all the little bones together. I wasn't impressed by the surgeon's referral, but it turned out to be an important doorway. He sent me for a special ultrasound to check my ribcage. The sonographer found not only was my cartilage inflamed, but the moving lump seemed to be a callous formed around a crack in a rib.

I hadn't told the neuropsychologist that I had been keeping a list of symptoms and questions, that I kept adding to, for almost two years by then. I knew it looked bad. It looked like thinking too much about my symptoms, which CBT wants us to think creates our symptoms. Reading it back is painful. My terror, my frustration, too palpable. It is three A4 sides of bullet-pointed symptoms, some with dates and specific examples where they had got worse, some tracing back years. Looking at them now I know what every single one of them was, was caused by, could have been improved by. But then I knew nothing, except what it was to be *very painful to the touch.*

To be very weak and shaky. To be suddenly allergic to being alive. To have specific localised pain that no one would address. It is particularly painful to see how I describe my rib pain, at the top of the list in September 2013:

> Constant localised upper abdominal pain. Epicentre under left ribcage, but pain radiates around upper abdomen and often into back. This has been continual since May 2012, but worsening in stages – worsened dramatically in late October 2012 after (possibly coincidentally) a week's treatment with propranolol, when my abdomen also became very distended. Worsened again seriously in June 2013. Sometimes the pain becomes more acute for brief periods (moments to days) – normally after activity has irritated it or someone has pressed on it, or during tachycardic episode (as below). Sometimes this is so bad I semi-pass-out. This has taken me to A&E a few times (e.g. Nov 2012 they thought I'd burst an ovarian cyst but this came to nothing). Now I try to sit it out if possible, as the hospital trips have ended up being very stressful and unhelpful in the long run (even if they have been able to give me better pain relief for the day/night).

I had cracked a rib. Without an accident or particularly noticing, though when I looked back, I knew exactly when it had been.

Before my diagnosis could make sense of my abnormal blood pressure readings as a by-product of the blood pooling and overcompensation common to EDS, I had been given beta blockers to try and bring my alarmingly high blood pressure down. Apart from the regular side effects – revolving slowly backwards through each day – my stomach ballooned. It hurt, but I know the exact moment when it snapped from a usual kind of pain to something more. I was sitting on the sofa in our old house, facing the large window that looked onto a field. Watery yellow autumn sun was almost managing to slip into the dark room. We were about to go out, and I coughed. I coughed.

I'd be waving a piece of paper with the date on in front of each doctor I saw since it happened. October 2012. The week my abdomen inflated.

How strange that I identified exactly where the pain was, but no one thought to look at my rib itself, not until it made itself big. It had to build itself up and reach out to be noticed.

In the months that followed, the pain got worse and worse. The pain was so bad I couldn't wear a bra or bear any trousers or skirts that pressed on my abdomen. I went to the doctor: they wrote it down as *epigastric* pain. This wasn't incorrect, exactly, but it sent us down the wrong corridor. It's odd now, looking back, to think I spent eighteen months unable to lie on my belly or endure the slightest pressure on my abdomen and just learnt to accommodate it. I was wearing clothes two sizes too big to try and limit the pain. Consultant after consultant pressed my abdomen until my eyes leaked and I felt my face grey, and said they felt *nothing*. There was nothing wrong. I sat in consultants' rooms and cried, desperately and uncontrolledly.

I refused to leave until they found out what it was. That was why I got accused of wanting to have cancer. They misdiagnosed what I was asking for.

No one thought to look at my ribs because no one – really, not one – had really listened to me when I told them exactly where the pain stemmed from. They kept asking the wrong question of my body, and when it came up with a blank where the answer should be, took this as confirmation.

The problem was there was nothing, nothing the matter at all.

*

Once my broken rib was discovered, like a lost continent, I spooled out my history of fractures to my GP. I was sent for a bone density scan. The scan confirmed my bone density was low. This was not a surprise.

My GP referred me to physiotherapy to see if they could help the pain.

Going through my long, long patient story, the physiotherapist casually asked, 'And who do you see for your hypermobility?'

The ground shifted, cogs whirred, and the whole labyrinth rearranged itself into a welcoming passage. She opened the door: I walked down.

*

We cannot be diagnosed if we cannot be seen. If people refuse to see us for what we are. In 2017, new diagnostic criteria for EDS were issued to try and simplify the diagnostic procedure. When I began to write this paragraph in 2014 there were thirteen recognised subtypes, each with distinct characteristics. By April 2018 there were sixteen subtypes. Within the community, there are mixed feelings about these changes. Some see them as making diagnosis more accessible, others as making it even more complicated, as a kind of gatekeeping.

Hypermobile EDS (hEDS), the kind I seem to have, is the only one which does not yet have a recognised genetic marker, so diagnosis is by clinical examination and medical history only – there is no blood test or laboratory test that can confirm it. This means diagnosis of hEDS relies on informed interpretation of clinical findings: variability of presentation, combined with the subjectivity of the diagnostic process and failure of current criteria to represent systemic aspects, leads to diagnostic errors. Studies have found physicians at all levels consistently fail to recognise hypermobility in patients or to 'establish its clinical importance'.[39] Hypermobile EDS is categorised as a rare disease although some experts believe it is nothing like as rare as supposed, but rather massively under-diagnosed. American EDS specialist Dr Derek Neilson suggests that rather than the assumed figure of 1 in 15,000–20,000 people, the incidence of hEDS might be 1 in 500, or even higher, a figure replicated by a 2018 study conducted in Wales.[40] Specialists argue that hEDS is 'the most common, though the least recognised, heritable connective tissue disorder'.[41]

A doctor who lives in the same village as my parents has told my mum multiple times she does not believe in EDS, that she thinks it's a fad, a fiction, a complaint about nothing, despite knowing about my story. Sometimes I say 'just let me at her'. Sometimes I say, I'll send her this book. But what good will it do if she has made up her mind? If she is convinced we are all unicorns?

*

Diagnosis is not a single moment: it is ongoing. It is a continual process of learning. Of asking questions and analysing answers. Diagnoses unfold one from another like paperchain people. This is another reason why getting it right is important. A wrong diagnosis breaks the link, and suddenly nothing makes sense. A wrong diagnosis drags the whole lot of them down. Say a diagnosis is a door, it leads to a path, or a corridor, and you follow it, and that route leads to another door, another diagnosis, and you can open it. It is the labyrinth of the body that you are trying to work your way through. Diagnosis is chronic too.

The process of diagnosis – of learning, of seeking – never ends. Like all other parts of the chronic life, it moves in cycles, in repetitive arcs. A correct diagnosis allows the arc to expand into a spiral, to keep moving and evolving. A wrong diagnosis keeps you stuck on a locked circuit, going round and round, going nowhere.

*

In October 2022 I am introduced to a toffee apple tree. It is Apple Day. W and I have gone to meet up with friends at a country estate in North Cumbria with a seventeenth-century hall and grounds packed with plants gathered from around the world over many generations.

We are told we cannot think of leaving before we see the toffee apple tree that grows behind the hall. At this time of year, and this time only, the tree gives off the scent of caramelised apples.

We smell it before we reach it. Walking along the back terrace of the garden, we hit a wall of sweet and buttery fragrance. The tree stands a little by itself, right at the end of the walkway, its gold and pink leaves vibrating with luminosity against the damp green of the lawn and the heavy grey of the sky.

The scent, like lychees and butterscotch, floral and sharp and sweet, is so delicious I want to bathe in it. I climb over the wall of the terrace to stand in its drooping branches, amongst the heart-shaped leaves, and breathe it in.

That night I google *toffee apple tree*. All the time we were being told about it I was hearing Toffee Apple Tree as a personal name, particular to that specific tree I would stand under, as though it were one of a kind. It did not occur to me it was the common name of a species. Because I'd never heard of a toffee apple tree, I could not understand what I was seeing, smelling, feeling.

Toffee Apple Tree is one name for katsura, *Cercidiphyllum japonicum*. Others are caramel tree, toffee tree, candy floss tree, gingerbread tree, cake tree. We can't agree what it smells of but we can agree it smells amazing.

The next afternoon I walk up the old road as usual, past the overgrown duck pond, towards the coffin path, as I have done on so many days, over so many years. This time a newly familiar scent stops me. I can smell the toffee apple tree. Now I know it, the scent is unmistakable. Ripe honey mango dissolving on the tongue. Burnt sugar and peaches. I stand in the road in the mizzle sniffing and sniffing, and then I see it, just over the wall of a nineteenth-century garden. In the mizzle the yellow hearts of its leaves glow with information.

Two days beforehand as I walked there with W I had stopped at the same place, wondering what tree had dropped the soft buttery leaves on the dark tarmac. Hundreds of times I have passed that spot in autumn, smelt the honey lychee scent, and not known what to think of it. I have walked on, knowing nothing about toffee apple trees. I could not turn their presence into meaning.

Once katsura grew throughout the Northern Hemisphere. There are fossil records of katsura going back 1.8 million years. But in the Pleistocene its territories shrank back so the only remaining trees flourished in China, Japan and Korea. Katsura thrives in moist, temperate regions. Of which Cumbria, I suppose, is one. It has been admired and cultivated for the scent and colours which drew me to it, and for its fine-grained, pale wood.

In the nineteenth century it was imported by plant collectors from China and Japan to America and Europe, first by Thomas Hogg, who sent katsura seeds to his brother in New York in 1865. It reached the UK in 1881.

The house that my katsura grows in was built between 1862 and 1864, blasted out of the rock to the design of Anna Deborah Richardson, the eldest daughter of a family of wealthy and well-connected Quakers. Anna is remembered for campaigning for women's rights and education, and her role in supporting the foundation of Girton College, Cambridge.

Anna was also chronically ill. Her family traced her health problems to a fast she undertook as a teenager in 1847 to raise awareness of the Irish Famine, after which she was never entirely well. In her late thirties, she developed new symptoms – numbness in her right arm, sickness. In October 1871 she became ill enough to travel to London, seeking a more modern medical opinion than she could find at home. Before this all doctors had told her that her 'troubles were from the liver'.[42] The doctor she saw in London blamed her illness on poor diet and 'years of non-assimilation of food', prescribing a rich diet of two large, protein-heavy meals a day, expensive wine, rum, cream, and crushed wheat porridge. The diet does not cure her, unsurprisingly. By November she is so weak she can barely walk, and cannot leave the house. The London doctor's experimental diets make her worse, not better. In April 1872 she is examined by a doctor from Hawkshead who diagnoses Bright's disease or nephritis, like Emily Dickinson. She dies that August, aged forty.

Grasmere was a refuge for her: somewhere she could live independently and peacefully. After her death, one of her friends tries to explain what the landscape of the lakes meant to her, how the 'mountain magnet drew her' to them, recalling how Anna herself wrote 'living here in this indescribable country I feel perpetually bathed in a glad sense of continually revealed blessings'. She had a motto carved on the fireplace in the dining room – *ubi caritas ibi claritas* – translated in her memoir as 'where there is love there is clearness; or as we might say, where there is charity in judgement there is to be found clearness of perception'.[43]

The garden of the house she designed is full of species from around the world. Vast rhododendrons of many colours, unusual jasmine varieties. I don't know which that remain now were her choices or those of later owners, but her letters describe her love of the garden and her plans for planting, from foxgloves and ivy her father transplanted during the building of the house, to friends planting 'little pine cones and cedars and four crimson rhododendrons' in the garden for her, gifts of alpine plants, of juniper and ferns, and her favourite clematis azura growing round the porch. When Anna died in Grasmere in 1872 it was almost a decade before the katsura is supposed to have reached these shores, but I can't separate the katsura in her garden from what I know of her, from something about clearness of perception.

Katsura is a long-lived species under the right conditions. As it ages, the trunk does not just expand outwards and upwards as one body, but sprouts new stems from root, giving the appearance of a forest bound in the circumference of the base. Thousand-year-old trees with diameters of sixteen, seventeen feet grow in ancient forests in China and Japan, the towers of textured and turned bark looking like mystical woodland cities.

In 1910 plant collector Ernest Henry Wilson recorded a katsura with a diameter of seventeen and a half feet in a forest in Sichuan Province, standing by itself in a deforested area. It was the first seeding katsura he had seen. In 2017 a team from the North America–China Plant Exploration Consortium returned to visit the same tree, and found the katsura surrounded by other vegetation and tripled or quadrupled in size. The trunks were ancient and hollowed out, dying from within, as they had been when Wilson saw them, yet the trees kept growing, kept replenishing from new stems.

In Japan ancient multi-stemmed katsura hold monument status. It is a sacred tree, linked with deities of moon, mountain and water. katsura trees are places of meeting, of the gods with the mortal realm, of the gods with each other, of the mortal realm with higher realms. Legend tells that a great katsura grows on the moon and a man of exceptional beauty tends it, trimming the golden leaves which shrinks the moon's orb as it seems to us to wane each month. The light of the moon is leaf-light, tree-light. The caramel light of katsura in autumn. The dark of the moon is the absence of leaves. The dark shapes we see on the surface of the moon are the shadows of the katsura's great canopy. If you stare too much at the moon Katsura Otoko will beckon you to join him. The longer you stare, the more years he takes from your life, pruning them as he does the branches of the tree.

In Chinese legend it is a woodcutter or perhaps a magician, Wu Gang, who chops each month at a tree which grows back even as he hacks it down. The species of tree varies, as does the reason he is there. The task is impossible, a punishment of futility. We see his work done, and his work undone, as we gaze up at the changing phases of the moon. Leaf-light, tree-light, absence of leaf.

Not everyone can smell katsura's delicate, sweet fragrance. It is the chemical compound maltol mixed with sugar released from the turning leaves that makes the distinctive aroma in autumn. But maltol, used in food and perfumes for its caramellic properties, is not perceptible to everyone. To people who lack the scent receptors, the katsura in autumn is just a pretty yellow-leaved tree, nothing more enchanting. It could easily be mistaken for a linden, with its own string of legends and enchantments, its own autumn gold. You could walk past the katsura a million times, and not know it for what it is. As I did, before a chance encounter elsewhere unveiled it to me. You will breathe in its distinctive perfume but if you do not know a tree can give off scent like that you will file it away in your mind as incidental. This is also a story about diagnosis. You can see something every day, but unless you have the frame of reference to recognise it for what it is, you will misidentify it, overlook it, year after year, no matter how carefully you think you are paying attention. You will assign another cause to what you observe, thinking you are being logical, working only with what you know to be possible. You have to know something exists in order to find it, right next to you, where it always was. To give it its proper name.

*

In October 2015, a year to the day after my diagnosis with EDS, I found myself sitting in another consulting room, in front of a different doctor: a gastroenterologist I had been referred to to help manage my EDS symptoms.

She had ordered a lot of routine, but very thorough, tests. All of the lab tests came back normal, except one. The levels of ferritin in my blood – one measure of how much iron we have in our system – was very high. Over 1000, when the normal range is below 250. She explained this might mean I had a second genetic condition, a metabolic disorder called haemochromatosis. She referred me back through my local hospital for gene testing, and in January 2016 it was confirmed.

People with genetic haemochromatosis absorb too much iron from their diets. You might think this would be an

118

advantage – we are constantly being told that iron gives us strength and energy, aren't we? Like anything, though, the dose is the trick. Too much iron, and you get just as tired and weak and achy as someone with far too little. Meanwhile, the iron is slowly poisoning you, and the body cannot get rid of it. Too much iron is building up in my body – far too much – deposited in my joints and stashed in my skin and my vital organs.

By the time I was diagnosed the iron had been building up in my body, in all of my organs, for more than half a lifetime. No one could see it, but I could feel it. I could feel myself slowly rusting, although I did not know what it was I was feeling.

If I had not been diagnosed with EDS, I would not have been diagnosed with haemochromatosis. One diagnosis gave me back control over my life; the second saved my life. One would not have happened without the other opening the right door. Diagnosis is a chain. Link to link. It can drag you down or give you a lead to follow. When the doctor recognised my high iron levels she said something I had thought for a long time – that many doctors, when faced with a patient with a clear history of one condition, choose to put every single thing the patient complains of down to that one pre-known condition, and don't do the appropriate investigative work. It is a deliberate, if subconscious, looking away. It is easier to not keep on asking questions, it is easier to stop looking for answers.

In January 2016 I begin the slow process of de-ironing my system, of drawing the iron deposits from my organs back into circulation, and out, away. This is the standard treatment for haemochromatosis, simple and archaic. Month on month pints of blood are taken from my body. Removing blood limits available iron, so the body is forced to release more from its stores to make new red blood cells. This is the economy of rust.

*

There is both a definite gene test and simple blood tests that should make diagnosis with haemochromatosis unequivocal and easy. Yet, as with EDS, the literature and general understanding is limited and often outdated. As with EDS, a large proportion of haemochromatotics are dismissed, ignored, or misdiagnosed for decades before they receive the correct diagnosis.

Despite my own diagnosis, my mum became one of them, fighting for five years through increasing heart damage to get treatment for a disease she already knew she had, that was proved by consistent blood results and gene tests. It is unclear exactly how many people may be living with haemochromatosis without knowing it because of failures in the diagnostic processes, just as with EDS. Recent estimates put the probable number of people with haemochromatosis in the UK at 1.2 million, based on the prevalence of the three genetic mutations which most commonly require treatment. Yet only 20,000 of us are diagnosed.

Some of this gap is down to basic misunderstandings and ignorance around symptoms. The excess iron can be stored in any organ in the body, so symptoms can vary dramatically. Textbook symptoms include joint pain, abdominal pain, fatigue, headaches, and either bronzing or greying of the skin. But this is the tip of the iceberg. Left to do damage, the iron may disrupt all sorts of bodily systems, disrupting hormones, causing thyroid and parathyroid diseases, diabetes, liver disease, heart disease. These individual damages have their own multiple symptoms. There is no single presentation of haemochromatosis, no standard, no typical. We are common as horses, but we appear in so many shapes – manatee, porpoise, peccary.

My ferritin had been flagged as high back in 2011, but haemochromatosis was never considered. There is a misconception I have seen repeated again and again that menstruation counteracts iron loading. But iron loading can stop or inhibit menstruation, so even if a person starts out self-regulating, they may not continue to do so, as their iron levels slowly, silently, disrupt their hormones.

These misconceptions explain why the neurologist who referred me to Neuropsychology tested me for rare Wilson's syndrome, but not for common haemochromatosis, although either one could have explained my symptoms.

As far as he was concerned, the problem was I was too female, and too young.

*

I have no problem with a doctor who says, 'I don't know what is wrong with you.' No one can expect one doctor to know everything. But it is important to be able to admit what we do not know. Too many times, I have seen *I don't know what is wrong with you* transformed into *I can't see anything wrong with you, therefore there is nothing wrong with you.*

What none of these doctors knew as they judged me too female, too sensitive – just an over-clever girl over-thinking, just a woman with women's problems somaticising – is that I had struggled all my life to recognise myself as a woman, as a girl. Most of the time I was grappling with what it might even mean to feel human. Most of the time I was just trying to get through the day. So often I had been seen by others as not appropriately feminine. I sensed it as a child; I knew it as a teenager. I was told in so many different ways I was not a proper girl. I was delicate, but in the wrong ways: breakably, messily, bloodily, not endearingly. I was too small, and then later, I was too fat. I didn't have to intuit this. The other children told me, repeatedly. And then there was my personality, the way I reacted to things. The same things that made me fail as a girl made it impossible for me to be a boy. I cried, too much, all the time. I wasn't brave. When I bumped into things, it hurt. I was too afraid to climb things, I was too weak, or afraid I was too weak. I was too loud and too awkward to be a passable girl and too silly and too soft to be a passable boy. I didn't decide this myself. I saw how I was seen. I listened to my peers and the names they called me. I saw myself in context and knew I was out of context.

When I was fifteen I cropped my hair, for the first time since I was eight. I was cast as the male captain of a Russian Icebreaker in a play in my local youth theatre group, about some whales stuck in ice in Alaska. I got to wear a big military coat and shout, 'Let's cut some goddam ice!' in Russian. I could live with it if that's how people saw me.

But at school I was cast as the creature in a class production of *Frankenstein*. I was grateful for the lines – I never got lines at school – but I knew it was meant as a curse, not a gift. They made me wear a green clay face mask, one of those that cracks as it dries. The girls who cast me said they'd given me the part because of my hair, because I looked like a man. But what they were saying, very clearly, was that they thought of me as a monster. That I was not like them. That I did not belong.

And yet so many doctors looked at me and diagnosed me as pathologically womanish. They looked at my body, looked at my notes, and saw the problem of femaleness. I had never felt so firmly placed inside a box.

*

Correct diagnosis saves lives. Correct diagnosis makes lives bearable. It gives you access to the right treatment. It gives you agency. It gives you the language to describe your realities to others in ways they will understand. It gives you back trust in your own interpretation of your body's weather. It gives you back trust that someone in the medical profession has seen you, heard you, acknowledged you, not dismissed you. It gives back hope.

Some people ask what is the point of seeking a diagnosis for a condition for which there is no cure. I've heard this said by ordinary people, by medical professionals, by members of my own family. To them I repeat: you're mistaking no cure with no action. No cure with no help. No cure with hopeless. There may be no cure, but there is treatment, there is management, and there is understanding: none of these can be achieved without a correct diagnosis. Diagnosis makes change possible. Diagnosis makes survival possible.

What a difference knowing not just about EDS but about haemochromatosis at seventeen could have made in my life, the years of pain and terrifying symptoms I could have avoided. The spells of deterioration, the downward spirals. The periods of unshakeable mental gloom, the periods of medical despair, the periods of damaging myself trying to push through, because *there is nothing wrong.*

I think about damage that might be irreversible, and what it would be like to not have it, to have avoided it. I think about all the pointless, invasive tests and wrong medications I have had, the insulting and patronising consultations, the doctors who have told me I need to *stop.* How all this could have been avoided, if only the right questions had been asked at the right time. If only someone – just one person amongst the dozens I saw – had known to ask the right question, known how to interpret the answer. Known how to turn the answers into change.

I think not just about the physical damage, but the emotional damage. The years of uncertainty and mistrust that could have been avoided. The trauma that could have been avoided. The panic I contend with every time I go into a doctor's office. The constant fear of dismissal. Of not being believed. I wonder who I would be if I weren't continually worried about not being believed.

I think of all the moments when a door opened just a crack, then was slammed shut. How much of me was crushed each time.

I think about the parts of my life that have been put on hold, deferred because of mismanaged illness, again and again and again, and how none of this needed to have happened, if someone – just one person – had only asked the right questions back in 2013, 2009, 2004, 1997. 1995. 1994. 1986. 1984. 1982.

Genetic

There is a feeling I get sometimes on a walk, especially on a long, slanting path, threaded with trees and tree roots and with a gully perhaps to the side, a feeling of deep atavistic dread, a kind of soundless humming of terror, in my body but not in my body. It's like I'm picking up a message on an inaudible wavelength that's coming off the land or the path itself. A kind of leaching of a bad past, of a bad history. Reverberation through the trees. I'll think something bad happened there, or that it is angry. I'll think I don't belong there, that there is something important I don't understand, and I will come to harm. I know it's silly, but I'll feel it, and I won't be able to rationalise it away.

When I feel like that, I think of Creswell Crags. It is the feeling I associate with the place. Maybe I felt it first there, maybe not. But it is the first time I remember feeling it, the first time I associated that feeling with a particular place.

Creswell Crags is a limestone gorge on the border of Nottinghamshire and Derbyshire. One side of the gorge is in one county, one in the other. There are tall walls of limestone on either side of a flat-bottomed ravine with water in the centre. We were taken there on a school trip when we were seven or eight. Ancient people and beasts lived there in a labyrinth of caves in the rock – creatures it was hard to imagine so close to town – cave lions and woolly mammoths, and huge aurochs and giant elk. In the caves things lingered, preserved, unearthed. People were already digging them up in Victorian times, blowing them out of the caves with dynamite in suits and bustles. They were still digging them up in 1988.

*

To recognise yourself as ill is to meet yourself again, to meet your past self again, with a new understanding, to meet your future self again, with altered expectations.

You might realise you have judged yourself harshly, as you have judged others, as others have judged you. You were not, after all, not trying hard enough to be well, or making yourself sick, thinking yourself sick, for some reason you couldn't quite reach but everyone else was convinced of. You learn to trust your body's signals again, to trust your own belief in them.

To know your sickness as genetic is to know yourself not to be alone in your difference. You know yourself as a mutant, not as a sole occurrence, but as one of many. Genetic illness is a matter of heredity. It is a matter of belonging. There is a long line of you, or people like you. You belong to them, and them to you. To know your sickness as genetic is to know yourself as plural, as many. You can see yourself, the individual at the far corner of a billowing family tree, your new family, your mutant family, but you can also see yourself repeated in all of the other leaves.

To try and understand the significance of a genetic condition is to turn your gaze backward, down the line of time. You squint at something in the far distance, hoping to catch a glimpse of your origin. Or else to recognise yourself in one of the points in between. Are these the people you came from? Are these people mutants like you? Was it this one who passed on this mutation, or this one? Did any of them feel like you do? If they did, how did they live?

Meaning doesn't just arrive one day in the post like a diagnostic letter from a doctor. It accumulates over time. It lives in the sedimented layers of fragments, snatched thoughts or phrases that seem inconsequential alone, but together become a body of knowledge.

Genetic

After my diagnosis I turned backwards and saw everything differently, with a strange vertigo, like standing on a thin path in a dark cave unsure what your next step may lead to.

*

Genetic haemochromatosis is caused by various mutations on chromosome 6 of a gene known as the HFE gene. Its role in iron overload was discovered in 1996; around the time I first started showing the symptoms of iron loading. Twenty years before my diagnosis.

The two most frequent mutations are known as C282Y and H63D, though it is believed many different mutations may play a role in the misfunction of the gene that causes a person to load iron.

For a long time it was thought the C282Y mutation originated in Norse or Celtic populations, that it was spread by Vikings along coastlines. There is a logic and an intuitive sense to this. Even now, the greatest frequency of the C282Y mutation is found in places where Norse people settled. There is a kind of historical romance to it too: an appealing narrative that fits a notion of national and transnational identities. When you are feeling weak, unfitted for the physical sphere, there is comfort in thinking yourself descending from notorious warriors. From warriors and artists, storytellers, poets.

*

A few years before the Creswell Crags trip, at my first school, we had been reading about cave people. We were learning about them through stories about a brother and sister who lived in the Ice Age, and had a woolly mammoth for a friend or a pet. I remember it as a picture book we read together in class, though I may be rewriting it. I can't find a record of it now, whatever terms I search with. The brother and sister were kind and courageous. I drew a picture of them for homework, placing them either side of the fire in the mouth of their cave. I spent a long time colouring it in, to make the shadows around the fire, and the texture of long ago. Mum had a friend round for coffee that day, and when I went to show it to Mum, her friend said, 'I wouldn't like to meet those two on a dark night!' She said it in a tone that suggested it was meant to be funny, but real, that the cave people were scary. I was mortified and indignant. I felt the wounding insult not to me, but to my Neanderthal friends. Was it the failure of my artwork? Had I failed to communicate their goodness? The shared sanctuary of the cave?

*

Creswell Crags was a dark place and the dark was gunged up with all the time and dead things. Too much of it to keep the numbers in your head. 5,000 years. 50,000 years. At Creswell Crags I slipped off an underground path in the dark when no one was holding my hand, and fell into a chasm so deep it threw me all the way through history and out of it. I fell into the Ice Age and lay there, immobile and broken, until I starved to death, and my body was never found. This is exactly what they said would happen.

*

To consider a genetic mutation is to consider a history of immigration, invasion, both. A history of settling, a history of conquering. A history of intermarriage, or a history of assault. It is dark down there, in the pit of history. It is hard to be certain what is happening.

Haemochromatosis is often called the Celtic Curse. It has been believed to disproportionally affect people from the traditional Celtic nations, though where exactly is meant by that is debatable. Haemochromatosis is most concentrated on the island of Ireland, where it is said it affects 1 in 83 people. There is a strange pride in the notion of the Celtic Curse, a sense of belonging, a sense that haemochromatosis is part of the Irish story, a key part of an Irish identity. That if you have haemochromatosis at the very least you are part of a Celtic diaspora, but you might be part of the Irish story too. I've wondered myself if my pair of C282Y mutations is enough to claim citizenship or arts council funding.

Science too has been attached to this narrative. A 2006 study aimed to prove an 'Irish origin of the C282Y mutation [and] point to dissemination of the C282Y mutation by Viking raiders and colonizers'. I've read research papers that put the age of the C282Y mutation at 1,200–2,000 years old, but in 2004 a team argued that mutation age had been misinterpreted – that it must have 'occurred in mainland Europe before 4,000 BC' and been imported into Ireland. Some studies claim the origin point as Scandinavia, that it spread from there.

What does it mean to be able to claim ownership to the origin of a mutation that has spread across the globe over thousands of years of migration, invasion, colonisation?

H63D is older, and its origin remains mysterious. In its highest densities, it is 'found in countries bordering the Mediterranean, the Middle East, and in the Indian subcontinent'. I've seen it called the Iberian mutation, though it may be more likely to have originated in North Africa. It has also arisen entirely independently in Sri Lankan populations – mutation as a response to external pressures.

I've heard people refer to them as the Viking mutation or the Spanish mutation, with excitement and pride, that thrill of finding a people you didn't know were yours, a long lost family. A blood connection with a past brought close, made suddenly human, made suddenly yours.

In an article in *The Atlantic* in 2013 Bradley Wertheim wonders about the origin of the mutation, the first person to carry it: 'We cannot yet ascribe an identity to the founder or the world he or she lived in. Exploring the roots of this illness from proton to population, it seems that nearly every answered question spawns far more unanswered ones.'[44]

Yet even as he says the search for a founder is impossible – a waste of resources that should be spent on supporting people living with haemochromatosis today – he still calls up her heavy ghost.

*

The trip to Creswell Crags was one of those where they ask parents to come along to help. My mum came, and though I think I remember being excited about this, that it was my mum this time, I don't know now if that was because of what happened in the cave; if I was really, before the trip, a bit displeased she would be there, saying things mothers say in a non-mother place, being motherly, being my mother in particular. We travelled to the crags by coach, and by the time we got there, one of the girls was sick. She couldn't go into the visitor centre, being sick like that, so someone had to stay behind on the coach. The teachers looked around in that kind of voiceless plea, and my mum volunteered, or was chosen. Perhaps it was because she preferred the idea of staying on the coach, not liking the idea of walking into the caves, or maybe it was just that she's good at looking after people, and knows it. Either way, we carried on to the visitor centre without her.

So when we left the visitor centre to walk along the gorge to go into the caves, to experience how it was to live in the caves, to journey into the Ice Age, shuffling and holding hands in a single file line behind a guide with a single torch, there was no one particularly checking I didn't lag behind, dragging my feet, tripping over my feet, falling down.

*

On the way back north after my diagnosis with Ehlers-Danlos syndrome in October 2014, I wrote about it as an *unveiling of what has always been there.*
I wrote about family.
I wrote:
What it will mean for the future remains to be seen. What it means for the past is everything.

*

I was born and raised in Nottingham, which is a city built on caves.
Its history is enabled by caves, and those caves are part of its living history. It is impossible to resist writing *they stretch out under the modern skin of the city like veins and arteries.* They carry the city's history from chamber to chamber. A hidden network. No one knows how many caves there are, or what might be cocooned within them.
People lived and worked in the caves for thousands of years.
Nottingham people are a people of caves. You could call us troglodytes, which is used as an insult, mostly, to suggest *cave people* in the sense we used to describe the people who stayed at Creswell Crags. It is used to mean backwards, regressive, prehistoric, atavistic. It is used to mean ignorant and basic.

There are famous caves and passageways like Mortimer's Hole, named for Roger Mortimer – usurper of Edward II, lover of his wife, Queen Isabella – who was eventually deposed and tried as a traitor and murdered by the young Edward III after Edward's men entered Nottingham castle through the caves.

There are hundreds of anonymous caves.

Our school locker rooms were built down into the sandstone, like the basements of all older houses in the city. We called them *the dungeons*. There were grated off sections we couldn't enter but we knew what the grates meant: the dungeons were the tip of the underground iceberg, the upper chamber of the labyrinth. The caves went on, deeper and deeper, connected by passageways running under the innocuous classrooms and playgrounds.

When we travelled to Creswell Crags to shuffle, one in front of the other, down through time, to be thrown back by it, we did so from a city of caves. We left a school assembled over cave mouths to another cave mouth. I never connected the two.

I saved a quote by a city council archaeologist from *East Midlands Today* at the top of a draft of a blog post I wrote about my diagnosis:

> It's amazing how many cave owners assume the city council are aware of their cave.[45]

It was coincidental. At the time, I didn't think the body of the city had anything to do with my body, with its hidden connections, its locked off histories. The labyrinths of it. But I was just like the owner of a house built on caves, assuming everyone knew what lay beneath the innocuous surface, the house piled up into air mirrored by the home dug out from stone. For so many years I had unconsciously assumed that if my body contained caves they would be obvious, to myself, to anyone looking at me. I would feel the absences and presences, the hollows and the gatherings. I assumed the correct authorities would be aware of them, that there would be maps and regulations. But how could anyone be aware of the networks burrowing under my skin if I was not myself?

*

In June 2016 when my EDS gastroenterologist told me I had high ferritin levels, I surprised her by having already heard of haemochromatosis. Just the week before my mum found out she too had raised ferritin levels. She had looked up what it might mean for her, and we had talked about it, about what it might mean for all of us.

Later that year a gene test confirmed I had the C282Y mutation on both chromosomes. I had inherited one copy of it from Mum and one from Dad, which meant at the very least they were both carriers of the mutation.

Knowing what we had learnt by then about the theory of the Celtic Curse, it didn't surprise any of us that Mum's test came back saying she was heterozygous C282Y-H63D – that she has the C282Y mutation on one chromosome and the H63D mutation on the other, that she inherited one of each of them from one of each of her own parents. With a long family history in the south-west of Scotland any kind of Celtic Curse made sense.

But my dad's test also came back heterozygous C282Y-H63D, meaning he inherited one of each of the mutations from his parents too. His parents with hundreds of years of ancestors in Nottinghamshire, a county often called the most landlocked in England, far from any Norse ships or any early Irish interchange. What were the mutations telling us about our family history that we didn't know?

*

It was like this. A narrow pathway of stone, barely visible by torchlight, falling down at both sides into unfathomable dark, and the guide, somewhere too far forward, saying, 'At this point in the cave you'll notice a pool to your left where we found the bones of a child, who must have fallen in there and died, tens of thousands of years ago, unable to climb out, wounded and starving, and to your right, a cave so deep, no one knows how far down it goes.'

I understood this was how death came: a certain fall, or an uncertain fall. Did I step forward in the dark, now, unhooked from my line, not knowing whether I might put my foot an inch too far left, an inch too far right? It was hard enough to keep myself upright and my feet on the ground in the light. What if my feet kept taking me forward, back into the twentieth century, but the rest of my body lost balance or snagged on one of these loose bits of time, and I fell anyway? How many centuries till they came for my remains with their little trowels and brushes?

Till they named me Creswell Girl?

*

In 2015 a team of archaeologists from Queen's University Belfast and geneticists from Trinity College Dublin collaborated to sequence the genomes from four people who lived in Ireland four to five thousand years ago: a Neolithic woman and three Early Bronze Age men.

The woman's body was excavated from a passage grave at Giant's Ring henge in 1855, and she was named Ballynahatty Woman. Her genetic make-up told researchers she had dark hair and eyes, and had Near-Eastern ancestry. She also carried the H63D mutation.

The men tumbled out of a collapsed cist burial in a pub car park on Rathlin Island, carrying genetic heritage from the Pontic Steppes. One of them carried the C282Y mutation.

The team's research paper calls this 'the first detection of a known Mendelian disease variant in prehistory': the earliest proof of a hereditary disease caused by a mutation in a single gene. The earliest proof, not just on the island of Ireland, not just of haemochromatosis, but at all.

Their work has overthrown previous ideas about where and when Irish culture and language originated and developed, as well as previous ideas about haemochromatosis.

Both the C282Y mutation – the 'Viking' mutation – and the H63D mutation – have been in Ireland for over 4,000 years, long before Norse raiders and settlers spread their genetic material down the coastline.

Whilst Ballynahatty Woman was farming the land south of modern-day Belfast 5,200 years ago, H63D was already being woven into the Irish story, over a thousand years before the next wave of mass migration brought C282Y to join it.

Publicity pieces from both Trinity and Queen's call this project 'embarking on a type of genetic time travel'.[46]

*

Go back a few centuries and my ancestors were farm labourers. Labourers of similar kinds in different fields from Wiltshire to Nottinghamshire to Lanarkshire to Dumfriesshire. Some moved off the land when the land had less to offer them, and became cordwainers, became different kinds of labourers, became engineers and inventors. Some moved to the city to join the police. Some moved to town and became painters and decorators. Some came back from a war with their lungs broken, and couldn't paint any more. Some spent their lives in bed. I scan through them, the ones I know of, and ask *was it you? was it you? was it you?*

I look over family history for clues. I pore over early deaths.

On my father's side, there is Granny Pycroft, who lived in bed. My dad, as a small boy, would be let in to see her. Her name was Lilly. She was the mother of my own grandmother, Rowena, my dad's mother. Lilly went once to Switzerland, to a sanatorium, bed to distant bed. When she returned, still sick, she went back to the place she came from; spent the rest of her life in bed.

Everyone had stomach problems, everyone was sick.

I am trying to get him to remember for me, to find clues. Lilly had three children: Leslie, Margaret, then Rowena. Dad remembers Margaret as, in his own words, 'fey'. He calls her fragile, says 'she was a long thin drink of water, very skinny, delicate looking'.

We wonder together if what he means is that she was marfanoid – that she had the particular narrow and disproportionally long-limbed body type linked to EDS – but what he knows is that she died of TB. Only when he had the test at school and found he had antibodies did they realise the family were infected.

I suspect the Muirs – my mother's father's family – with a run of sons dying in their forties, and my grandfather himself, with his childhood osteomyelitis, his pancreatic cancer that spread. But I know the Blacklocks with their narrow marfanoid jaws and their long marfanoid arms to be carrying something forward too. They with their heart failure and their diabetes, early and late.

My grandmother Peggy, the third youngest of nine, who would let me ride her back like a horse around her front yard, who made the best home-made chips, who would let me climb into bed with her in the morning when she was visiting and would teach me to draw. Who lost all her teeth. Who cracked her dentures again and again because they were not moulded to her high, narrow palate. Who added inches onto the pattern of every jumper she knitted to cover my mother's wrists, my brother's wrists, my wrists.

I ask Mum about her mother's family, and she tells me about the nine of them: Jake, then Tom, then Jean, then Jessie (Type I Diabetes), then Nan (Type I Diabetes), Mary (Type II Diabetes), Peggy (Type II Diabetes), Davy and Phia (Type I Diabetes and Epilepsy). Tom, the second eldest, was diagnosed in adulthood with 'disseminated sclerosis', now more widely known as multiple sclerosis. He walked with crutches and used an Invacar – a single-seater motorised mobility car. Phia – Sophia – was a bit unwell always.

How Peggy – my grandmother – and her mother Jessie both had heart attacks at seventy-nine. How they both had Type II Diabetes. How Jessie lived in the country all her life, with no running water or electricity. She'd make soda scones on the fire on the griddle with milk from the farm.

David, my grandmother's closest brother, had a sudden heart attack in his late sixties. Their father, David Hendersen Blacklock, had died of a heart attack at seventy-two.

I see guilt, or complicity, on all sides. I see familiarity. Those I suspect the most are also those I feel the most natural sympathy with. I suspect them because I think we are alike, more than familiar, that we are a sub-family within the family. The mutants and double mutants hiding amid the rest.

Was it you?

*

I'm not sure I believed it when we came out of the cave's lumpy throat and into the daylight, and everyone was still there, except my mum and the girl who were on the coach. Everything still looked like 1988, and no one had been gored by a woolly rhinoceros or a scimitar-toothed lion. Nobody noticed I was still in the cave. One creeping thought was that we didn't come out of the cave, or that I didn't, that everything that followed was ridiculous enough it could only be a dream after, or during, the long moment of falling.

*

I keep coming back to that word *fey*. What does it mean to describe someone as fey, to be described as fey?

My first thoughts are to do with fragility, vulnerability – that to be fey is to be not for or of this world.

When I'm not sure what to think of a word or why I keep thinking of a word, I look up its history, the lost and buried meanings it trails behind it. The etymological dictionary tells me *fey* comes from Old English *fæge* and Old Norse *feigr* – meaning timid, feeble, cowardly, but also doomed to die, fated, destined. It is linked to a sensation of elation that comes before death. To be fey is to be disordered in the mind, like one about to die.

The dictionary tells me the word 'foe' evolves from a shared root. That which is doomed to die is also our enemy. That which is otherworldly is also doomed to die, as our enemy. It displays unearthly qualities because it is no longer of this place, or of us.

Unless we are it, unless we are the fey, in which case we are so close to death, we can see behind and through it, and so resonate with palpable unearthliness.

I begin to wonder if the sick are intrinsically fey.

In *Pain Woman Takes Your Keys,* Sonya Huber calls those who dwell in the kingdom of the sick 'the good and bad witches, the double-sighted'.[47] We know things, have seen things, can see things coming.

In July 2020 Alice Wong established the Disabled Oracle Society, after tweeting 'disabled people are modern day oracles' in response to the failure of the protective response to the spiralling pandemic. During the pandemic our oracle powers have come not from the supernatural, but from experience and knowledge. We know how precarious states of health can be; how tedious and terrifying it is to be seriously ill. We know that even simple infections with known diseases can catalyse cataclysmic effects in susceptible bodies. We know that health is not to be taken for granted, is not a virtue, is not controllable. That anyone is only one accident or infection away from disability. As Wong expands in an essay: 'Disabled people know what it means to be vulnerable and interdependent. We are modern-day oracles. It's time people listened to us.'[48]

In *Ask Me About My Uterus* Abby Norman writes about her conviction that there was something the matter with her when all her doctors dismissed her as like the myth of Cassandra, who 'couldn't even use her sight to save herself'.[49] I have used this appellation so many times of myself. These last few years I have called myself a Chronic Cassandra, plagued by visions of health consequences, unable to stop them from coming to pass. All of our warnings, all of our pleas for caution are treated just like our symptoms are, as hysteria. What good is double-sightedness if all it does is appal the normal? If we can't use it to save ourselves, or others?

Michele Lent Hirsch suggests people cannot bear illness because it reminds them too much of their own mortality, reflecting on how as a young disabled woman her 'palpable connection' to death became visible to others. She became unsavoury to the well: her '"deathyness" was showing', she writes, and no one wants that, wants to be reminded of that. She describes walking around with 'a small cloud of deathyness [. . .] wafting around' her after a near-death experience, and how it would make other people talk to her as though they were talking to a ghost.[50]

Sometimes I think if I were a ghost people might take my warnings more seriously, might trust my arcane gleanings. But I have felt like a ghost of myself drifting disconnected through my own life too. I have felt the cloud of deathyness, a fug that separates me from the simply living.

Mum has said, more than once, that we have the sight in our family – in her family – and I wonder what that really means. Is a visionary simply someone who has a complicated relationship with time? Someone more or less fey? Or someone who lives, at least partly, in the other kingdom, the double-sighted sick? Too deathy for life? Someone who can see down into the recesses of the cave because they are also there, have also been there, know what it is to fall.

*

There is a tired family joke that we must be related to Rob Roy, because Rob Roy had notoriously long arms, like we do. There is a photo of my brother by a statue of Rob Roy taken as proof. Rob Roy and his long arms reaching down an illegitimate tree to touch fingertips with my teenage brother, the auburn waves of his nineties curtain haircut and his outsize limbs proving him to be the rightful heir – both men's long arms outstretched to reach through time to mine. We want to own all the heroes, lawful or no.

I tell this to N early on in the process of our bonding over poetry and our mutually excessive arms. Despite our different countries of origin, our different ancestral narratives, we know ourselves to be sisters of the long arms, cold-blooded salt-seekers. Years later, when I know our arms are pathological, and not just quirky, I repeat the diagnostic procedure at home, asking her to stand and face the cottage wall, measuring fingertip to fingertip to confirm our relation. In an echo of my own diagnosis, I have to do hers twice to trust the enormity of the disparity, to trust my calculation. She has the longest reach of all.

When she visits the house of the poet Du Fu in China she sends a photo of her posed alongside his statue: the elongated sweep of her lyrical arms met perfectly by his. She emails: 'See his arms, he's pretty Marfan, isn't he?'

We are sisters of the long arms, and we are descended from poets and swordmasters and folk heroes.

I know, I know, these are only statues, not records of the men, not replicas of their proportions, but our hearts as well as our arms tell us they belong to us, and us to them. Can't we have them as one of us?

We want to see ourselves in history, we want to belong to something, and something to belong to us.

I look up Rob Roy Long Arms and fall to weeping with laughter. The first entry I find tells me he had 'arms so long that it was said he could tie his garters without stooping'. The next details 'extraordinarily long arms'. The next tells me 'his long arms were said to give him an advantage' in sword fights. The next one begins to make sense of the legend of the excessively long arms. It was Sir Walter Scott – famed in our parts for escaping out the guest room window of Dove Cottage in a quest for a pub breakfast when the Wordsworths' porridge-based regime got him down – who secured the image of Rob Roy as marvellously well-endowed in the arms in the public consciousness.

W. H. Murray puts this down to Scott's inability to understand a Highland tendency towards comic exaggeration, but the belief in the arms is strong. On one website dedicated to the Scottish Clans, I find them described as his 'inherited long arms'.

In his famous novel on Roy's life, published in 1818, Scott gives us a Roy whose frame disrupts the rules of symmetry, the Golden Mean, the canon of proportions:

> Two points in his person interfered with the rules of symmetry; his shoulders were so broad in proportion to his height, as notwithstanding the lean and lathy appearance of his frame, gave him something the air of being too square in respect to his stature; and his arms, though

round, sinewy, and strong, were so very long as to be rather
a deformity. I afterwards heard that this length of arm was
a circumstance on which he prided himself; that when he
wore his native Highland garb, he could tie the garters
of his hose without stooping; and that it gave him great
advantage in the use of the broadsword, at which he was
very dexterous.[51]

Scott turns to his own reference points, using the language of
archaeology and folklore, so that Roy becomes a remnant of
something non-human, something pre-human:

> this want of symmetry [. . .] gave something wild, irregular,
> and as it were, unearthly, to his appearance, and reminded
> me involuntarily, of the tales [. . .] of the old Picts who
> ravaged Northumberland in ancient times, who [. . .] were
> a sort of half-goblin half-human beings, distinguished, like
> this man, for courage, cunning, ferocity, the length of their
> arms, and the squareness of their shoulders.

Roy, in Scott's version, becomes a late manifestation of an
ancient phenotype – a creature out of time – atavistic, deter-
mined by its lineage. The latest in a long line of mutants.

Pict, or goblin.

Is it any surprise that Rob Roy has caves named for him,
where he is supposed to have hidden himself and his tremen-
dous, terrible arms from the normalising law of the day?

*

In 1893 folklorist David MacRitchie proposed that Fairies were
real before they become myth, a forgotten race 'transformed
into an unreal impossibility, within a period of two centuries or
so'.[52] Fairies are like Picts, he argues, not magical beings but real
peoples whose identity and culture were usurped, swallowed
by history. Stories of Fairies and related seemingly 'absolutely

unreal' creatures are misrememberings of lost ancestors or lost tribes driven into fiction. This wasn't a new idea: James Cririe had suggested it ninety years earlier in his popular verse tour of the Highlands, but MacRitchie makes Cririe's theories sound plausible, leaning on Scott for evidence.

Much of the argument is based on how Fairies and Picts are both said to live or have lived: underground, in dwellings dug into the earth and turfed over. Faery we know is entered by going down through the earth, through caves. Down, down into the other place, the shadow kingdom. In Caithness, the remains of Pictish houses are called wags, a word derived from a Gaelic word meaning 'little cave'. One Gaelic name for pictish houses MacRitchie translates as 'house beneath the ground', though these drystone buildings are no more caves than my traditional lakeland cottage is, built half below the old road as it is.

MacRitchie reminds his readers 'both in Gaelic and in English, the word "cave" is by no means restricted to a *natural* cavity'. A cave could be a built environment, just as what we read as a natural cave may be a long-abandoned dwelling, formed not by geologic processes, but by its past inhabitants.

The underground labyrinth of Faery is made uncanny not by its inhabitants but by what those who followed did to unsettle them. Who do we belong to, Faery, or the newcomers who pushed them into shadow? What are we recalling when we go down into the earth?

I always thought *fey* as in unearthly, as in doomed, was the same as *fay*, as in fairy, as in magical being, as in dweller in Faery, but now I read it's an accident of sound, of variant spellings. Fairy comes from fae, from fata, which is fate, which is oracle.

The Fay are literally otherworldly, incredible, visionary. Maybe also doomed to die, or else locked into an eternal battle of rights over the places that used to be theirs.

I read a tweet that reminds me of something I'd forgotten, but once knew well: that the Fay can be killed with iron. In later myth the iron becomes silver, so that silver can stop witches and warlocks and werewolves.

Now I think *did the Fay have haemochromatosis?* By which I mean, is killing the Fay with iron a way of remembering the longevity of haemochromatosis in the isles, of remembering the people who carried the genes before the people who came to tell the tales? Of Bally-nahatty Woman in her passage grave, the Bronze Age Chieftain of Rathlin, and all their kin? Of all those who went underground, remembered only in legend and in genetic heritage.

*

Fifteen years before Scott published *Rob Roy*, Dorothy Wordsworth brought the legend of Rob Roy's long arms back to Grasmere. During her 1803 tour of Scotland with her brother William, they hear many tales about Rob Roy, and she writes them down in her journal. On 27 August 1803 she records how the landlord and landlady of the inn where they were staying became teary-eyed talking about Roy, 'a good man'. Amongst many stories they tell her:

> He was a famous swordsman. Having an arm much longer than other men, he had a greater command with his sword. As a proof of the length of his arm, they told us that he could garter his tartan stockings below the knee without stooping, and added a dozen different stories of single combats, which he had fought, all in perfect good-humour, merely to prove his prowess.

Dorothy recognised these as archetypal stories, comparing Roy to Robin Hood, but she takes the comment about the arms literally. They appear in her brother's poem almost as an aside, 'wondrous length and strength of arm'.[53]

Maybe Scott long-armed the story of Rob's long arms from Dorothy's tour journal, or William's poem. Maybe it had already become an agreed fact and he learnt the story the same way they did, from the people who claimed to remember the man as he was, alive, in all his long-limbed glory.

Kate Davies dedicates a chapter of her 2018 book on craft and knitting in the highlands, *The West Highland Way*, to Rob Roy's arms, concluding that 'Rob's long arms never really belonged to him'.[54] She calls them 'figurative devices, tropes lost in translation, errors of understanding passed down through the centuries'. Davies sees the genesis of the long arms not in Rob's genetics, but in the genetics of a joke, a Gaelic colloquialism for a thief, literalised in English. She supposes that the legend stuck because it served a purpose: 'We wanted our Highland legends bigger, braver, stronger, even verging on the grotesque.' In the grotesque hyperbole of 'arms longer than those of any man' she finds impossibility and the failure of one culture to understand another. I find myself thinking *was it you?*

*

In February 2018 I held a writing residency in Hawarden, a village in Flintshire, on the borders of Cheshire.

At the library we could ask for a special permit that allowed us to walk through the Gladstone Estate woods, marked on the map as the Bilberry Woods. These woods were not at all like the soft, mossy, dappled spaces above Town End where bilberries flower each spring amongst bluebells and wood anemones and wood sorrel and dog violets. The first time I visited them, I came from the public footpath through the wide, rolling green parkland alongside the old castle. You enter this path through a red door in a large red gate in a crenellated gatehouse in the centre of Hawarden. It has the look of a magical portal, especially when the door is left open a fraction, and you can see a slice of grass and sky from the road.

It was a bright afternoon, after a morning of snow flurries and hail. I had wanted to explore the castle. It was surrounded by a low wall, and beyond the wall, thick waves of snowdrops, with primroses glowing amidst them. But the wall was topped with barbed wire, and punctuated by signs reading PRIVATE and CCTV IN OPERATION. There was a gate in the wall, but the gate was locked. From the lower, shaded ground of the park, the squat round tower and separated arches of the castle against the blue sky looked like they were in another season, or another time. I had half a thought they were in Faery, and half a thought to cross over when I walked the perimeter of the wall, and found a tumbled section that had clearly been breached before. But I thought of the permit folded up in my pocket, and the Bilberry Woods, and the peculiar responsibility of being a Writer in Residence, and I went back to the path.

As soon as I left the park, and dipped down to the permit-only area, I felt the error. There was no sun there. The path was an estate road calf-deep in churned up mud and dankness and disquiet. It led over a stone bridge over a turgid, brown stream, then up along the edge of an open swathe of park estate, scattered with occasional trees. There was a pine wood to the left of the track, and the pines were croaking in the wind. A buzzard circled above them, appearing and disappearing in the sway.

Ahead was a cattle grid leading into the woods. You knew which way to take at each turning, because one route would have a tree with PRIVATE: NO ENTRY tacked to it, and one would have a tree with PERMIT HOLDERS

ONLY. I followed the PERMIT HOLDERS ONLY trees, but I felt myself drawn further and further into the woods, not closer to the village. The path turned back somehow and ran alongside a stone wall which bordered that open piece of parkland. There was light over there, and twenty-first century industry on the horizons. Smoking towers and glistening houses. In the wood, there was vertical time and a peculiar darkness. It began to hail, lightly. The mud was so deep my hips were rocking out of their sockets with each step. Going forward was painful, but to go back might be further still, and it felt bad, it felt wrong, like I could slip off at any moment and down into one of the stagnant pools that lurked between the trees.

But it was the last part in particular that gave me the Creswell Crags Feeling. The woods came to a halt again after a slope down towards a noirish pond, two tyres floating in it like corpses. The path carried on along the side of the stone estate wall, but to the left of it was a kind of dip, like the edge of an ancient earthworks, or an old ha-ha, and beyond that, a hilly field. Trees had grown up on the banks of the dip, throwing their roots into the path. Larger, older trees made the path shuffle round them. Sludgy water sat in the bottom of the dip, undecided whether to be a stream or a drain.

I was in pain. Much pain. I had begun to worry I'd gone wrong at the signs in the mud somewhere, and this path wouldn't take me back at all, that it would keep going on and on in the wrong direction, until I couldn't move myself through the mud any more. My left foot was dragging, which I knew made me more likely to fall. But it wasn't any of those things that did it. It was something to do with the line of austere trees, the gully, the boggy core, the light.

*

After that first walk in Hawarden, I avoided the woods for weeks, particularly the centre and the village end of them, the public footpath end of them, with the stagnant pond, the compacted earth and root path between the wall and the tree-lined gully, and the ruined mill at the bottom. It is along this stretch, running along the old estate wall, that the Creswell Crags Feeling was strongest. I could hear it like the soundtrack of a crime drama.

Even from the park side of the walk, on the wide, open hilly swathe by the old castle, I could hear it. The path through the park runs parallel to the woods, with the river through the old mill at the bottom of it. The bad noise seemed to cover that line of woods, the muddy valley, like the clusters of crows and jackdaws. Even on a bright day, when the sun was warm on my face, when I looked to the woods, that was all I could think.

*

In the library, I look up Creswell Crags online. This isn't the first time. Last time I thought to look it up it must have been years ago. I couldn't find much. Now there is a visitor centre website and plenty of images, including satellite images, and an artist's reconstruction of what it might have looked like in the Ice Age, with a woolly mammoth walking down the centre of what is otherwise entirely recognisable as the modern-day gorge. I say recognisable, because in the library, scrolling through the images, I begin to understand that my fear is visual: a lingering memory of a wooded gorge with water at the bottom, and paths of sandy earth running along and through it.

There is another image which layers a contemporary photograph with a superimposed Victorian couple, admiring the industry of archaeology. There are images showing the paths. The pictures that show the mouth of the caves are mainly on sunny, summer days, and it doesn't look so frightening. There is one picture of the gorge in deep snow, looking like Narnia.

It is described on the visitor centre website as *Home of the Ice Age Hunter*. A Durham University webpage tells me the caves are 'Britain's primary resource for Upper Palaeolithic archaeology, and the richest cluster of Middle Palaeolithic archaeology in the north of England'. They contain the only Upper Palaeolithic cave art in Britain:

> simple, incomplete engravings including a cervid (probably a young red deer), a bovid (probably the extinct wild cattle aurochs), a horse, several downward-pointing triangles usually interpreted as vulvae, and enigmatic elongated forms which could represent incomplete long-necked birds or highly-stylised human females.

This cave art was only discovered in 2003. Before that, there was no evidence of cave art in Britain at all. The engravings are believed to have been made 13–15,000 years ago.

What I cannot find is any mention at all of a body in a pit or a pool, and a steep drop on the other side. I read people's accounts of visiting on their blogs; I read the current education guides.

Did I misremember the whole story? Was it an animal that fell, and not a person? Was there really a drop on both sides, or did my imagination make one from the dark and the cold feeling of the long past listening in? Did it matter?

*

One of the first excavators of Creswell Crags was a local man from the village of Creswell, urged to do so by his wife, who had a dream of buried treasure in the caves. The treasure turned out to be the bones of extinct beings.

*

In a biography of King Alfred – which may or may not have been written in AD 893, during Alfred's own lifetime, by Asser, Bishop of Sherborne – Nottingham appears as *Tigguocobauc,* Old Brythonic for the house of caves, cavy house, cavy dwelling.

In Asser or pseudo-Asser's account, an army of Danes 'leaving Northumbria, invaded Mercia, and advanced to Nottingham, which is called in Welsh "Tigguocobauc" but in Latin "The House of Caves" and wintered there that same year'.[55] The year was 868.

I think about those Norse in Nottingham, and the C282Y mutation in my father's family tree. Maybe they'd been carrying it forward from that first ninth century overwintering, or from the early tenth century, when Danes manned the garrison at Nottingham alongside Saxons, or AD 939 when Olaf Guthfrithson, Norse king in Northumbria and Dublin, conquered Nottingham, and became its ruler too.

*

In the cavy house you grow up walking on streets built over caves, going to friends' houses in which the cellars connect to underground passageways, going down every school day into the subterranean locker rooms. Trying not to think of the vast unseen underground network of them; the things they hold. Running past the barred entrance way, its cool cave breath, the sense it might swallow you, or cough something up into you. You understand this as a kind of haunting. The hairs raising on the back of your neck, the chill, you know signifying deathliness. Signifying the return of the buried, the past. Uncanny. The creeping of the skin analogous to the feeling you get when you say *someone walked over my grave* and its bending and folding of time. You are already down there, under there somewhere, and the unknown unknowable feet of the future are stepping lightly over you, and you are also there, in the present moment, tickled by the invisible fingers of the long dead. You are you, your ancestors, your descendants. Your ancestors are grazing the back of your neck, lifting your hair up to blow on your goose-pimpled skin, and you are the ghost, reaching your fingers out to touch the fingers of the future carrier of your strange, bad genes.

*

The Creswell Crags trip is tangled up in my mind with another school trip: one to Dovedale in Derbyshire a couple of years later. There is a record of this trip to Dovedale in a school project I did afterwards. The project was on rivers, and I had chosen the speciality subject of the Amazon. I made my project into a little booklet, bound together with pink ribbon, in a cover of red card decorated with a wonky pencil crayon drawing which is clearly meant to be The Amazon. It's one of those pieces of schoolwork that keeps turning back up. I don't know how, but it keeps moving house with me. I found it again in December 2017, clearing some boxes we had moved from the old house two and a half years earlier and never unpacked. I was surprised to find my photos and notes on the Dovedale trip in there alongside the special section on the Amazon. I'd only remembered the Amazon part, which was largely plagiarised from the *National Geographic*, but included a drawing of an ocelot that I was particularly proud of. The teacher's note at the back says *You have researched well but I am not so sure that all the words are written in your own way!* Probably the whole point of the Dovedale trip was the rivers project, and the Dovedale part was more important than the Amazon part. It seems odd to me now that's not how I've thought of it.

The project dedicates a page to Lovers Leap, where we stopped for lunch. There is a photo of us, eating our lunches on rocks by the path overlooking the River Dove. Our clothes are peak 1990: shell tops and colourful, batwing-sleeved tracksuits. Some of us have compasses around our necks. There are others in the background, including the teacher, Mrs P, looking away.

There is a photo of ducks on the River Dove. There is a terrible poem I have called 'a poem on rocks'. There is a map I have drawn of the route, and a bunting's feather stickered below my five-book-Bibliography. I only know it is a bunting's feather because I have labelled it. Like much of the project, it has a faint, pencilled tick next to it, and a little pencil star. There is a postcard of Dove Holes caves taped in. All the tape has rotted away now, and the photos and postcard are loose. It does not mention how we wandered off, how they searched for us, how they panicked, how furious they were, how much trouble we got in.

*

It was like this. We were walking and talking, D, H, and me. We had got ahead of the others, somehow. Maybe they had stopped whilst a teacher explained something about rivers, or rocks, or maybe someone had tripped or was doing up a shoelace. We saw the entrance to a cave. I suggested we go and look at it. We went. Time passed. I couldn't say how long.

When we came out of the cave, we couldn't see the rest of the group. We called out, worried we'd been left behind, then started up along the path again, double-quick, almost running. I knew the way, it was easy. You couldn't go wrong. Dad was a keen hiker. Before his feet became too painful and Mum's knees became too painful, we would go into the

Peaks some weekends, the three of us. I had my own little hiking boots that year – the same hard, implausibly uncomfortable brown leather as grown-up ones – bought from the Scoop shop on Central Avenue. I remember finding them on the shelves so vividly but not whether I was embarrassed or pleased to have the correct gear, only that they never softened. I retrofit my smugness and certainty about the route. You just followed the path to the tea rooms, which was called Polly's Cottage, which was both funny and embarrassing.

When we got to the end though, the rest of our group weren't there. We checked the car park, and they weren't there either. We waited.

*

Back at school, in the brown classroom, held behind or called in especially to be shouted at. Mrs P's classroom, not my form room. Mrs P saying over and over again, 'But why did you stray off the path, but why?' Probably she didn't say 'stray off the path'. It seems unlike her. Maybe she said, 'Why did you go into the caves?' The 'but why' came over and over. She seemed to be focusing her interrogation on H, maybe because H was crying so much, maybe for some other teacherly reason. We knew she, as a teacher, could not be trusted to have impartial feelings about us. She had made her mind up about each of us long before the trip. It felt like she was physically shaking H as she shouted 'but why but why but why but why'. What I remember most is both their faces, red. Mrs P's hot and red and angry. H's red and folded into the bad kind of sobbing you got mocked for. Did I cry too? Probably. I always cried when someone shouted.

What I knew, and no one said, was that it was my fault. We were all being shouted at like this, being asked to explain ourselves, because I called my friends to look at the caves. Maybe I don't remember the rest of what Mrs P said because this is what she said. Not 'why did you leave the path' but 'why did you follow her?' Have I forgotten because I want to forget that she expected better of the others, but not of me?

Did I tell them no one would notice? Did I say it didn't matter? I don't remember, but it's likely.

What I remember is *but why but why but why.*

*

I call up my mum on FaceTime. It is March 2018, and I need to know what she remembers about two school trips almost thirty years earlier. The first thing she says is that Dovedale was her fault. She was with us. How didn't I remember that? It makes sense, thinking about the photographs. There are photos of me, which means I wasn't taking them all. Only D and H and I are looking at the camera, and Mum knew them, because we all played together often. Is that what ties the trips together, not just the paths, the caves, the trouble, but the presence of my mum?

She says it was her fault, Dovedale, because she was with us, and she let us walk on ahead. There were no instructions. Everyone was walking in small groups, she says, and no one had been told anything, so we just carried on. She doesn't remember the caves.

She also swears she has never been to Creswell Crags. She would remember, she says. She remembers every trip. She starts listing them. I try to argue, 'But you didn't actually go, you stayed on the coach, because a girl was sick.'

She shakes her head, adamant. 'I would remember that.'

*

I am thinking about all this in the woods in Hawarden, against the backdrop hum of the terror sound, trying to gauge its pitch.

Passing another PRIVATE: NO ENTRY sign nailed to the flaky bark of a pine tree, I wonder if the answer we couldn't give then is what ties the Dovedale Trip and its wholesome cave to Creswell Crags and its awful cave of deep, hungry time.

It is human to wander off, and more than human. It is natural, animal, deep in us. The compulsion to cross a line you've been told not to cross, to climb a wall you've been told not to climb.

That is why we have desire lines; why they're called desire lines. The grass is always greener, the flowers always more beautiful and the sun brighter on the other side of the wall, or beyond the tree with the PRIVATE: NO ENTRY sign on it.

But to stray from the path is dangerous. There are wolves off the beaten path; there are faeries. There are bog creatures and will-o'-the-wisps and a hole you might fall down to the centre of the earth and never be found again, not even after 10,000 years.

People will not wait for you, and they will be angry. People will wait for you, and they will be angry. You will not be the same you when you return.

*

I started excavating my schoolbooks for evidence of Creswell Crags and Dovedale. I need to know more about what happened on those trips, why they keep resurfacing. What am I trying to tell myself with these partial rememberings? I go down in the basement with Dad next time I'm home and we come out with a box of jotters and exercise books. But everything got muddled when they moved house in 2010.

There are books from senior school and some from junior school, but none from quite the right times.

I read through them and through them and find some clues, about Dovedale at least. There is a piece at the very end of one book dated 21 June 1990 about Lover's Leap, which doesn't mention any of the difficulties and fallout of the trip, just tells a story about climbing a peak, and looking over the edge. I called it 'The Thousand and Five Foot Hill'.

The story – let's call it that – is nothing about caves or getting lost or getting in trouble. The drama is all in the setting – 'Lover's Leap, which is a bit of quite high ground, with a massive jagged rock jutting out above the River Dove, which looked like a sheet of glass' – and the narrator's fear of heights. They get to the top, join their friends, and achieve a view the narrator calls 'the most impressive thing I had ever seen'.

The teacher has ticked the margins at various points and written 'good, a thoughtful piece of writing'.

There is no evidence of anything to hide or be forgiven. I have buried the misdemeanour under a spectacular panorama.

*

Sometimes I like to tell myself that my compulsion to stray from the main path – to walk where the spirit takes me, to trespass – is genetic. I blame my great grandfather John Henry Pycroft, who co-founded the first Methodist chapel in Nottingham with my great grandfather George Herbert Atkin and walked miles to it every Sunday from the other side of town, as the crow flies, as god wanted him to, irrespective of traffic.

I blame it on my dad who is always striding ahead, who can't sit still, my mum who does what she thinks is right whether there are instructions or not.

But these are both simplifying narratives. A way of explaining, or excusing, behaviour. That my fear is around the question of conforming/not conforming, and that the reason I can't conform is hereditary, that it's *not my fault*, that it's inborn, ancestral, which makes it beautiful in a way. A way for me to wriggle out of the responsibility for my trespassing/transgressing. A way to explain it to myself. A way to explain away the bad noise of it, the fear of that fall. A way not to get in trouble.

The problem on the Dovedale trip, where the trouble came from, was that we hadn't fallen behind. We had diverted from the path for a short while for just a few metres. When we didn't come out to see the tail end of a crocodile of our classmates and teachers, we assumed we'd been left behind.

Our classmates and teachers, still behind us on the path, assumed we had already fallen behind. Afraid to lose us, they waited.

Afraid to lose them, we hurried on.

*

There are two sets of caves along the route in Dovedale.

There is Reynard's Cave, high up through a limestone arch, named after a seventeenth-century highwayman who was said to live there, or hide things there. His name links him with the trickster tales of werefoxes and fox spirits that span the globe.

In 2014 a hoard of Roman and Late Iron Age coins were found buried in Reynard's Kitchen, the smaller cave next door, after some visitors to the cave uncovered four of them. Three of the Roman coins date from earlier than the Roman invasion of the British Isles, raising questions about how they got there, who they belonged to, what they represent. It is the only time coins from these different cultures have been found buried together.[56]

How long those coins rested there, waiting to be uncovered, as so many visitors clambered over and around them, their unacknowledged history of travel and trade.

The other caves, a pair known as Dove Holes, are easier to access. Smooth-sided round caves like an inner ear. At nine I was already long averse to falling, hesitant with risk. It must be these caves I led my friends into.

Dove Holes, like the caves at Creswell, gave temporary shelter to hunters around 13,000 years ago. By four and a half thousand years ago they were being used as tombs by Neolithic tribes who farmed the surrounding landscape, who buried their dead in caves and man-made dolmen, who may have built the Bull Ring henge near the village Dove Holes, which takes its name from the caves.

I check my rivers project for clues. The last entry before the Bibliography and the feather is a postcard labelled 'Dovedale' which shows the caves, though it does not name them. I have labelled it Dove Holes.

It seems now like a deliberate provocation. I made that teacher tick a picture of the caves I took my friends into, that got us separated, that caused all the trouble.

*

M comes to visit me at the library, in the last week of my residency, and drives us to a nearby castle in a wood. I've been told about it, because it's a mystery. No one knows why they built a castle halfway down a gorge.

We stand on the parapet with snow flying horizontally past us. She says we remind her of the Stark sisters standing on the battlements at Winterfell and I tell her about my own list, all the doctors who have wronged me. It is a joke, but also not a joke.

Below the castle, there is a river, a rocky, mossy river of just the sort dippers love. We see a tree-creeper flit from branch to branch along the shoreline, but no dippers, though we look out for them. We carry on up the side of the river, and suddenly we're in a sandstone alley, and it comes on, as soon as I see the cliff walls, the low buzz of the Creswell Crags Feeling.

I try to explain it, and why I'm writing about it. How I think that vertigo of deep time might be the same feeling I get when I think of genetics, that same sense of looking down or out into something unfathomable. She abbreviates the Creswell Crags Feeling, names it the CCF.

Later, after the slow walk around the castle in the woods, after we have driven back to the library and talked more over tea, I try to explain how the CCF ties to proprioception, that loss of the self in space and time. But I can't quite get hold of it; it keeps slipping from me, me from it.

*

My grandfather Nichol Strong Muir developed osteomyelitis in his leg when he was five. They managed it by scraping the bad bone away, in those days before antibiotics, weakening his tibia. If he fell, it would break, and he kept falling. He played football, though he was told not to, because he loved football, but the wrong move, the wrong contact and his leg would break, again. Every time it broke the remaining bone weakened, healed less completely. It kept breaking.

Nicky was known all round the hospital because he'd been there so often. He had type O blood – the universal type, acceptable by anyone – so whenever there was an accident and they needed a transfusion, they'd call for him and hook him up. His breakable body saved lives.

When he was eighteen, they wanted to amputate his leg after yet another break. His father had given permission but he wouldn't accept it. He sat in a hot bath and soaked his plaster cast off. He kept his leg, but it was bad. A sinus developed, a tunnelling wound from the outside down to the damage beneath. A kind of living sinkhole. Bits of bone and other matter would tumble out of its mouth, the body's own archaeology thrown to the light. He lived with a perpetually open wound, perpetually infected.

When war broke out in 1939 he was passed A1 to enter the army, fit for overseas duties, despite his open, glaring wound. He was sent to train in Chesterfield, but found he couldn't walk in the heavy regulation boots. He went to the army doctor, who allowed him to train in shoes instead, but it didn't help. His leg was so bad by then, the pain unbearable. He went back to the doctor, who charged him with malingering. In preparation for court martial, he was examined by a different doctor, who took one look at his oozing leg, declared him unfit for active service, and sent him home, and to hospital. Once his leg had recovered as much as it could, he became an ambulance driver.

This is the legend my mum grew up with, into. To break was a feature of living. To fall was inevitable. No hurt can be buried when our past injuries tunnel to the surface, or the surface gives way, exposing the cavities. There is a version of my family history that can be told through fracture, not just mine, but generations of it, generations of falling, injury, hurt, continuation.

Nicky was in and out of hospital all of his life. In the sixties, when my mum was working as a radiographer in Carlisle, he fell at work and broke his other leg, the good one. He persuaded the ambulance drivers to take him not to Dumfries Infirmary, but to the Cumberland Infirmary in Carlisle, so Mum could see him. This fall changed their lives. He got industrial compensation, no longer had to haul his body through work that was destroying it.

I remember the cut away part of his leg as smooth and shiny, like Bakelite jewellery. It's a memory of a memory, uncertain and probably garbled. I was so little when he died, all I remember are snatches of images and my love for him.

I can't know if he was particularly susceptible to breaking, anyway, like me, regardless of the osteomyelitis. If he was particularly susceptible to falling, too.

I can't know for certain if his generosity with his blood also kept him well for longer, if he was unknowingly self-managing haemochromatosis those years he gave up his blood for others. But I can see how it bought him the time that let me know him, what his story would have been if his bad leg hadn't brought him into the fold of the hospital, made it part of his life, for better and worse.

I can see what my mum's story would have been, and how it would have ended. When she was nine, she became very ill. She had terrible pain in her abdomen, a temperature so high she hallucinated creatures in her room through the days she lay there in bed, vomiting and delirious. When they took her to hospital on the instructions of their doctor – a friend of Nicky's from football – they found she had pneumonia. But treating the pneumonia did not make her recover. She lay in hospital in pain, confused and frightened.

Nicky was the one to drive their doctor, another medical friend of his, and the local chemist to the Queen of the South match that week. At the end of the game, they lost the doctor. He'd spotted a consultant he knew in the stand and gone to talk to him about the troubling case of a wee girl he knew, who wasn't getting better.

That evening the consultant examined my mum. She had an enormous abscess on her appendix. They put a drain in, gave her antibiotics. She had to sit upright to let gravity do the work, let the decay flow out of the cavern of her belly. She spent six weeks like that on the ward, recovering, and six months later returned to have her appendix removed.

Without the consultant's intervention, without the doctor leaping across the stand, without Nicky – friends with everyone – my mum would have died then, in 1952.

A history of fracture and wounding and a shared love of football saved my mum's life. It saved her future. Let her live, pass on that history and everything buried deep in her cells.

*

My other grandfather used to dislocate his shoulder and knees and pop them back in by pushing against the hood of the car. I didn't know this until after my diagnosis. Dad had never thought to mention it. I think about Grandpa Atkin's physical awkwardness, his terrible varicose veins. He was not an easy person to be around, to love.

It made me feel differently about him, when I learnt about his dislocations. He and his sister Gwyneth both had a marfanoid look. So much suggests a connective tissue disorder, but what else lay under the skin?

I was a teenager when Grandpa Atkin died. Dad talked then about how through his life he had episodes of fever and disorientation that he blamed on malaria he had caught during the war. Back in the nineties, Dad wondered aloud if malaria was a helpful cover to conceal episodes of depression. Now I wonder what role iron overload might have played in his mood swings, his temper. I think of his constant tan, haemochromatotic bronze. I think *was it you?*

*

On Thursday 5 February 1998, in the peak of my teenage illness spiral, I wrote in my journal:

162

Genetic

On Monday night I slept for 13 ½ hours and in my dreams the cemetery on Wilford Hill came creeping to my garden, so that where the wall is instead was a short wall fading into a slight incline studded with uneven row upon uneven row of snow-shrouded grave-stones.

I could not shake this dream, this vision of the graves and their inhabitants in our garden, under the turf we lived over, creeping closer and closer to us. Those graves inching down the hill, like their inhabitants had picked them up and moved the stones. They were so close to the surface. We thought they were gone but they still lived with us. They were growing with us, overlooking us, undermining us.

In the years before the dream, four members of my family had been cremated at the cemetery on Wilford Hill. My dad's dad, two of my dad's uncles, my dad's mum.

My relatives weren't literally buried there in that ground, but it was the last place their bodies were taken, and in the dream, it was them who picked themselves up and shuffled themselves closer. They came down with a message, but I couldn't hear it. I couldn't understand what they were trying to tell me. I couldn't put together the cave of the grave, their presence, my own sickness. Not when I was awake, at least.

＊

In the heatwave of summer 2018 drowned villages rose up as the waters drained away from the reservoirs that hid them, and the invisible histories of the land became visible, as the shapes of old waterways and earthworks pushed through the grass like bleach marks; even the outlines of flagstones in Roman villas along Hadrian's Wall. The Ghost Garden of Gawthorpe Hall shone through the years, a dull yellow-brown. Pictish carvings on a symbol stone, forgotten for centuries, rose up as the River Don sank down. The Internet was full of them, these suddenly apparent histories.

We live alongside these echoes all the time, though we do not see them. They aren't ghosts any more than you or me are ghosts. They live alongside us, the living descendants of our past: solid, tactile. They are stone and grass, they are earth.

*

When you go down into the earth you are going down through time. You are stepping down through layers of time, like an infographic, or fairytale.

You are stepping down into an earlier version of your life in dwellings, atavistic, devolving into your ancestors.

In the cool of the cave – any cave – you feel your ancestors step into your bones. Your bones unbecome, rebecome, in the cavy house of the body.

If you go down far enough, or in the right place, maybe you can step into the moment your genes mutated. First one, then another. Or both together, a new species created with one twist. You could be there, at that moment when you became what you will become. Oracle. Fated. New and ancient.

Chronic

Waking is resurrection. Day after day you come to in the same concrete body you drift from in the night. The shock is always new. Sleep is one kind of effort. The end of sleep is another kind of effort. This is chronicity. You have to resurrect yourself every day.

No one can help you. There are nights your body will not let you go, and keeps you stuck in it, feeling everything, hearing everything, seeing the light from the hallway through the back of your eyelids. It keeps you squeezed in its cramped muscles. There are nights you untether yourself, wriggle out through a chink somewhere, and dream of swimming, or flying, unhindered by its vigilant pains. There are mornings you have to pull yourself back up from somewhere deep and unthinkable. You pull yourself back up through the magma, through the earth's crust and the sedimented years, through the layered remains of the bones of your ancestors, through the foundations of your house and the concrete floor and the underlay and the carpet, through the ceiling and the floor below you, its warped board under worn carpet, through the box of tights and socks and the mattress, indented as though you have been lying there all night. Then you have to persuade it to move. You do your manoeuvres. The ones by which you greet gravity, your frenemy, and by which you hope to appease it. You wiggle your toes and rotate your ankles, pumping your calf muscles until you think it might be safe, or safe enough to raise your upper body to drink the necessary water. Part of your mind is working, as always, on the long calculation of how much energy and time it will take you to get to the bathroom, and if you have the strength for the clenching your pelvic floor requires.

*

Chronic comes from the Greek *khronikos* (of time, concerning time) from *khronos* (time). From the fifteenth century it was being used to refer to diseases which lasted a long time. The literal sense of chronic, 'pertaining to time', has long since been swallowed up by that other sense, of long-termness. Of something that goes on, or goes and comes back. The worst house guest. A pest.

*

A chronic illness is an illness which belongs to time. But it doesn't just last a long time: it changes time, eats it. It takes you into time, and changes your relationship with it. A chronic illness is the end of time. Time as you knew it dissolves into chronic time, as life as you knew it dissolves into chronic life.

You learn all the kinds of time in the chronic life: clock time, experiential time. Time meted out by calendars and cogs, time as passed through the body, as a thin water the body floats through. Horizontal time – or vertical time. Chronic time.

*

In my bed in my attic room in my first year in Grasmere, tucked into the eaves, shaken by high speed jets and chinooks as they fly low through the valley, I learn time like De Quincey described it: repetitive and elastic, folding back on itself, endlessly, drawing distant times and their places together, dragging close times and their places apart. A palimpsest in which 'everlasting layers of ideas, images, feelings [. . .] [seem] to bury all that went before. And yet, in reality, not one has been extinguished.'[57]

Chronic time makes a palimpsest of everything. It reveals the folded nature of time. The arbitrary nature of time. It shows us time as experiential, not as we agree to pretend it is: not linear, not progressive, not leading from one moment to the next and the next and so on, but all at once, a pile up of time, a mess of time. Time as plaster cast. Time fraying underneath.

One night I lay there in my bed under the slates and I swear I fell through every bed I have ever slept in, before that night and since.

*

Spring 2020. All year a novel coronavirus has been spreading across the world. They have named it Covid-19. I have been watching its progress anxiously for months by the time a lockdown is declared here to try to break the chain of infection. The world is stilled, becalmed. I have never known this kind of quiet in Grasmere. No contrails cross the sky, hardly any traffic on the roads. The sounds of nature are turned up as the sounds of human activity are muted.

Every evening now, W and I walk on the common. We walk in the gap between work and dinner, which gets longer as we move from March towards midsummer. We almost always walk clockwise, checking the duck pond for frogs or herons, before moving slowly up the path under the trees, past the metal bench without touching it, and along the last strip of tarmac to the end of the overgrown pond we think of as the heron's pond. In the wet months the heron is always there, stalking through the reeds, or pretending to be invisible under the weeping tree, or hiding behind the wall of rhododendrons.

Here most evenings we take the path up round the crag opposite the tarn onto a boggy moor with craggy knolls dotted over it like sleeping trolls, the hundred paths winding between scattered trees. Sometimes we climb a troll and look down towards Rydal Water, which has been creeping further and further away from us these last weeks as we move only on foot. We follow one path, or another, skirting the crags like we are circling a moat, and emerge from behind the wall of an enclosed wood, rejoin the road, pass by the duck pond, and back down to our house.

Every walk is the same. Every walk is different. A circular ritual, designed to keep us apart and together.

Sometimes we are especially tired or the weather is bad, and we only go as far as the end of the heron pond, and return on the old path parallel to the tarmac, raised and half-hidden in the trees, that once was the road, before a different route was favoured. The ponds either side have dried up in the strange spring drought. They are leaf-pits now, strewn with weed which dripped from branches in the ceaseless rain of February, and has dried into grey-green curtains of moth-eaten lace. I call it the autumn path, because the ground is old leaves and beech mast all year round. As the weeks roll by we have to stoop further and further to creep under the branches of the big trees as they green.

We are not alone when we walk. We cross paths with neighbours and greet them from a distance. Sometimes we disturb a deer at the beginning of the walk, in one of the gardens of the large, empty second homes along the road before we reach the duck pond and turn up, or along the path that rises from the pond to the bench. More often we see them on the way home, sleeping in the bracken, or grazing in a clearing. A strange dell sinks and rises behind the duck pond that also has a raised path through it, another old portion of road that has lost its purpose. This dell, like the duck pond, was created when one of the large houses was built in the late 1880s. Trees were felled, and the fellside scooped out to build the house and its walls. It is wasteland that has re-greened itself into segments of bog and meadow and swampy grove, perfect for deer to hide themselves in. One rainy evening we see a roebuck just standing there in the dell, beyond the raised road, next to a tree we once watched a barn owl hunt from until it got dark around us, and all we could see was its white face like a moon. The roebuck watches us watch him and does not run.

We see red squirrels leaping from one side of the road to the other, or running along a wall, or chasing each other up the garden trees in their cloisters or the feral trees on the path. There is a tawny owl who hunts along the same route we take. We disturb it day after day without meaning to. Sometimes it sits in a tree and blinks down at us; sometimes it keeps three trees ahead of us. We meet Herdwick sheep who have fled their fields to exercise their historic grazing rights on this land that used to be theirs, who watch us cautiously, checking whether we have come for them before they relax. We see birds we are learning to identify with a bird song app that records their voices as we stand and listen, trying to fix cadences in our minds, and we see ones that we cannot mistake: fighty jay, shouty wren, cuckoo cuckoo cuckoo.

We can walk out from the house, and if we time it right, meet no one once we get beyond the road. There are no gates or stiles to form barriers or disease vectors. We rarely meet other people, only animals, insects, amphibians, birds. You can sit on the common, cocooned in uninterrupted birdsong, and imagine this is what Lakeland sounded like two hundred years ago.

*

When you are diagnosed with a chronic illness, you are expected to go through a cycle of emotional responses. When I was shown this cycle, I recognised it as the same used for grief counselling. We were told it was alright to grieve for our former lives. Our lives as unsick, as productive citizens of a healthy world.

There are stages, we were told, that we would go through. Five stages: denial, anger, bargaining, depression and acceptance. We were shown them drawn into a graph, whose dips and plateaus seemed more than usually arbitrary.

But all of us in the room had been living with our pain, our chronic bodies, for so long already we had moved beyond the expected stages of the cycle. Some of us had moved so far beyond it, we had forgotten a time before acceptance. Some of us were not sure we had ever been at the corner of health where the graph was supposed to have begun.

When was I well? When did the cycle start? Before I had daily pain? So, when I was eight, maybe, nine? Before daily pain and injury and fatigue stopped me from participating in activity on a daily, crushing basis? So, when I was ten, eleven maybe? Or before I first thought I might be ill and not injured, or just quirky, so when I was sixteen? I was certainly angry then, angry and afraid, and also depressed and anxious. Frustrated. Expectant. Or before I first realised I couldn't work like other people, and would have to find an alternative career path if I was to work at all. So, when I was twenty-four, twenty-five? Or when I had to admit I could not work full-time at all, when I was thirty-five, and newly diagnosed with chronicity, and a year into my first full-time academic job, and on a course being told it was normal to grieve for health I could not remember owning. I was in the throes of a kind of grief then, grieving for a career I realised I couldn't compete in, despite all the years of training. I cried for it. Or was it when I was eighteen months old, and first broke my leg, and the trajectory of my body's life changed?

Or was it when I first put my intoeing feet to the ground to stumble forward into the world, or when I had my first wide-spread allergic reaction when I was first given cow's milk, or was it already set, from the moment I started to grow from my mutated genes?

Had I been grieving all my life for the shroud of the normative body that kept being lain over me? If so, what kept me grieving was the lie, not the body: the expectation, the insistence that my body was not my body, that my experience in my body was not true.

*

Chronic time is time like Woolf described it in *On Being Ill*, slowed right down, almost to pause, so that the sick 'float with the sticks on the stream; helter skelter with the dead leaves on the lawn, irresponsible and disinterested and able, perhaps for the first time for years, to look round, to look up'.[58]

And the slo-mo sky:

> This incessant making up of shapes and casting them down, this buffeting of clouds together, and drawing vast trains of ships and waggons from North to South, this incessant ringing up and down of curtains of light and shade, this interminable experiment with gold shafts and blue shadows, with veiling the sun and unveiling it, with making rock ramparts and wafting them away – this endless activity.

This is time snapped into fragments, into disconnected phrases.

Time running through the body as repetition. Time 'setting us to wait, hour after hour, with pricked ears for the creaking of a stair'.

Time as chronicity.

*

Chronicity is repetition – the repetitiveness and boredom of waking up each day feeling as bad or worse than the day before. The body's complaints vary, but it always has complaints. In its difference, it is the same. Doing your exercises, trying to get outdoors, taking your medication at the allotted times. On a bad day, waiting for it to be over. On a busy day, waiting for it to be over. On a better day, wondering when it will be over. Gritting your teeth and breathing through it until it is over, counting the threads on the blanket, or the birds outside the window, or watching an entire box set, until it is time to try to go to sleep again, to try to keep asleep again. Repetition with variance. The effort of lasting the day versus the effort of lasting the night.

*

Time becomes an endless, looping condition experienced through the body. The body is witness to the erasing and overwriting of times; the sick body is witness to the over-layering of times, able to see all the layers as present at once.

*

Time like Harriet Martineau described it in *Life in the Sick-Room* – deep, complex.

Time of the sick room, in which 'history becomes like actual life; life becomes comprehensive as history, and abstract as speculation'.

When you are sick, all rooms are sick rooms. Simply by crossing its threshold, a sick person can transform a healthy room into a sick one. They freeze all clocks with their terrible breath. All time becomes the time of the sick room. All time, the time of pain, of fragmented moments of pain, 'that condition being made up of a series of pains, each of which is annihilated as it departs'.[59]

Time invalidated, unspooled by the ongoingness of illness, so:

> Not only does human life, from the cradle to the grave, lie open to us, but the whole succession of generations, without the boundary line of the past being interposed: and with the very clouds of the future so thinned, – rendered so penetrable, as that we believe we discern the salient and bright points of the human destiny yet to be revealed.[60]

In the sickened room the sick person opens their mouth, and instead of words, the past and the future fall out, all jumbled up into each other like Scrabble tiles tipped from the box.

*

We don't have a language or narrative for talking about long-term, non-terminal conditions. Everyone reaches a terminus eventually but it is the length of the journey that decides the terminology. We go long-haul, as they say now of those unre-covered from Covid-19.

Chronic illness is a full-time job, is a community action, is a way of life. It is carrying on. It is enduring. It is unendurable.

*

As April 2020 tips into May and the evenings lengthen, we go out later, shifting our wandering hour with the deers' and the daily Covid briefing.

Sometimes we follow the stony bridleway instead of the thin path, going down past the old quarries, and back along the river to the shores of Grasmere, through the mossy woods, bluebells ecstatic in the low light. Halfway down we stop and look for evidence of the hutments we know once stood there: a shanty town that housed workers on the Thirlmere to Manchester aqueduct.

In January 1886 various papers ran the same bulletin:

> The plant for commencing the Thirlmere Waterworks is rapidly entering the Lake District. During the past few days cabins for the navvies have been constructed on White Moss Grasmere, and labourers are swarming into the district.

There are photographs that show the hutments, bare and functional against bare crags; Dunney Beck at the lower boundary; a pale rough road leading up from them towards the tarn, the tarn itself is unseen. The common looms over the hutments. It's hard to place now, standing at the same point. The tree growth is so immense, it seems a different landscape entirely.

We stand on mossy cushions on rocky outcrops and try to picture the huts, the scene un-greened, un-treed. We examine remnants of wall, smashed pots and glass bottles along the beck. Evidence of habitation. Of working lives.

In 1890 it is estimated that there are 450 of 'the pipe track people' living in Grasmere.[61]

Many, though not all of them, would have been living in the shanty town on the common, where now bluebells sway under pine trees broken by their own weight, and deer weave between beeches and birches, and squirrels skitter from high in oaks that sprout out of rocks and look as if they have always been there.

But they haven't. This is an ancient wood, and a new one. Cleared centuries ago, regrown through generations of un-use, of abandonment. Natural and not at all.

You could look at the common and think it a wild place that has always been wild, but it is edgeland, industrial waste-land, domestic margin.

In 1802 it is a through-route, grazing ground, useful and used. Dorothy Wordsworth writes about being driven from the path 'by the horses that go on the commons'.[62] She describes it as 'a place made for all beautiful works of art & nature, woods & valleys, fairy valleys & fairy Tairns, min-iature mountains, alps above alps'.[63] But it is an inhabited fairyland, not an empty world or a private one. In her next sentence, she tells how, 'Little John Dawson came past us from the wood with a huge stick over his shoulder.'

People worked there, slept there, wandered there, camped there, begged there, let loose their horses and got fines there. People fell into the quarries and died there. People lost their eyesight to quarry blasts there. A man was stabbed in the leg by a young girl there. People foraged and harvested the growth of the land. Commoners fought for their rights and landowners pushed at the common's edges to make space for themselves and their plans.

Walk there now and you may see none of this, only fairy wilderness. If you look closer – fairy ruins.

In 1829 De Quincey describes it as a place of 'swamps', apparitions of the air, and the 'silence of ghosts'.[64]

You might be trespassing on some temporary home when you cross it, some borrowed belonging.

*

Time like Sarah Manguso describes it, ongoing, co-present. She writes: 'I've never understood so clearly that linear time is a summary of actual time, of All Time, of the forever that has always been happening.'

How she comes to think her anxiety about her chronic illness 'derive[s] from a fixation on moments – an inability to accept life as ongoing'.[65]

*

Everywhere we walk during these locked-down weeks we find treasures of old waste, as though the ground is pushing them up just for us. A lemonade bottle. Shards of porcelain. Thick glass annealed by a fire. Glazed pottery. One path is so strewn with fragments it looks like mosaic.

It seems the floods of February followed by these long dry weeks have uncovered old dump sites. In the 1890s the tarn we pass daily was used by the council to sink waste in, until a campaign to protect it as a site of Wordsworthian associations, with plantlife of particular note. The rubbish is dug in further, covered over. A promise is made to move the dump and save the view and tourism. The boghole becomes a destination in itself.

The problem of rubbish on the common shifts but it does not go away.

In 1957 the *Lancashire Evening Post* reports that the common 'has been littered with dozens of rotting cabbages, bedding and mattresses, carpets, broken furniture and old prams'.

We think of all of this – as we walk the common in 2020 – of the ghost lives, the feet that have walked before us. Who dropped the ginger ale bottle that glints like a green eye from under a log. These pasts keep resurfacing, whether we want to notice them or not.

*

Time is passed through repetition. Time in a chronic life is a palimpsest of tedious repetition. Linear time loses meaning, or substance. We see it for the cheap lie it is. Time is a looping bandage with sticky moments of repeated action/repetition squished together. It cannot be stretched out into something that looks like chronology/chronological. Time is a pill box with the days of the week marked out for you, which you refill and consume over and over again. Even as I think it, as I write it, I realise I am using this word – chronological – to mean something it doesn't. That time is progressive, that it keeps moving forward. That one moment ends and another begins and then that moment ends and another begins and so on. This is a lie, but it helps us to move through it. A chronic life gives the lie to the progression of time.

*

To live with illness is to live with uncertainty. To live with illness is to live with disruption. The only certainty is that disruption will come. All planning must circle contingency. Everything circles.

I think of this as we circle the bluebell ocean of the common in May 2020, as I stop to catch my breath, or watch a bird, or click a joint back into place, or to rest, or to listen for the deer whose unseen watchfulness has raised my hackles. W and I talk about risk, how ill and disabled people must account for risk and plan for contingency and can never forget it.

I am realising fully in a way I never have before this pandemic – not in my body, in the risky fringes of the body – that there are people who have never had their life disrupted by illness. Who have not been forced to accept uncertainty as one of their life's guiding principles. They have never known the boredom of illness, or the repetition. How living with illness is living with a different relationship with time.

I try to remember how I felt as a teenager to realise my body would take priority over any plans I made for it. How every time I broke a limb or ligament I would cry with frustration, convinced my life was over because, it was on hold for six weeks, eight weeks, twelve weeks. Months spent at home, half-years lost waiting for tests which yielded no useful results, half-decades lost chasing wrong diagnoses. I remember all this – how it felt to think halting the usual progression of my life for mere weeks would be ending it – and try to feel empathy for those who feel that way now.

I remember how it felt to finally find out why my life was like this. I hadn't been imagining it, or wishing it, as I had been told so many times by so many doctors. I could stop pretending to believe I could manifest a life uninterrupted by sickness. I could learn to live with disruption, diversion, repetition.

In the looping dream-walk of the common, I try to find toleration for people's anger at lockdown.

In early May, Miranda Hart compares living with chronic illness with living in lockdown. She posts a video note on Instagram:

> Chronic Illness is lockdown, it is quarantining. Anyone who is finding lockdown hard, imagine being the only one in lockdown [. . .] Imagine having dreams for your life, then being told to go into Lockdown: that is Chronic Illness.[66]

Chronic illness for many is a kind of permanent lockdown, but the lockdown most people experience in 2020 is nothing like chronic illness. It's more like breaking a bone. It's horrible, it's inconvenient, it changes your short-term plans, but it won't last forever. I can already see what this will mean. As lockdown eases, their boundaries will expand. For me and millions like me, who cannot normalise the risk, they won't. They will shrink back further, as the risk of moving through the busy world only increases. I struggle to imagine any ground we could share – any common land that could take us all. I tweet *I've been in plaster casts that have lasted longer than this lockdown.* I try to imagine how it would be to fear the itch more than the falling.

*

Chronicity emerges in 1829 to mean a 'state of being of long continuance'.

My state of being is of long continuance. *I am tired morning, noon and night.*

When they ask how you are coping you are not supposed to ask, 'What is normal?' You are not supposed to say, 'I have been walking in the dark woods amongst your soft-sleeping brothers and sisters; across the high moors among the sweet-scented ghosts of my brothers and sisters long dead; under the grey sky through the dreams and murmurs of my brothers and sisters yet to come.'[67] You know this would mark you as deathy. You know this would mark you as not-quite-human.

*

Chronicity is repeating yourself over and over to doctor after doctor, nurse after nurse. You get better at telling each story, or worse. You get bored of your own voice saying it. You miss out details or become unable to distinguish important details from less important details. Do you tell them the stool you broke your toe on was bought from a charity shop to help you manage in the kitchen, so you don't have to stand when you're preparing food, but you bought it years ago, before you knew why you couldn't stand, and it doesn't fit in the kitchen in the house you live in now, which is why it was in the lounge? Do you tell them it is that orangey colour of cheaply stained pine? Do you tell them you hate it now? You hate it even more now it has broken you?

Every time you tell the story, you change the wording slightly, you edit yourself. Or repeat whole phrases. The phrase takes the place of the memory, and if you have told your story wrongly, this is what you are left with, the telling of it, not the event itself. Who can say what really happened anyway? You begin to think you sound like a parody of yourself, and entirely untrustworthy. If the story is too smooth it sounds rehearsed, which is dangerous. If you seem to be enjoying telling it, or not enjoying telling it, they will be suspicious. If the story sounds rehearsed they will be suspicious. If you hesitate, it makes it sound like a lie. If you are too articulate, your pain must be a lie. Everyone knows what a really sick person sounds like, looks like. Everyone knows pain cannot speak. If you speak without scrabbling for words it makes it sound like a lie. You need to make the story sound spontaneous. You add a few ad libs each time. They accumulate. They become part of the story. You begin to self-edit mid-story. *It feels like a spear thrust skewering me to the bed, no it feels like a javelin, that's it, a javelin.* You need to tone down your metaphors. They sound too clever, too thought-through. Suspicious, like you've been thinking about your pain, like you've been talking about it. Everyone knows what that means.

*

In February 2018 I read a new healthcare guidance page on so-called medically unexplained and functional symptoms that claims the quest for diagnosis 'promotes chronicity'.

Promotes chronicity, as though it is a lifestyle choice. As though it is addictive. As though anyone would choose it if they could.

In 2021, in the midst of a pandemic that is disproportionately affecting disabled and chronically ill people, the BBC airs a documentary about 'illness fakers', based on a notorious subreddit which accuses people with chronic illnesses of fraud. The central premise is that people profit from presenting themselves as chronically ill. Where are our profits, we ask?

Over the following year the illness fakers discourse becomes increasingly mainstreamed. There are newspaper articles. A bestselling novelist makes a chronically ill young person the antagonist of their latest thriller. Articles speak of the 'secondary gains' to be made from identifying as chronically ill. We are called a cult. We are accused of promoting chronicity by talking about chronicity.

Still no profits! we complain. We have been professionally ill for decades, we declare, and no one has given us any profits.

*

Every time you go in with a new injury, having to repeat it, repeat it, then spell it out *E H L E R* . . . trying to explain it in brief and simple terms, hoping they listen, hoping they're not insulted, hoping someone might understand the significance. You get used to saying *hypermobility?* like it's half a question, so you're not saying outright, 'Have you heard at least of joint hypermobility?', which is what you mean. So you're not saying *have you really not even heard of this, not even seen it written down once, never once, in your medical career, in your time in emergency medicine, ever once come across another patient whose injury is because of or complicated by.*

You try to save your energy. Don't waste resources on anger, not there. It can't help you. Anger proves your injury is psychological, or you are seeking drugs. Be sure to refuse drugs, if you can. If you can't, be conspicuously reluctant. Say, 'Well, if you think it's the best thing.' Whatever you do, don't appear eager. For drugs, for treatment, for attention. Don't seem relieved, which can be confused with eagerness. Don't smile too much, or you can't be suffering. Don't suffer too much, or it's not convincing. Don't be too articulate. They will know you're one of those women: too clever to live without invention. Don't slur, don't repeat yourself, don't stammer or lose your thread. They will think you are drunk, or high. Don't forget to answer them. Don't answer back. Don't risk alienating them by knowing something they don't, not now. It's not like they'd listen to your suggestions, anyway. It's not like they'd trust what you say.

*

Chronic is used to mean not acute, as in *intense* as in *severe but of short duration* as in *coming quickly to a crisis.* Acute comes from *acutus* meaning sharp, pointed – or, figuratively – shrill, penetrating, cunning. Acute is finite, curable, not concerned with time. It will be over. It will sharpen, rise to a piercing peak, then fall.

*

On Monday 9 February 1998 I wrote:

> I'm now hoping & wishing & praying that I'm only going to get better now – that things can only get better – and I'm not going to slip back down that icy sticky slippery pyramid or fall into some hidden pitfall or gorge along the way. Most likely if I were to regress it would be to fall from standing.

I have always been so good at falling from standing.

*

The introduction to the copy I own of Harriet Martineau's *Life in the Sick-Room*, a scholarly edition produced by Broadview Press in 2003, places Martineau within a nineteenth-century 'culture of invalidism', produced when 'a variety of social and historical forces converged [. . .] to *enable* invalidism to assume this cultural status'. The editor, Maria Frawley, clusters Martineau with Elizabeth Barrett Browning, Charles Darwin, Alfred Tennyson and Robert Louis Stevenson as the public faces of a movement of hundreds who '*believed themselves* to be invalids'. The emphasis is mine.

Here, she might as well say, is Martineau's own account of her illness, but she cannot be trusted. She was a member of a culture, a cult, of invalidism. She went into a room and made it a sick-room. She was *promoting Chronicity*. She believed herself. She believed herself to be. She believed herself to be invalid.

In detailing the extensive discussion over whether Martineau's illness was physical or psychological that took place within her lifetime and afterwards, almost two centuries of medical gaslighting are repeated and replayed.

This, too, is chronicity.

*

Time like Sonya Huber describes it: 'slippery, recoiling, eelish', impossible to grasp or keep in hold.[68] Time slithering out from between your clutching, seized up hands. Time stopped, magnifying. Huber writes of how 'pain shatters time into a mosaic', of the 'up-close view of the glinting tiles of each moment' that results from this shattering. Of 'awe at seeing up close the gaps in time's connective tissue, watching as the self emerges in a shadow blur despite being blasted into fragments'.

I wonder if it is the difference in my own connective tissue that makes me more aware of the difference in time's connective tissues? If there is a recognition there, of what is seen as whole, as directional, but is actually nothing but a bundle of disparate moments or matter bundled together.

*

'Cute' as in clever (1731) as in pretty (1834) is a shortening of acute. Only a disease which leaves can be clever or pretty. That which stays is something else entirely.

*

When it is especially difficult to deal with normal daily life, when a week seems impossible, people say, 'Take each day at a time.' They mean one after another, each day consecutively. They don't mean all at once. But that is chronic life. The same day, over and over again, with no progress, with variation, but with no sense of moving forward. A body-horror *Groundhog Day*. Every day layered over every other day, and all of them chronic.

*

On 3 November 1997 I started a new journal. I know because I wrote my name and the date on the inside cover, recto. It has an Escher print on the front, of fish becoming geese as they rise up through the pattern. The image is called 'Sky and Water I'. In the inside cover, verso, is written, 'A piece of me', and in a different ink, below it, I've written out the poem 'Love not me for comely grace'. On the doubled endpaper, 'My luve is like a red, red rose', which I've helpfully attributed to Robert Burns. This is in the same pen as 'Love not me for comely grace'. On the next page, two stanzas of 'The Road Not Taken', and on the other side of that, undated, the following:

> I've been looking over my old diaries, and how very apt and very ironic much of them were. If only I'd analysed them as I do now, I could have saved myself so much shame, pain and waste. I can't write a lot. Last Wednesday I dislocated my right knee in the kitchen, fell over, and broke the head of my right radius. At least, that is what I have deduced must have happen[ed]; I remember very little. "It all happened so fast". I will have very much to write when I am more able, but my arm aches now so I can't.

*

Is the worst of chronicity the endless stretch forward of it, day after day to get through, one after another, or the endless repetition of it, event layered on event? Is it the vertical or the horizontal? Drugs to be taken over and over, pain to be gritted against. I get so bored of taking my medication, of having to think about it, of how it loops a thread around one day and another. Sometimes I wake up and think, can it really be time for that again, already? But it is, it always is.

*

In English lessons Mrs J taught us that you can remember the difference between continual (repetitious) and continuous (constant) if you think of the sssss of continuous as a stream running running running.

This was in sixth form, not long after the fall and break. I can see very clearly the room we were in, the low shelves around the perimeter full of battered copies of old set texts. I can almost feel the movement of the air as Mrs J walked behind us, talking. I could be back there, my leg stretched out under the desk awkwardly in its cast, my right arm hooked up in its sling. If I reach my foot out I think I could kick the metal leg of the table.

*

On 21 January 1998 I reflected on the previous six months:

> Time has slipped by me & I've learnt nothing [. . .]
> I've been so tired that the days – or most of them – have just passed me by in a blur, without hardly touching me. The things that have filtered through slightly more reasonably stick out like landmarks in the haze.

If I remove the details I list that I can remember, the landmarks, I could be describing any six months since. And yet some moments are so clear I can taste them. This is time in the Chronic Life. All slipping, haze and islands of time.

*

I keep using this word *chronic* but really I mean lifelong, I mean inbuilt, I mean part of me and indivisible from me. I mean often acute. I mean not dyschronic – unhooked from time – or a-chronic – timeless. I mean not finite. I mean going on, on, on.

I mean genetic. I mean stemming from every part of me.

*

Every night, lying in bed, trying to relax your muscles, trying to align your limbs and joints. Trying to let go of the body in pain. The way it tethers you to wakefulness. You are well practised at this, but you have to learn it from the beginning every time, every time, every night. Hoping once you sink your-self down there or rise up into a flying dream, that you stay there till morning. *Let me not have to think till morning. Let me get through the night and let me not remember.*

*

That time two servings of a new medication gave me Par-kinsonian symptoms. They came on halfway down the M6, on a drive down to Nottingham. Now every time I go past Knutsford I think of the stop we made there, how I realised as soon as I tried to get out of the car that something was very wrong. How the steps to the overpass seemed to roll away from me, get taller and taller as I tried to move my feet up them. Trying to raise a glass to my mouth in my par-ents' kitchen. Stuttering through phone call after phone call back to the doctors at home, trying to assess my condition remotely. *Nnnno ittttt hahahaasssssn't gggggg ooonnnnnne awayayayayay yetttt.* Stuttering and shaking through a con-sultation with a doctor at a drop-in centre in town, who recognised the problem, and the solution. *You need an anti-cholinergic, but I don't have one here.* Being sent on to A&E at the Queen's Medical Centre: the setting for so many scenes from my childhood and teens. Oh nostalgia. I am thir-ty-three and I have cycled back to these same plastic chairs. I can't escape them. The service has not improved. Stuttering and shaking through layer after layer of triage. The triage nurse who turned to W midway through, and said, 'Does she always speak like this?'

Driving back north again, because the three young doc-tors who come to look at me don't believe these symptoms can be caused by the medication. I struggle to tell them that both my GP and the drop-in doctor said that they were, that it was a known problem, that there was a known solution.

Watching them talk to each other as though I wasn't in the room; cluster round the desk to google *adverse reactions: Domperidone.* Finding nothing, bafflingly. Watching them decide there is nothing to treat. Watching them send me away.

Explaining to another triage nurse in another hospital etched over with previous visits. Finding another doctor who recognises the problem, who knows the solution. *You need an anti-cholinergic, but I don't have a bed I can put you in here, and I don't want to give it to you and send you away.* Being sent back down the motorway again, the way you have come, to the bigger hospital in Lancaster, carrying an envelope with vials of your own blood in it, and a note from one doctor to another.

Explaining to another triage nurse in another hospital etched over with previous visits.

This time, you have found the right formula. Some time in the small hours you are given the injection. Immediately, the shaking stops.

Good, the doctor says, it's a fifty-fifty chance whether it works straight away, or not at all.

Repetition, and the disruption of repetition.

Never knowing which you will get.

*

Doing your exercises, trying to get outdoors, taking medications. Trying to get outdoors. Doing your exercises.

*

When I was seven or eight, I forgot how to tell the time.

I was too ashamed to tell anyone.

My parents had given me a wristwatch to mark moving to a new school, and they had had my name and the date engraved on the back.

But it itched my wrist when I wore it, and worse, when I looked at it, I couldn't work out what it meant.

It was like everything I had learnt about clocks, about time, had been erased from my memory. I taught myself by copying, by working it out. I counted round each number each time. 1, 2, 3. 3 and a. 4 and a.

I had lost clock time, or clock time had lost me.

*

Outside school, my best friend and I would play the time game. I say game, but it wasn't play. It was training. We were training ourselves to recognise time as it moved, without the clock. We were training ourselves to feel time moving through our bodies, through our environment. To let it move – until we were ready, then pounce – catch it, pin it down. We understood time was evasive, cunning.

We would stop play, put down our Action Force or Sylvanian Families, and guess the time, aiming for as accurate an estimate as we could make. We trained like this for years. We became excellent time-tellers. We told the time from all sorts of tiny clues that a clock-watcher would never notice.

We learnt to slip in and out of clock time like currents in the water. We could become entirely lost in the flow of time, and then hook ourselves to the second.

We taught ourselves about the trickiness of time. Its many faces.

We played intense. We entered our play worlds and things worked differently there. When we were playing, we were in the expansive, malleable time of dreams – hours could pass in a moment, moments could stretch to hours. We were unmoored in time then, in another place. We could surface out of it and feel like we had lived whole lives, like decades had passed.

But we also learnt to play clock time. We learnt to dip into the current and pick out a moment.

I don't practise enough now, but I can still do it. Most of the time I am floating loose in dream time, in the ongoing moment, but if I want to, if I need to, if I concentrate hard and use all my training, I can feel the clock turn.

*

Martineau in 1841 writes about the inbetweenness of chronic illness – 'under sentence of disease for life' – of the uncanny relationship a body develops with permanence and transience in pain.

In an essay first published in 2013, 'A Day in the Grammar of Disease', Huber writes, 'I am neither well nor doomed. Sometimes I watch your soft bodies not in pain and can't remember. I push forward, each day of appointments a wager.'

This is chronicity. It goes on, not just through one lifetime, but through many. We are all the same body in pain, spun out in an infinity mirror. Continuous. Or is that constant?

*

I measure time between repeat prescriptions, between blood tests, between venesections.

The first year of my haemochromatosis treatment consisted of monthly venesections, a pint out every month. The first bad month I am dizzy to insensibility just sitting upright. I fall off a pavement trying to move between classes through the horror of the upright. A nazgûl moves through the wall next to the rented bed I struggle to sleep in between teaching classes and points its deathly arm at me from the clothes rail. From the next month, I get a pint of saline in at the same time as the pint of blood comes out. The blood out one arm, the saline in the other. A kind of circuit in itself. The cycles of the body.

The first week after each pint out is dead time, time stopped or slowed down to almost stopping; time spent lying on the sofa, trying to remember to keep my feet raised, trying to drink, eyes leaking through the pain of the muscle spasms, trying to remember not to raise my head. As the months pass, the recovery becomes easier, some of the time. A day lost, or two. Sometimes I'm fine the day after, and it lands on me on the second, the third day. Sometimes it hangs around my neck almost until it is time for the next blood test, or the next pint, making every step an incalculable effort. I reach bed every evening panting from the horrific ascent of the stairs. Every time I go into the day ward and take up my now familiar place on the bed in the corner, I am making contingency calculations, wondering how much time it will take from me, and when.

*

Repetition blurs everything. If I remember anything with clarity it is only because I wrote it down at the time, or because it comes back in the darkness, in the folding of time. Writing is a spell against chronicity. It fixes time. It captures the present as it turns to dust. As it becomes the next moment, and the next, and the next, all indistinguishable from the last.

*

On Wednesday 15 October 2014 when I leave UCLH with my new diagnosis I write:

Hello body. Old pal. Old companion. Old antagonist. Bane of the wee small hours. Torturer. Broken Vessel. Poorly built ship. Wrong Trousers. All that I am. All that I ever was. The cells and [corpuscles? corridors?] of me. The valleys and planes of me. The disproportionate wrongly-made faulty parts of me. The disorder connections in me. The mutant gene.

This body – hello body – makes sense so suddenly & gloriously – sense of a kind it never has before. This rectangle palm of mine. This long bony wrist & its need to click click back into joint. This twisted frame of mine. This pain.

A marfanoid walks into a bar . . . Why the long face?

I go back through everything I have ever known through my body. And reread. And rethink.

34 years of not-knowing.

34 years of variable levels of unknowing suffering.

Struggling in the dark alone.

Professor G said 'no one needs to suffer with this from not knowing'.

I wanted to say, 'I think you have saved my life.' I think I did say, 'This is revelatory.'

Yes. It is the unveiling of what has always been there. What has always been known, but not a known known – felt but not acknowledged – the face at the window of an empty room.

Hello arms 10.5 cm longer than they should be. Hello meaning. Hello meaning through the pain.

Professor G asked questions. Many many questions. All round the body. All around the history. Joint by joint; error by error. Then he measured. Fingertip to finger, arms flat against the wall; body pressed against it. '11 cm' he said – 'that can't be right' and measured again – '10.5 cm. Well, you've lost 0.5 cm but still.'

Disproportionate is the word we are looking for. Not ape-arms. Not child-of-Rob-Roy.

Then the bending & checking of the joints. Hips, shoulders, elbows, wrists, hypermobile. One knee – but maybe not the right any more – hypermobile. Feet flat.

Hello strange and terrible mutant. Hello body. We have been ignoring each other for a long time.

Chronic

I write:

> And I'll get help. Help with talking to you, body. Without
> screaming, without breaking down, without breaking. We
> will get better together – we'll be better at being together.
> At least now, we know who we are. Now, at last, we know
> for sure what species we are.

*

In an article on books about chronic illnesses, titled, 'The
Ubiquity of Chronic Illness', I read:

> What exactly constitutes an 'illness'? Why not use a less bi-
> omedical term instead: 'disturbance,' 'problem,' or simply
> 'condition'? And how are we to understand 'chronic' –
> simply as the flipside of 'acute' or 'curable'? Would not
> 'long-lasting' better evoke the temporal dimension implied
> in the drawn-out experiences of ongoing treatments and
> embodied suffering?[69]

Doctor, there is a disturbance in time. I think it's stuck. I
think it's glitching.

The glitch won't stop. The glitch is long-lasting. It is a
problem. The ongoingness of embodied suffering from the
glitch is a problem.

The authors of the article do not find answers to these
questions.

*

Ellen Samuels recognises the dyschronic effect of illness as
disrupting time to the point it creates something like time
travel. That dislocated from consensus reality – socially
accepted time and place – we move backwards and forwards
in time, freed from the lineal, from time's arrow:

Crip time is time travel. Disability and illness have the
power to extract us from linear, progressive time with its
normative life stages and cast us into a wormhole of backward and forward acceleration, jerky stops and starts, tedious intervals and abrupt endings. Some of us contend with
the impairments of old age while still young; some of us are
treated like children no matter how old we get. The medical
language of illness tries to reimpose the linear, speaking in
terms of the chronic, the progressive, and the terminal, of
relapses and stages. But we who occupy the bodies of crip
time know that we are never linear, and we rage silently –
or not so silently – at the calm straightforwardness of those
who live in the sheltered space of normative time.[70]

*

On Tuesday 6 November 1997 I write:

What I do remember is remembered as if only a dream
– blurred snatches and detached sensations. I was in the
house alone – Mum and Dad had gone to their initiation
rite at Rackets – the new gym. I had been revising biology
at the kitchen table, had gone for a drink to take my St
John's Wort with. Crossing back across the kitchen to Ella
Fitzgerald, I must have twisted; I fell. I fell at the end of
the surface with the toaster on it, at the end of the Jam
cupboard, next to the old black scales. I was wearing my
short sleeved fluffy pink jumper and my blue rifle jeans. Toe
nails painted green and a white T-shirt on underneath. I had
just been raiding the fridge again – eating habits I am de-
termined to dissolve, from this day and forever more. I fell.
It hurt. Maybe I clutched my knee; I remember taking my
hand off and right patella being even more right than normal and going 'shit'. Through my jeans feeling + seeing mis-
shapen knee. Not my leg, but a special effect. It wasn't real
and it wasn't me. Futilely I tried to push it back into place. I
realised I had to stand up – there was no other way. I had to
be strong and stand up, and I did, with the intention of call-

ing 999 then the neighbours (who I later found out where [sic] at 'Hercules' anyway so its good I didn't need them!). However, on standing my knee clicked back into place. I rested against the end surface – trapped between the dining room door and the worktop. I steeled myself to reach the phone – so close – so far. I had the phone, but then I realised that if I did intend for the neighbours to phone me save me, I needed to open the door, and I might as well get the moving over and done with. I moved. I opened the door, burning alive inside my skin, Ella Fitzgerald still playing. I rested there while crying more in frustration and anger than pain. It ruins everything.

By 6.30 p.m. we were at Casualty. We got back at 1.13 a.m. It was a long day. Everything is ruined; but life goes on. It must. There lay the pity of it.[71]

*

Synchronicity is when you take a break from writing about chronicity, and sit down with your coffee next to a man with ME and PoTS. You don't know this at first, of course. You are both slumped down low in your seats, your feet up as high as possible. You begin apologising to each other, then realise you are slumped for the same reason.

It is February 2018 again and you are in the library. You have begun to understand that writing about your experience of illness is writing about your experience of time.

You have come out of the library to go to the loo and get a coffee, and to warm up next to the fire. You are struggling to sleep here. There are lights you can't control in the corridor and every night you seal yourself into your room, pinning the blackout curtain you have learnt to travel with over all the gaps around the door. Every morning too early housekeeping clunks along the corridor, dragging a vacuum cleaner *clunk clunk clunk* through the dream you feel like you have only just entered. It makes it harder than it should be to be upright once the day comes. You are feeling sick this morning, your blood pooling away from your head and making you feel unusual. Except it is usual. It is bad. That is usual.

You take your coffee into the common room, to the sofa by the fire, and slump into it, your feet propped up on the big, rectangular footstool. You are trying to bring your head as low as possible, your feet as high as possible, to counter the blood pooling, without drawing attention to it. You have become a master at this manoeuvre. The slump just enough to make an onlooker tut about your posture, not enough to make them tell you off about putting your feet up, or bother you with their concern. You'd be better lying on the floor with your feet on the seat, but it attracts too much attention, and you end up explaining yourself over and over again, which is exhausting and unhelpful. Also, it is hard to drink down there, and you need to drink.

There is a man on the sofa at right angles to you in the same position. When you begin to talk, you learn it is for the same reason. The dysautonomia slump.

It is good to talk to someone without having to pretend to sit upright, or keep apologising. The solidarity of shared symptoms, shared trauma.

You talk about chronicity, about being mistreated and misunderstood, about mistrusting yourself, about the cyclical nature of the chronic, about how you circle back on yourself, about the peak and troughs of 'flare' and 'recovery', about how you never learn, or never learn enough, about the shrinking circuit of a home, a room, a bed. You say something about learning to accept different limitations, or expectations.

I am thinking about something someone said about managing frustration by dreaming, by really entering one's dreams, by really feeling them, by feeling them as real. Of travelling by dream.

He says, but then you come to the problem, what is the compromise I make with reality to make this bearable?

I tell him this is an important point, and I will put it in the book.

What is the compromise we make with reality to make this bearable?

*

I spent most of my last school year asleep, or sleepless. Sleepless at night or dreaming fitfully. Falling asleep at inappropriate times, in the day, in the pub.

On Tuesday 5 February 1998 I write of the cemetery on Wilford Hill creeping to my garden in my sleep, the snow-shrouded gravestones on the lawn. I write:

> In the same dream, the last before waking, my room was full of beautiful clothes in beautiful colours, draped over chairs, hanging from the window and curtain pole, strewn across my bed and piled in heaps on the floor. And me, desperately trying to tidy and try on before I was forced to give at least some of them up.
> I slept for 13 ½ hours (or 14 ½ perhaps).

Deathiness was coming for me. I was running out of time to savour the beautiful clothing of the life I imagined, the future selves I had to give up.

*

On Friday 6 February 1998 I write:

> I feel like I'm sleepwalking now – very tired and haunted by last night's series of very lucid and very strange dreams. There was one where, Nikita-like, I was forced to become a spy or a government agent, and one where C and I took

turns driving her quad bike through puddles like small lakes, up and down hills between trees in a place we called the Arboretum but was more like a tropical swamp. The last was post-Jurassic Park, only I don't remember if the future world we inhabited was only film-fiction or if we thought it was real. But I remember coloured velociraptors with tempers, on our side, which talked, deserted houses, watching part of Jurassic Park while taking tea with a pair of blue velociraptors who had found me in the attic explaining – they work in pairs – they thought everyone had left – and perhaps a red and green pair who arrived late. I remember being attacked by an outside force and having to run through the backyard trying to help the children first over the fence & into vans to escape, and seeing while climbing the wire fence another truck by the side of the house belonging to an opposing faction. This meant the attack, appearing to be dinosaurs – the planet's nature rebelling naturally against our presence with no purpose except natural urges, was in fact a staged attack – a release of animals by 'the enemy' to make it look as though our habitation attempts were failing through incompatibility with the planet's own ecosystem. We drove & drove & ended up back in huge cities unknown to us, but the fear remained. These dreams never left me on waking & have been following me around since on top of the image of the garden transformed by the encroachment of Wilford Hill cemetery a couple of nights before.

*

On my last morning in the library, in 2018, I am woken at 6.55 a.m. by housekeeping banging along the corridor, then slip back into a dream in which a storm destroys the road south out of Grasmere. It seems incredible to everyone, watching the road crumble apart, that this could happen so soon after Storm Desmond washed away the road along the side of Thirlmere, the only route north out of Grasmere. In the dream, W has set off early somewhere on the bus, and doesn't know about the road. I set off later, in the car, and I am on the road when it starts to come away and apart. There are many of us on the road, and we keep driving, through Low Wood as it tumbles down into the lake, and past Ambleside as it breaks apart like melting icebergs. We drive frantically over islands of tarmac drifting further apart. I abandon the car somewhere near the lake and take shelter in a waterside cafe, where everyone is watching the water rise outside French doors. It is up to the level of the balcony. In the dream, the water is Windermere, but the cafe, I realise later, has borrowed its aesthetics and geography from a waterside cafe in Salcombe, in Devon, a feature from my childhood. Through the French doors, someone in the cafe catches sight of horses struggling in the water. I open the door to take a look, and the proprietor shouts at me. The water will come in, and then we will be like the horses. I remember I saw horses from the road, earlier, swimming in the swollen lake, trying to find land. I have to help them, but by the time I push down through the crowd on the slipway next to the cafe, one of the horses is fully submerged: still, white, its mane flowing with the water like reeds in a river. I ask if it is drowned, if we can't yet help it, and the crowd says it's drowning, but it won't move, it has lost itself. I start to take my clothes off to get into the water, to try to coax it out somehow – how can I not try? – but even as I do so, it appears, with its fellows, on the slipway, transformed from a white horse into a long-haired fell pony, its thick brown coat matted with wet, and shivering. I am still patting it warm when I wake.

It only happened in my sleep, but because it happened at the library, it belongs to the library, and somehow therefore also to the caves. It belongs to the horse's head carved on that rib bone, the first piece of Palaeolithic art found in Britain. The rib from which the Creswell Crags I visited was built. The hooved animal of myself. Not a zebra, not a unicorn, but a fell pony. Resilient, persistent, self-reliant – the latest link in an ancient lineage.

*

Chronicity is returning to the same place at different times and realising you've moved everywhere and nowhere. You return to the same room years apart for different procedures. The same waiting room in different decades. Chronicity is being introduced to the sonographer who is going to help guide the injection into the nerve overgrowth in your foot, and realising you've met before, when she guided a needle biopsy in your thyroid in a different part of the same hospital the year before. You feel both the terror of repetition and the relief of difference. You tell her, and the consultant, laughingly, about how awful it was – the needle bouncing on your carotid artery – the young doctors' nerves – the repeated failure to get enough tissue to test. You tell them how you counted the blobs on the ugly ceiling tiles to try to stay calm and keep breathing. You know that though this will be bad, you did keep breathing through that, and that was worse.

You don't tell them that as you are saying this, you realise you are in the same room where you had an ultrasound of your ribcage in 2014, the ultrasound which confirmed a suspected inflammation of the cartilage in your ribs, but also showed that you'd broken one. The ultrasound which opened the door just a crack to show the corridor that would eventually lead to diagnosis. Odd to think you'd not been back to that same room in between, though you have been having ultrasounds of your liver every year, and when they dig the wand in to get a good picture of your liver all you can think about is your ribs, how tender they are, how you forget sometimes now you can wear a bra again what it was like

Chronic

when they were screaming all the time. Your bad rib starts to pulse a little in sympathy, or memory.

Chronicity is hoping you won't be back in that particular room too soon, but knowing you won't evade it for ever.

*

On Sunday 16 March 1997 I draw a picture in my journal of four circles, with arrows, in a kind of petal shape, and next to it, in the white space, I try to describe how I see the world:

> Circles, you know.
> millions of them
> all interweaving so much
> some of the time you can't even
> tell they're there, but they are.

Maintenance

It is an early evening in early May. I go for a swim in the lake and it is glorious. I go in feeling sad and defeated, and the water does what it does – it holds me up, it shows me myself with a filter of sunlight and the odd clarity of lakelight – it reflects me back at myself, shows me flying above the fells and through the blue sky, how the sky is also in the water. It reminds me the body breathes in the inbetween, in the neither one nor the otherness of the warmer water just below the membrane of the lake's surface, that the body breaches this surface, links water and air. That the body is only one creature amongst many. That the body is permeable. The leaky cup of the body overflows and is refilled by the leaky cup of the lake. That permeability is life.

What it doesn't do is heal me. What it doesn't do is *make me better*.

Swimming does what it always does: it moves my muscles and joints, gently, and without the drag of gravity making my blood pool in my hands and legs. It allows me to move more easily, less painfully. It lets me feel joy in movement.

What it doesn't do is erase the pain. Not during the swim, certainly not after.

*

In *Brilliant Imperfection*, Eli Clare describes the ambiguity of cure, how 'cure is slippery', how 'cure saves lives; cure manipulates lives; cure prioritises some lives over others; cure makes profits; cure justifies violence'. That it is

202

'embedded in understandings of normal and abnormal, natural and unnatural'.[72]

That 'cure requires damage' and locates the damage only in the individual.

That 'the belief in cure tethers us not only to what we remember of our embodied selves in the past but also to what we hope for them in the future'.

Cure relies on undoing the abnormal, the invalid, the defective, and restoring the healthy, the whole, the natural.

Depending on your relationship to the past and future, cure is either a fantasy, or a threat.

*

Every time I crawl out of the water it is like pushing through a stage of evolution again, when that evolution only makes you unfit for purpose. Discussing this with E – a year-round swimmer, a genuine lover of the cold – she says that knees prove the implausibility of intelligent design. They aren't fit for purpose.

Every time I come out of the water, gravity falls on me so hard I'm not sure I can get myself upright: to pile one joint back on top of another. Standing, the pain of downward pressure re-establishes itself. The pain in my hip, or my foot, or my ankle, or my shoulder. Ah yes, this is my body after all.

*

My relationship with Grasmere is a relationship with water.

I was sold on the Lakes, as William Wordsworth described them in his *Guide*, as a miniaturised Switzerland: an idealised landscape of glacial mountains, meadows and cool, clear lakes.

My first year here I felt myself leaching away in the rain. I felt the rain refilling me, with everything it brought from its journey. I understood my body as permeable, and the things held within the thin membrane of my skin as in flux, moving within a greater system, in a way I had not quite grasped before. Not as anything other than a strange, distinct moment. Here I understood this to be life, to be the state of our daily existence.

When I waded into the peaty brown water of Easedale Tarn on a hot day in my first month living in my attic bedroom, it sealed the contract I had already made with the Lakes. It had been a long time since I had swum in fresh water. I had risked a lot, given up a lot, changed things that made me frightened and uncomfortable to be there, but I felt what I had to gain.

I thought that Grasmere was curing me. I fell for the lie, without even articulating it.

I ignored my body's mutterings. In my first spring in the north, just a month or so before I moved into my Grasmere attic, I walked the Langdale Pikes with a group from my university. It was my first fell walk in years. I thought I was going to faint or throw up on the ascent. I had to keep stopping to catch my breath. Afterwards my knees swelled up like overripe persimmons. But I was amazed at myself, and at this place I had come to. I thought I was making myself better, that Grasmere was making me better.

I thought if I walked and swam I would keep getting better. I would get stronger. Grasmere was my physiotherapy. Someone told me about a yoga class that turned out to be the best class in the world, and I started practising yoga for the first time in years. I felt good.

In the winter, I walked the coffin path every afternoon after I finished work in the museum or cottage, drawing circuits around Grasmere and Rydal before coming in to work on my doctorate by the fire. In the summer I went on walks with friends that lasted into the long gloaming, and swam, and laughed.

Grasmere was my medicine. I believed in it. I had faith. I had love.

When it began to fail me, I thought I just needed more, more tree, more lake, more mountain. I couldn't understand why it wasn't working any more, why I was getting sicker and sicker, despite the mountains, the water, the trees. Even after all those years, all that sickness work experience, I still fell for the oldest line. I still fell for the impossible pill.

*

Clare unpicks cure to its root as restoration, as an effort to turn back time. That 'it grounds itself in an original state of being, relying on a belief that what existed before is superior to what exists currently'.[73]

A few years ago I worked on a collaboration with a climate biologist, for a poetry project on climate change. The scientist told me you can never truly restore a habitat, just make a different one. She was talking about fenland restoration. She used the phrase 'not better, not worse, just different'. Or that's how I wrote it down. One set of insects will have died or dispersed as their old habitat was removed. After restoration, a new set comes in. Different. Not better, not worse. Never the same. 'You can't go backwards in time,' she told me.

Cure assumes there was a time when things were unproblematically well to go back to, when the body was benign, polite, did as it was asked with enthusiasm and courtesy. I don't have such a time to return to, not in my body.

Say the body is a body of earth – a small planet in which we live like a molten core, or, no – a mycelial network in the soil – what is there to be restored?

The ideology of cure makes a cultivated garden of the body, a smallholding, a landscaped park. It wants the body weeded, the soil enriched, the pests controlled. It wants the high yield of the body. The neat verges of the body. The municipal lawns of the body, mowed into tidy stripes. The flowerbeds of the body, tulips blooming in intricate patterns just as planned.

But the body was never a garden, unless by garden you mean the beginning of everything. Our first and only home. The place we have been sent out of. Though I don't believe in this origin story.

Now I see talk of rewilding the body, but this too is only an attempt to restore a health you think you lost when you put up all those fences, when you pulled up the growth you designated unproductive. You think wildness will save you. You think nature is essentially good and fair.

Nature doesn't care about the integrity of your wild body.

If it restores you to wildness, it will be through feeding you into the earth.

*

Maintenance is the name for the stage reached in the treatment of haemochromatosis when the levels of iron stored by the body have been reduced to a level deemed safe. It is the level they want to keep you at, for your own good. They want to keep you level. They want you well maintained, like a sports ground or a shared-occupancy building.

As with anything, deciding when to stop is vital.

There are many ways to measure the amount of iron in circulation and in storage in the body, but for haemochromatosis the most important indicators are the levels of serum ferritin and the transferrin saturation.

Ferritin is a protein that stores iron in the body's tissues, releasing it as required, but a much smaller amount in circulation in the blood acts as a transporter for iron, carrying it to organs. Iron is bound to the protein, carried through the blood, and released at receptor sites. Ferritin is a courier. The amount of ferritin acting as a courier is what is being measured in a test of serum ferritin.

Serum ferritin rises as the amount of iron in storage in the body rises, but it can also be raised by inflammation, so alone cannot be used to diagnose haemochromatosis. Once diagnosis is made, though, it is a good indicator of the quantities of iron in the body.

Serum iron is another measure of the iron content in the body, combining the amount of iron circulating carried by ferritin, and the amount carried by transferrin, another protein which transports iron around the body. The total iron binding capacity is a measure of how much iron the body can carry through these proteins. Transferrin saturation is a percentage calculated by dividing the serum iron levels by the total iron binding capacity. It shows how much iron is currently bound to these carrying proteins.

In most people, you would expect the transferrin saturation to hover around thirty per cent. When I was diagnosed, mine was in the high nineties, meaning almost all the iron carriers in my body were being used. My couriers were all occupied, on zero hours contracts.

Until June 2018 there was variance in what was considered maintenance in the UK, but new guidelines for diagnosis and treatment are seeking to standardise therapy. The most important change in the new guidelines is to insist on measuring maintenance not just by the levels of ferritin in the blood, but also by transferrin saturation, keeping both below fifty: fifty micrograms per litre of ferritin, and fifty per cent transferrin saturation.

Both ferritin levels and transferrin saturation are relatively clumsy ways of trying to guess at iron storage and toxicity. They show one tiny part of a much larger picture that many haemochromatotics will never get to see. Although some people are given access to a special kind of MRI scan – a FerriScan – that shows the iron stored in organs – most aren't. Most of us will never know with precision exactly what damage has been done where, how reversible it is, how reversed it has been as our levels have come down.

Maintenance is what it says it is: not a remission, but an attempt to keep things steady. An attempt to preserve what is good in the present, as best we can. It is a holding pattern, nothing more.

*

Moving my body on land is like dragging a dead body after me. My own dead body. It is a dead weight pulling me back downhill, downstairs, down to the ground. Sometimes I help myself by lifting a leg with my hands. Sometimes I ask my partner or a friend to push my back, to take some of the weight. It is as though I have two bodies and one of them is abnormally responsive to gravity, or an empty skin stuffed with rocks. I am a light thing and I have to carry it, and it is carrying it that makes me so tired, that makes me stumble and fall.

Gravity is my enemy.

Water is the enemy of my enemy.

Water is my dearest ally.

*

Sometimes, I limp all the way to the lake. I say 'all the way' and it makes the walk seem epic. To the abled it would seem a tiny distance, not worth thinking of as a walk, even. But when each placement of your foot on the ground triggers shooting pain in a foot or a hip, when carrying just a towel and a water bottle pulls too much on your shoulders and back, even a few metres becomes a marathon. Sometimes my legs aren't too bad but carrying my bag feels like lifting the planet. If I didn't live so close, I wouldn't get there at all. This is the grace of proximity.

Getting there hurts, but I know being in the water will help. Short term, as it lifts me up into its kinder element, its more forgiving physics. Long term, as it keeps my joints moving, lubricated, and helps stop my muscles from becoming weaker and weaker. Some people believe the secret to managing EDS is to keep the muscles as strong as possible, that they will keep the joints together where the ligaments fail. But even our muscles are different, and respond differently. All I am certain of is that water is better.

When I step into the water – when I wait until my legs have remembered the water, and my sore ribs say they are ready to go under, when I have loosened my difficult shoulder as much as I can, when I dive under or glide along its surface – I slip out of my skin and into another one that looks the same but feels completely different. It is agile and confident. It is trustworthy. It trusts its environment. It trusts itself.

*

The Nature Cure is a distraction technique. If it works it is because it takes you out of yourself, the circuit of thought you have become trapped in, reminds you of something outside, bigger, more. It takes you out of yourself and puts you back in, differently.

The Nature Cure is a coping mechanism, a method of self-soothing, the kind you might be taught in CBT class or by a neuropsychologist, the equivalent to listing everything you see out the window, or counting, or pyramid breathing. It is a tool of management, of de-escalation.

The Nature Cure is Distraction Therapy with a greenwash, trailing all the colours of the rainbow, all the colours of the aurora borealis, all the colours of the sunset/sunrise.

*

Cumbrian poet Kate Davis describes swimming as an equaliser. She lives with permanent effects of childhood polio, which she wrote about in her first poetry collection *The Girl Who Forgets How to Walk*.

She tweets:

> Being in open water is such a good feeling. I'm not brilliant on my feet, I trip and stumble a lot, fall sometimes. But you can't fall over in water, it takes away my physical problems and makes me equal to other people.[74]

You can't fall over in water. This echoes so much of what I think about my own relationship with water, about my body in the water, and out of it.

I am fast in the water, often faster than my companions.

I know even as I enjoy my slick speed that it is internalised ableism that makes me relish the fact that in the water I can outmanoeuvre friends who are fitter, stronger, more agile than me on land. Friends I am always trailing behind, or apologising to for being so slow. It is internalised ableism – mine, not theirs – that makes me apologise, that makes me embarrassed by my awkwardness, my pain, by the time I have to take thinking about where and how I place my feet, the turn of my ankle. I know it comes from something that hurts me, that hurts us all, but to glide away in the water, to outpace them . . . sometimes it is too sweet.

*

In *Waterlog* Roger Deakin writes, 'When you enter the water, something, like a metamorphosis happens. Leaving behind the land, you go through the looking glass surface and enter a new world in which survival, not ambition or desire, is the dominant aim.'[75]

But none of these is my dominant aim. To see swimming as a way to remind the body its aim is survival requires that the body isn't constantly struggling for survival, which the sick body is. Which my body is. I never leave survival mode.

This has to do with risk, with what is at risk when.

I swim to avoid risk, not court it.

Sarah Jaquette Ray has recognised that, 'At the heart of adventure sports is the appeal of personal challenge. The individual – usually male – pits himself against Nature and survives.'[76] This acknowledges the dominance in nature writing of the figure Kathleen Jamie famously called 'the lone enraptured male' – 'here to boldly go'.[77]

Jamie suggested, 'It's only recently that we, with our (almost) guaranteed food supplies, motor engines, vaccines and antibiotics, have begun to make our peace with these wild places, and to seek recreation in land which was once out to kill us.' Jamie's lone enraptured male is also necessarily 'bright, healthy and highly educated'.[78] Ray calls this figure the 'wilderness body ideal'.[79] Stacy Alaimo recognises it as 'the abled, hyperfit body' that dominates environmental writing and thinking, and is clearly at the centre of the major-ity of nature writing.[80]

For people who are in continual pain, the relationship with bodily risk is different. Pain is not a healthful by-product of healthy exertion or impressive effort: it is a constant companion. You want to limit your time with pain, not encourage it.

For people who live with fatigue, the relationship with effort is different. Exhaustion is not a healthful by-product of healthy exertion or impressive effort: it is a constant companion. You want to preserve yourself from fatigue, not create it.

Ray asks, 'If getting close to nature is about risking the body in the wild, what kind of environmental ethic is available to the disabled body?'[81]

When being outdoors becomes about survival instincts, about risk, those who experience risk differently are sidelined, erased.

It's a lot easier to think of bodily risk as an adventure, rather than a crisis or a bad thing to be avoided at all cost, if you are healthy, resilient and able-bodied. If you might shiver all day after you get out of the water, but not if you shake so violently you slip a rib out of place, and spend weeks in agony, or wake up unable to move a limb the next day. It can seem beneficial to push your body to the point of pain through sporting endeavour if you are not in pain every moment of the day. If you don't dislocate joints or break bones just walking across your living room, or packing shopping at the supermarket.

Ray finds 'the only place for the disabled body in the wilderness ideal is as an invisible, looming threat – symbolic rather than actual'.[82] The body the literary swimmers are splashing away from, as they round the bend of their fantasy river.

*

I have to be careful.

I choose places I know I can enter and exit the water without undue risk of injury. There is no frisson for me in the notion that I could break a toe, or more: I know what that feels like. I know the cost, short and long term. I've done it. I've done it just crossing a room, time after time. I know the frustration of having to unplan weeks. I live with the adjustments breaks have made to my gait, my strength, I live with their continual low hum.

The challenge is not swimming, but everything else. The risk is not swimming, but everything else.

I don't experience a cold water rush. Maybe my broken thermostat forbids it. Maybe my autonomic dysregulation undoes it. I get no high, no rush of dopamine, no intense feeling of aliveness. If anything, I feel the reverse – a deadening sensation after movement ceases and the unpleasant sleepy shutdown that cold of all kinds always brings – before the ceasing up begins, before the muscle cramps set in.

When I swim in very cold water, all my old breaks burst into loud, throaty song, as though they are new again. The cold unwinds time, peels apart the calluses I can feel under the skin. Cracks me open. There is no healing in this. Not for my body.

*

The Nature Cure is against treatment.

The Nature Cure embraces wellness.

The Nature Cure tells you all you need to do to 'get better' is to a) go outside more or b) be more active in a natural environment.

If you remain sick you are doing so because of your own lack of commitment to getting well. You have not embraced The Nature Cure. Maybe you are still taking your toxic medicines, maintaining your toxic connections with the contemporary world.

The Nature Cure looks both stern and sad.

The Nature Cure wants the sick to give up their pills and their patches, their bottles and syringes because the birds will make everything better.

The Nature Cure wants you to tell your friends, 'The Nature Cure is my only medicine!'

The Nature Cure forgets that it is cruel.

*

When our own bodies are presented as unnatural, as something to be corrected, both the word 'Nature' and the word 'Cure' take on sinister connotations.

The things that make me sick are genetic, are part of my own nature – written in and by the smallest parts of me, at the centre of my every cell, part of my diverse internal landscape – so how can any cure that wants to dig them out of me be natural?

Even if it were possible, which it isn't, cure would be my enemy. Cure wants to undo me. To unmake me, in the name of 'healing', in the name of 'wholeness', in the name of 'health'. In the name of natural and normal and well.

The dark side of cure is eradication. Cure wants to remove, to erase difference. Cure wants people like me to not be people like me.

*

Kate Davies, a maker and writer based in the Highlands, returned to swimming after a stroke. Her experience of disability is different to mine, but her words are words I could have written myself, have written myself: 'In the water, my body is supported.' In the water, she says, her body can move 'with something that feels like ease'.[83] On the land it is a very different matter. It is like being two creatures.

She is clear about the realities of what swimming can do for her and what it can't. She knows it has improved her muscle strength, that it is helping her. Swimming has therapeutic properties for her body and in turn for her mind. But it cannot turn back time. It cannot restore her to an earlier self, and there is no expectation in her writing that it should.

*

I swim because I like it. I swim because my body is lighter in the water, because I move more easily in the water. I feel competent in the water in equal measure to how incompetent I feel on land, always stumbling, off-balance, having to think so hard about where and how I place my feet. It is easier to be in water. It is easier, and it is beautiful.

I swim because through chance I found a painkiller that works enough for me, with few enough side effects, to allow me to get that far, some of the time: to reach the water, to move myself in it.

I swim because of all the ways I can move my body, swimming hurts me least. I swim because it is good to move. It is good for all of me, for how I feel, and how I *feel*. I am more myself in the lake than at any other time.

I swim because under the water I feel like my body and I are working together, that it might do what I ask of it, that we could be a wonderful being.

I swim because I have feelings for water. At any given time I would prefer to be in water than on land.

I swim because when I swim I am part of something bigger and wilder than myself. When I swim I swim alongside the lake's inhabitants. In the summer months swallows swoop over me and damselflies and dragonflies buzz around my ears. Ducklings cluster at my feet as I dry. The woods around the lake are full of birds – woodpeckers, treecreepers, fly-catchers, long-tailed tits. Grey wagtails flit from rock to rock, their yellow bellies shining back from the mirror of the water. In the winter a hunched-up heron and a black-headed gull in its snow-white hood watch from the shore.

When I swim we are part of one body, the body of the lake, and many.

The lake does not cure me. The water does not cure me. Swimming does not cure me. Why would it? It is asking too much of a body of water to fix this inconsequential human body.

I swim as a means of maintenance. To keep myself as level as I can.

*

I learnt to swim at Noel Street Baths, Nottingham. Opened in 1929, the Baths were closed in 2010, when a new leisure complex made them redundant. Now, half of the old Baths are occupied by Nottingham Climbing Centre, with the shallow end of the pool I learnt in repurposed as bouldering walls called 'the shallow end'. The other half of the building was taken over in 2017 by Living Faith, an evangelical mega-church founded in 1983 in Nigeria.

I remember my swimming teacher, her kindness and unrelenting insistence I conquer my intense fear of putting my head underwater. She used to make me hold my face in the water at the end of every lesson, but I hated it, I hated it. I tried not to be afraid, because of her calm faith in me, in her method, because of her determination, but it was only trying. I pretended it was helping, but nothing changed, not till much later.

I remember her face, her hair, her manner, but not her name – I have to ask Mum for that. Dad says she was boneless – if you shook her hand it felt like she had no bones under her skin at all. This could sound like an insult, but we know what he means, he means she was formed differently, that she was one of us. 'Polly is boneless too,' says Mum, stating the obvious. They argue about it a little. Dad insists she was more boneless than I am. Mum isn't so sure. It is unresolvable. I phase out for a moment and hear us from a distance. We are arguing about how far outwith the bounds of normal human structure I am; the woman who taught me to swim when I was four was. I don't remember this about her. I just remember how much I adored her. We all wonder aloud whether her different structure was what drew her to swimming. We are all as bad as each other.

Mum wanted me to have the confidence in the water she never had. In her childhood the sludgy waters of the Solway Firth receded miles through bogs and archipelagos of grassy tussocks a careless child could fall and drown in. It was not a friendly sea to learn to swim in.

She learnt to swim at Victoria Baths in Sneinton, in her twenties, after she met my dad. In the summer, they would sail dinghies at Nottingham Sailing Club. It was an older woman who crewed for Dad in his National 12 sailing dinghy, who taught my mum to swim. Once a week in winter they would go to the swimming baths and then for fish and chips, in holding for the summer's sailing.

There is a history of late learners in my family. May Antill, May Atkin, Dad's Nana, learnt to swim in her sixties. She decided she wanted to learn, and she did it. One more challenge to meet. She would take my dad and his sister to Arnold swimming baths, and they would walk all the way, walk through the cavy house of Nottingham to learn to swim.

*

In spring 2018 I enter maintenance for the first time. In this new detoxified stability I am able to begin to decode the signals my body has been desperately trying to transmit to me. I thought I'd never be able to unravel the fatigue and pain that have dominated my life into different strands, trace them back to their roots, but now I know what causes some of them, I can begin to tell them apart. I learn the difference between the zone-out blankness that means my B12 has bottomed out, and the mammoth unrefreshing sleep that means my brain is rusting up. I learn to distinguish continual micro-injuries of my joints from the pain caused by iron deposits around them. Most importantly, I find I can translate these signals into messages I can pass on, and those messages can be translated into appropriate actions. I know what I need to do to help us both.

By the summer my iron stores have begun to rebuild, and with them, their effects.

In the fortnight before my blood tests show the rise, I notice certain things. My hips begin to ache again, in a very specific way – a deep ache in the ball of the joint, and a pain around it. They are tender to the touch. In the night, when I roll onto my side, the pain of the pressure on them wakes me. It is only when this comes back that I realise it had gone, or had died down to background mutter, in the previous couple of months.

The first night I notice the pain around my hip joints, I think it is caused by swimming. There is a heatwave and I have been swimming most days in the lake. There hasn't been a day of rain in months. Some of the lakes have blue-green algae in them. Grasmere hasn't tested positive for it yet, but it is smaller and warmer than them. It seems at risk. I know one of the symptoms of blue-green algae poisoning in humans is joint pain, and I worry that my hips are telling me that the lake is eating itself. That they are warning me of environmental catastrophe.

Maintenance

I am used to feeling things before other people do. A canary in the mine of everyday life. I feel everything. Why not ecological collapse?

*

Blue-green algae is not algae at all, it's a misnomer, an error of categorisation based on appearance. They are bacteria, prokaryotes – single-celled organisms with no nucleus. This was only recognised in the 1970s, when they were renamed cyanobacteria. Blue-green bacteria. They are many, and ancient. Arguments about just what they are and how to classify them continue.

When cyanobacteria blooms in a body of water, under the right conditions, it can grow too quickly for everything else to thrive alongside it. It blocks out the light. Fish suffocate, drowning in the water for lack of oxygen.

I learnt this at school as a teenager, long before I lived here in this district of lakes. I drew and redrew endless diagrams of the cycle of eutrophication, drawing arrows to show minerals and nutrients leaching into a body of water, algae fattening on the riches, blocking sun from the depths. I drew fish swimming, and fish dying.

I was so haunted by the concept of eutrophication that I wrote a song about it. I identified with the fish. I felt I was like the fish, in some indistinct but compelling way. I too was suffocating in the element I was supposed to thrive in. It was one of a clutch of songs I was starting to make a recording of when I dislocated my knee that time in the kitchen and broke my elbow. I never finished. I was too sick by then, and there was too much else I had to do.

*

After a week of rising pain, I begin to realise it is a catastrophe of the internal landscape. The toxins are within me, not without. It is not a blue-green bloom in the lake, but the slow, scaling spread of rust that is hurting me.

As my earth rusts, as the valleys and lakes inside me grow in toxicity, I sleep all morning, fitfully. My nights are disturbed and unsettled. I cry at adverts and soaps. I feel despondent and strangely disconnected. Clock time is slipping away from me. I know it's there, but there is a thick film between us. I miss appointments. I feel sick all the time, much more than had become usual. I am a little outside my body, tethered only lightly to it. When I move bits of it, it is like moving a puppet. I stare at my typing fingers aware they are mine only because I can feel the faint pressure of their pads on the keys, and a tingling running up them into my hand, but it is unconvincing. I find it hard to persuade myself to eat, and when I do, I feel dizzy and sleepy. My skin is dry and itchy, cracking into tiny scales. My feet itch at night, and I peel the flaking skin off my heels.

As the hip pain grows, it spreads into my pelvis and lower back, so that by the time I have the blood tests, I am having difficulty sitting and difficulty rising. The day of the tests I think I must have got my painkillers confused, but when I check, I haven't. The whole lower section of my trunk from the small of my back downward is at a constant high throb of pain, leaching into my upper legs. I feel maudlin and unmotivated.

The pain replicates itself like bacteria, blocking everything else out, until the pain is all I can contain. The pain suffocates everything else. It is a thick curtain that blocks out the light. There is no air in me. The life in me begins to die back. The dieback makes the pain grow quicker.

When the blood results come back, I feel a strange excitement, something a bit like joy. It makes my eyes fill up with tears again to think *I know now: I know what these feelings mean.*

*

What makes me sick is also what makes me me. Not meaning I am defined by my illness, by my status as Sick, or by the impairments which direct how I experience the world, but that my symptoms are products of the genetic material out of which I am made.

Not only would I not be the same version of myself if I did not have the experiences that my illness has led me to, but that at the most basic, core, molecular level I would not be the same person.

There is no good or bad in it, it is just as it is. Cure would write me out of existence and replace me with an improved model without the errors in her code. She would not be me. She would probably be a disciple of The Nature Cure.

*

There is a woodpecker in the trees as I swim, percussion to my strokes. We've seen it a lot this spring already: later in the summer I will be walking back home from the lake and a pair of them will fly over me. From the water I look back at W reading on the bank and laugh as a family of treecreepers scuttle about around his head, visible to me from the lake but always just shifting out of his view.

But we saw on *Springwatch* a woodpecker just like our one eating a treecreeper's babies. This is nature.

It makes me happy to see the woodpecker, its monochrome speckles and red flash like Snow White mashed up, but it is a killer. The treecreepers will have more chicks. Maybe they

221

will live, maybe they won't. It is only natural. Is that what you want? How you want to live? Is this the cure you think you deserve?

*

Wordsworth wrote 'let nature be your teacher', not let nature be your only recognised healthcare system.[84]

*

In June 2018 as my iron levels rise stealthily, I hear Nuskmata give a lecture in which she talks about the poisoning of Quesnel Lake in Canada by the Mount Polley mine. Quesnel Lake is the deepest fjord in the world. It is a home to rainbow trout and sockeye salmon and char, grizzlies and black bears and bald eagles.

In August 2014 the tailings pond of the Mount Polley gold and copper mine spilled around twenty-five million cubic metres of wastewater into the rivers and lakes and forests below – toxic with arsenic, mercury, copper, lead, nickel.

Nuskmata is from the Nuxalk and Secwepemc peoples, and a member of the Xatśūll First Nation, whose unceded territories include Quesnel Lake and her hometown of T'exelc, or Williams Lake.

When the spill happened, it was just as the salmon should have been returning. Instead, their home was devastated. In an interview Nuskmata recalls: 'People were crying and talking about it like there had been a death. We did a ceremony you do in a time of grief, of great loss and that's exactly how our communities were all feeling.'[85]

By the time I hear her talk four years have passed and nothing has been done to either correct the damage or to prevent similar disasters in the future. Nuskmata became a water protector, founding the Stand For Water campaign with First Nations Women Advocating Responsible Mining to argue for the rights of the lake itself.[86]

She speaks of the lake as a family member, as a grandmother. For Nuskmata's community, the lake is not an inanimate accumulation of water, it is a living body – a person who is an essential member of the community. The whole watershed is alive.

*

Cyanobacteria are ancient, and manifold. There are fossil remains of cyanobacteria dating back at least two billion years. As of 2013 there were 2,698 identified species of cyanobacteria, all different in form and function, though it is supposed there are many more.

Some, like the ones we worry about multiplying in our waters, produce toxins, which are dangerous to humans and animals. They can destroy our nervous systems, our livers, the functions of our very cells. Exposure to neurotoxins produced by cyanobacteria has been linked to development of ALS, Alzheimer's and Parkinson's disease. Toxic blooms have caused mass dieoffs not just of fish, but of ducks, deer, bees, turtles, cattle – anything that lives in or by or drinks affected water or eats other creatures that live in or by or drink affected water. Who in this place of lakes does not know someone who has lost a beloved dog to cyanotoxins?

In May and June 2020 over three hundred elephants in Botswana died after ingesting cyanotoxins.[87] A 2021 study warns of the increased threat of cyanotoxins to endangered megafauna as climate change accelerates, calling this event an 'alarming early warning signal of future catastrophes'.[88]

But to see cyanobacteria only as poison is a mistake.

Cyanobacteria are special. They are life-givers and killers. They can be anti-inflammatory, anti-microbial, anti-viral, anti-fungal. They can shrink cancer cells.[89] They can modulate the human immune system. Some of them, like spirulina, have been part of the human diet for thousands of years. They are proposed as a solution to fuel crises, food crises.[90]

Cyanobacteria are the only oxygen-producing prokaryotes. They photosynthesise, making energy from sunlight, as plants do.

Cyanobacteria are also thought to have created the oxygen atmosphere of earth. They call this the Great Oxygenation Event, or the Rusting of the Earth. It happened around 2.3 billion years ago. The oxygen the cyanobacteria released when they transformed the weak light of the young sun into energy to live bonded with iron in the oceans and the air and the rock. Iron oxide deposits reddened the planet. Without cyanobacteria, humans could never have evolved. Without them, I would not be here thinking about them, writing about them. You would not be here reading this. They created the atmosphere we need to breathe, just as they can destroy the atmosphere fish need to breathe, just as they can destroy.

Cyanobacteria are everywhere, not just in the water. From sea spray they disperse into the air, like the Little Mermaid at the end of Hans Christian Andersen's tale. They are world travellers, circumnavigating the globe as aeroplankton before tumbling back to the water. They live in the fur of polar bears, turning them green.

They were here long long before us. They will be here long after we are gone.

*

Like blue-green algae, haemochromatosis is a misnaming based on a misunderstanding. In 1889 German pathologist Friedrich Daniel von Recklinghausen made the link between iron deposits in the liver, blood, and disease, but concluded the cause was a pigment that stained affected tissue. He called it the blood colour disease – haemo/chromato/osis. It wasn't until 1935 that it was recognised as hereditary. You have to know what you're looking for. You have to ask the right questions.

*

Nuskmata's call for recognition of the personhood of Quesnel Lake is mirrored by legal shifts towards acknowledging the inalienable rights of bodies of water, such as Te Awa Tupua (Whanganui River) in Aotearoa New Zealand and the Ganges and Yamuna rivers in India, granted legal personhood in 2017, and Muteshekau Shipu (Magpie River) in Quebec, Canada, granted personhood in 2021. All these campaigns have been led by indigenous people, in response to industrial damage.

In 2014 Aotearoa New Zealand recognised a former national park, Te Urewera, as a legal entity. It was the first place in the world to be awarded the same legal rights as a person.

I wonder how different our conversations about the lakes here would be if this national park I live in were recognised as a living being. This national park owes its existence in many ways to William Wordsworth, or at least to his legacy. But he held a sense of an 'active universe', in which 'every pebbly stone . . . the stationary rocks, the moving water and the invisible air' have as much agency as people, and the landscape is made of 'living stone'.[91] 'In all things' he writes in his *Prelude*, 'I saw one life, and felt that it was joy.'[92] I wonder what would he make of how this living landscape is exploited now in the name of green therapy, in the name of The Nature Cure.

*

Who of us can say we are truly, entirely whole? Who of us would not be eradicated were a universal cure to descend on us from the skies, or the trees?

As Clare does, I try to be honest with myself: would I feel differently about the notion of cure if I thought it was in any way possible?

I've said time and time again things like, 'I could take the pain, if it wasn't for the fatigue', but do I really believe that if I had the pain without the fatigue, I wouldn't say the same about the pain? 'I could take the dislocations, if it wasn't for the pain?' Take the pain away. 'I could take the bladder problems, if it wasn't for the dislocations?' I could take the bladder problems, if my gut hadn't shut down. Slowly I would unmake myself in thought, organ by organ, joint by joint until there was nothing that resembled me left. Until there was nothing left at all.

*

The Nature Cure is an ancient deity. It has been around longer than we have been human. It comes from a time before medicine, which is why it hates medicine so much. There were times when it was everything to us, and we would do anything to encourage its favour. It thinks medicine has taken its power.

*

In Grasmere there are several ancient holy wells. Holy wells, sweet good water, buried over, untended, largely forgotten. The words *holy* and *healthy* both come from a root that meant whole, uninjured. Holy and healthy were once the same thing. A holy well is a hale well, a wholesome well, a healthy well. A holy well is a well well. Holiness is linked to happiness, to good luck as well as good health. A holy well is a lucky well because health is luck. Wholeness is luck.

The most famous of the holy wells shares a name and dedication with the village church, St Oswald's.

St Oswald's Well is hidden, submerged and somewhat forgotten, in a field belonging to the National Trust and rented out with a house called St Oswald's, named for the well which it has usurped.

In 1866 Anna Deborah Richardson hears from her neighbour Miss Cookson, one of the Wordsworths' last surviving friends in Grasmere, of how the parish clerk used to speak of St Oswald's Well – 'a well of very beautiful water'. Third-hand Anna records how 'healing qualities were believed to exist in it'. Already, then, in 1866 it was lost to history, mislaid somewhere in a field behind Pavement End.

George Middleton wrote about it in his fantastically titled 1918 book *Some Old Wells, Trees, and Travel-tracks of Wordsworth's Parish*:

> Near the middle of the last century, with the object of evening the land's surface and winning a few square yards of pasture, the rude masonry about the well was removed and the cavity filled up and turfed.[93]

It is marked on some older maps, but there is nothing to see of it now, from the road at least, which is the closest public place to it. It is strange to think of something that had been so central to village life for so many centuries – from before the time of St Oswald, from before the Christianisation of good clean water – being covered over, being actively dismantled and buried.

*

In 1844 a hydropathic centre opened in Grasmere, cashing in on growing tourism to the area, and the legendary healing qualities of St Oswald's Well.

An advert run in the *Westmorland Gazette* in May 1844, under the title HYDROPATHY, promises:

> In the Romantic Vale of GRASMERE, Westmorland, an HYDROPATHIC COLONY is formed, and the *pure* Gräfenberg treatment practised by a qualified eyewitness, with every co-efficient of the Water Cure, conducing to the health entertainment of invalids, including Rowing Boat on the Lake, Gymnastic Exercises, &c. The fine mountains in the immediate vicinity, and the extreme purity of the air and water, render this beautiful locality peculiarly suitable to a successful course of this powerful remedial agent.

By September the doctor in charge, J. F. Paisley, MD, is declared in the Kendal Mercury as having 'separated from the Grasmere Water Cure establishment', seemingly fleeing with debts the centre refuses to answer for. The hydropathic centre seems not to have even opened by this point: the same notice assures that 'his place will be filled immediately by a first rate Gräfenberg Physician', that 'the buildings are all completed' and the 'baths are second to none in Europe'.

Nevertheless, it seems the cure is on hold. 'Invalids desiring accommodation are requested to apply to Lieut. PHILIPPS. RN', it says, but when they can expect their cold water treatment to begin is uncertain.

Lieutenant Philipps is the same Mr J. P. Philipps who, in August 1844, places a notice in the *Westmorland Gazette* that 'all claims and demands against the cold water establishment at Grasmere' should be sent to him.

I imagine the desperate sick arriving in Grasmere in seek of their cure, and finding a half-finished, unstaffed centre, and only the lake gleaming at them coolly.

*

Hydropathy as a medical science was invented in the early nineteenth century by Vincenz Priessnitz, a farmer in the town known then as Gräfenberg, in Austrian Silesia, now Lázně Jeseník in Czechia. He founded his own hydropathic centre by converting his father's house in 1822, when he was only twenty-two years old. The fame of his water cure was already drawing people from near and far to Gräfenberg. His method involved a mixture of cold baths and showers, wet bandages and body heat, and consumption of large quantities of water. He was taken to court by local doctors who reported him for fraud, but the courts found in his favour. In 1838 he was granted a retrospective licence for his spa and by the early 1840s he was world famous.

Although water cures of various kinds have been practised around the world since ancient times, Priessnitz's method quickly became the latest craze in nineteenth-century wellness culture. The Science Museum website describes Priessnitz as 'an illiterate Austrian farmer', as though that makes it especially amazing that his method became so popular.[94]

Priessnitz's story as told in nineteenth-century biographies as in twenty-first century ones is one of overcoming: overcoming poverty, overcoming illiteracy, overcoming having a blind father, overcoming injury, overcoming low social status. In some versions he purportedly 'discovered' the water cure after treating his own broken ribs, or a crushed finger, in some after a mystic medical encounter with a wild deer, as narrated by his follower Dr Charles Schieferdecker:

> Whilst he was engaged in attending the cattle of his father [. . .] he made use of the many opportunities which his situation offered, to observe the instincts of his Hock, and the wild animals that came near him. He was particularly attracted by the circumstance of a beautiful stag coming every morning to a spring near his pasture-ground, and, after quenching its thirst by long draughts from the limpid fountain, bathing its supple limbs in the cool water that surrounded the spring. Once, after having waited for his shy friend several days, he saw the animal limping, and evidently in a state of suffering, approach the spring and drink more plentifully and remain longer in the water than ever he had observed it formerly. This the stag repeated for several successive days, until the marks of illness had entirely disappeared, and it had regained its former supple-ness and vigour.[95]

In the cold water legend the stag cured itself by standing in a cold pond. The story of Priessnitz and the story of Priessnitz's stag are inspiration porn mixed with equal parts mind over matter: from this the very essence of The Nature Cure may be distilled.

*

In the darkest, deepest winter, on Burns Night 1845, the *Westmorland Gazette* ran adverts under the heading HYDROPATHY for St Oswald's in Grasmere, and a rival institution in Bowness.

Of St Oswald's, it claims 'this water-cure establishment, in the beautiful vale of Grasmere, is now in full operation'. The new 'superintendant', a Leopold Stummes, MD, is claimed to have been the personal physician to the Earl of Lichfield, and to have learnt the water cure from Priessnitz himself whilst Lichfield was under his care at Gräfenberg. There is no mention of Lt. Philipps now, only Stummes.[96]

Meanwhile Dr Paisley, unabashedly advertised as the 'founder and late Physician to the Grasmere Water Cure Establishment', is said to be continuing to 'receive invalids as indoor patients' in Bowness, with different rates for 'those of limited means' and free treatment for 'the poor'. Dr Paisley is proud to declare that 'during a practice of nearly three years, [he] has not had occasion to use a single grain of medicine in the treatment of the several diseases submitted to him'. The cure is nothing but cold water. The cold water cure is everything.

*

In August 1845 the *Carlisle Patriot* repeats the advert for 'the Water Cure Establishment in the beautiful vale of Grasmere', with all of Stummes's references, but attaches to it a letter of thanks to Stummes from a former soldier, John Johnstone, who claims to have been cured by him in Grasmere.

Dated 26 July 1845, the letter places Stummes next to God, 'the Great Author of all good' in Johnstone's gratitude. He claims to have been 'restored' by the treatment, that he writes 'to make public record of my cure'.

Handily, for the purpose of advertisement, he also makes note of 'three of the more remarkable cures' of other invalids he witnessed whilst in Stummes' care: a 'respected clergyman of Grasmere' who was cured of a 'sore throat of an alarming character', an unidentified person with a 'frightful brain fever' who was 'cured and walking about in twenty-four hours' and a person at the 'point of death' from a 'quinsey of the severest order' who 'was walking out of doors on the eighth day'.

Was Johnstone real, or fabricated for marketing purposes? If he was real, was he really brought so low by 'a life of arduous military service, and the baleful influence of the tropics' that the Grasmere Water Cure was his last resort? Was he ever really ill, and was he ever really cured?

His story is too convenient for Stummes. Under previous care Johnstone says he had been subjected to excessive bleeding – a failed blood cure – which had 'exhausted the springs of life'. Clearly only hale, healthy water could bring his springs back into spate.

All this 'without having taken a grain of physic'. Then, as now, any nature cure, be it by blood or by water, requires the setting aside of the evils of medicine, and everything it represents.

Instead, Johnstone is prescribed 'the purity of the air, the enchantment of the scenery'.

He ends his letter/advert: 'This sense of reviving spirits which I feel within me, will make me ever remember Grasmere as the truest image of the "Happy Valley".'[97]

*

In a history of the National Trust in the Lakes, Elizabeth Battrick records that the house called St Oswald's 'was built c.1851 on the site of a barn on land belonging to the Wray. It was intended to be a "Hydropathic Establishment" and was adjacent to St Oswald's Well, reputed to have medicinal properties. The Hydro seems to have been a joint venture of Lt. John Phillips Philipps R. N. and Thomas Helps of Chester, but did not flourish.'[98]

It 'did not flourish' makes it sound as if the hydropathic centre itself took sick, and died in exactly the way it was trying to prevent. That the cure was the poison too.

*

Priessnitz died in 1851, at the age of fifty-two, probably of scarlet fever. Ultimately, he could not cure himself.

This in itself does not negate his practice, as notated by Schieferdecker, which was based around the principle 'truly may pure water be called a genuine panacea for all diseases, in every degree, that are curable'.[99] Written into the very basis of the healing power of water is the acknowledgement that not all diseases are curable.

Priessnitz, whose life's work and fame revolved around the notion that pure, clean water was all the body needed to help it heal itself, that it tended naturally towards health, and only needed help to rid itself of sickening 'stuffs', still did not believe in a universal nature cure.

*

The Grasmere Water Cure Establishment was next to Kelbarrow, where Wordsworth's son-in-law Edward Quillinan said faeries lived, and where legend has it some unwritten king called Kel was buried in a barrow that no one has yet managed to find. Perhaps Kel was a Faery king and his barrow is in the other place: in Grasmere but not in Grasmere, locatable, but only if you cross the boundary between this world and theirs.

Or perhaps Kel is not a king at all but the well itself. Keld is a dialect word for spring, or well, a derivation from Old Norse. Maybe it is language itself that is buried there, history covered over, a swell of culture pushed underground.

It is its holiness, its wholeness, its haleness that makes Grasmere homely, that makes it a good place to settle and dwell. And yet I knew enough before I moved back here to know that holiness is close to uncanniness. That homely and unhomely are flip sides of the spinning card and that

Grasmere held both of these in its bowl and steeped us all in them.

*

Lieutenant John T Phillips Philipps R. N. started his naval career on HMS *Temeraire*, the gunship immortalised in J. M. W. Turner's painting *The Fighting Temeraire tugged to her last berth to be broken up, 1838*, two years after she played her vital role in the battle of Trafalgar. Turner, who had sketched and painted Grasmere forty years earlier; for whom the landscapes and light of the Lake District hovered close.

Philipps's obituary, in August 1875, lists the various posts and commands he had held, taking him from the English Channel and the Baltic to Lisbon, to St Helena, The Cape of Good Hope, North America, the West Indies and eventually becoming the commander of two steam packets, the *Lucifer* and the *Medusa*. His command of these ended in July 1844, a few months after the first adverts for the hydropathic centre had gone out, and though he didn't officially retire until 1860, I wonder if he saw the centre as a retirement plan. A way to make sense of his life on land, but with water. A way to try to recover something.

*

In February 1850, the entire contents of the house called St Oswald's are listed for sale by auction.

A sarcastic note on Dr Stummes's retreat and the closing of the centre in the *Carlisle Patriot* in December 1847 supposed that 'the learned doctor has discovered [. . .] that the piercing air, frost, and snow render Grasmere quite cold enough during the winter months without the appliance of the "cold water treatment".'

In her 1855 guide to the Lakes, Harriet Martineau walks the reader down Red Bank Road and past St Oswald's, noting how 'the Hydropathic Establishment struggled on for a time, but found the Westmorland winters too long for invalids'.[100]

Yes, Harriet, they are, too long and too cold. You know it, I know it, but something still keeps us here, still keeps us thinking it's the right place to be.

If you look up the definition of hydropathy it says 'not now part of orthodox medicine'.

Underneath it, on my search, *hydrotherapy* appears, with the short explanation: 'Formerly called hydropathy and also called water cure [. . .] part of alternative medicine, in particular of naturopathy, occupational therapy and physiotherapy, that involves the use of water for pain relief and treatment.'

The hydrotherapy I've experienced – gentle exercises conducted under the supervision of trained physiotherapists in a very warm pool – is a long way from the cold water treatment of Gräfenberg and Grasmere.

But the winter swimmers, the ice-crackers, the cold water addicts – are they giving themselves the cold water treatment? Has hydropathy actually been translated into a swimming cure?

*

Only after I understand haemochromatosis can I connect the unusual vigour I felt when I first moved to Grasmere with the heavy bleeding I experienced in the months around the move. Before I left London I had been to the doctor, who had passed me on for investigation because I hadn't had a period in years. I wasn't quite sure how many – three, four? – longer?

Something seemed to shift when I moved. I was still living in my seventeenth-century silk mill workers' cottage just to the south of Lancaster when it began. It was always only a holding pen on the way to Grasmere – I was always waiting for a room to be available for me – my life with lakes drifting towards me like a mirage – but it was a time that stays with me, the first time I had ever been sovereign over my own space. I knew the house was the one for me before I even saw inside it. It was made of sandstone and it smelt like a friendly cave. It smelt like home, somewhere I knew. Somewhere I could be safe alone. From its door – the short walk up that back lane dotted with cottages and Victorian villas to campus – past the field of cows, and the squat church sitting in the moat of its graveyard, lit from within on winter afternoons like a Christmas card. And the house entirely my own.

I knew my life and the patterns of my life had changed utterly with that move from East London to Galgate, but it is only with distance I can see enough of them to make any meaning from them. I used to refer to my PhD as a crochet hook that reached into the fabric of my life and changed the direction of everything. Instead of dragging my aching body down the road to a Tube or bus to work or classes or both every day, I was nestled in my tiny fiefdom, spending hours reading and writing, playing the tatty piano I had bought for myself for £6 as a present for being brave and moving, walking up the lane and back. I drove to town. I drove to Grasmere once a week that first month for the last of that year's weekly poetry readings. I walked the canal towpaths in the afternoon sun.

Did any of this have anything to do with why, not long after I moved, I went from having no periods at all to bleeding heavily every two to three weeks? I will probably never know. But what I do know now is that what I thought for years was a kind of mountain and water cure that Grasmere enabled was actually a blood cure.

I had never bled so heavily before. I bled out between the start of work and the morning break; I stood in the cottage talking tourists around the rooms, feeling the warmth bubbling out of me, calculating how long I might have before everyone could see it.

At the time I thought the bleeding was terrible. It felt like my insides were falling out. It felt like the previous five years' allotted blood all falling at once. I felt myself draining away with it.

And yet in other ways I felt better than I had done in years. My gouty toe was no longer gouty. I was moving better, I was feeling lighter, somehow, less like I was walking with my shins dragging through the ground, as though sunk deep into it. Blood cure, blood magic.

If I'd known about iron loading then, maybe I wouldn't have sought to stop the bleeding. But I didn't know. I intervened, and eight months later I felt I was walking around on the raw bone-stubs of my legs. I was in so much pain. I didn't understand. Grasmere was the answer, wasn't it? Hadn't I done everything I needed to do? Bathed in nature, breathed in the golden light, breathed out the rotten smoke, taken the cold water baths, communed with trees and rocks and all the chattering creatures? I had given myself to nature, why wasn't she giving me health?

*

I thought things would get easier after diagnosis. That having the right words to say would act as a charm, unlocking all secrets. In some ways they have, but the work of maintenance is exhausting. One doctor does not communicate with another, does not communicate with you, and everything falls apart. One test gets lost on a system, and extra admin, months of it, springs up like magic beanstalks overnight.

There is the euphoria of knowing what is happening and why; the despondency of not being able to act on your knowledge.

Diligent in my rust, I try to get my bloods checked monthly. My GP will send me a message: *iron high: request venesection.* It is my job to ring the Day Hospital to book a venesection, but each time there is a new problem. There is no clear instruction to venesect me. There is no instruction to venesect me at particular levels. They cannot take my word on the tests. They cannot see the tests on their system.

And yet I am doing exactly what I've been told to do.

I know the systems are imperfect. I know the systems are overloaded. But so am I.

Eventually a new regime is suggested and new instructions given. My levels will be kept lower. Instead of going to the GP for my bloods once a month, I will go to the hospital every three months. Instead of the hospital I have been going to, in the county town of the next county down, I will go to the smaller hospital in Kendal, which is now equipped to do venesections. It is marginally closer, slightly easier to get to, and definitely easier to park at. I swap a five-minute drive every month for an hour's drive every quarter. The hospital is happier: they can see my results. The problem is, I can't. I have no way any more to track my levels. The problem is the computer systems don't talk to each other. The problem is I do not control my data.

What a difference to my life it would make to be able to determine my own treatment. What a lot of time and pain it would save us all.

*

In the summer of 2022 Windermere makes the international news. Aerial photographs show feathers of toxic algae spreading over the surface of the water like ink on marbled paper. Green on green. The lake is dying, reports say. The water is unsafe. The largest lake in England is dying.

The park authority doesn't want visitors to be alarmed and puts out a press release saying that it's under control, under investigation. Reports of the death of the lake are greatly exaggerated. The explosion of algae is natural, they say, it happens every year.

Advocates for the lake say there is a problem with pollution, with septic tank leaks and sewage overflow. It has been getting worse for years. Now it is critical. They expect the mass death of fish. They expect catastrophe. The lake is dying and it will die if changes are not made, quickly.

The park authority says it is looking into it. It is collating evidence, working on long-term strategies, forming partnerships, taking samples. It is committed to improvement. The problem, it says, is that no one can be certain what the problem really is.

*

Every year when the first bloom of cyanobacteria is reported the same message goes out. You cannot tell from looking at it whether a bloom is toxic or harmless. You have to treat it as though it might be toxic. Don't swim in the water, don't let your pets by the water. But who knows how long it will be before they can come out to test it, to be sure, one way or another. All the same the visitors come out, with paddleboards and kayaks, to enjoy their water cure. Their well-being is more important than the well-being of the water. The tourist board tells them so.

I keep thinking of Quesnel Lake, how even in 2022, the mining company is permitted to release up to 52,000 cubic metres of mine waste into it every single day. How the mine predominantly feeds the renewable energy sector. The gold and copper mined in BC goes into solar panels, electric cars. Green energy is built on a foundation of dirty mining.

'Nature' and 'Cure' are both the product of false binaries, of a dualism that is damaging our bodies and our world. We separate things out, choose one lake to be our natural health service, another to be sacrificed in the name of a greener, healthier future. We see no irony in any of this. We are proud of the progress we have made in the name of health, of our bodies and of the planet. We will squeeze the last drop of sap out of nature to make sure we get our cure.

*

Rust, like cyanobacteria, is everywhere. Even the iron-rich core of the earth is rusting, and the earth is rusting the moon.

By the end of the summer of 2022 my iron levels have been under control for nine months – the longest I have lived without iron-toxicity in twenty-five years. I have almost forgotten what it is to taste metal in my mouth at all times, or that deep particular ache in my hip bones.

There is long-term damage that cannot be reversed. There are new problems that have arisen from the legacies of harm. But there are also damages that have been halted. In the reed beds of my brain, small creatures are beginning to flourish. A sandpiper has nested in my skull, curlews in my pelvis. Where a dark mass spread over the surface of my mind, smothering everything, I see sunlight, and the flicker of fish tails. Trout leap through my skin. I dream in a halo of damselflies. Tiny frogs cling to my toes.

I am also bleeding again, copiously, painfully. I lose a week of every month to it, but I haven't had to have a pint of blood taken out all year. I begin to think of it as werewolf time, an unavoidable transformation that is making the rest of the month possible. In maintenance, I am, at last, self-maintaining.

In my worst years of undiagnosis, I came to think of my body as a disabling environment. I felt like a fish floundering under my own surface, powerless to alter the course of our shared fates. Now I recognise my body as a precarious ecosystem. We are adapting together to find a new balance. There are some things that have been lost forever, others that may be restored. I am the lake and the char. I am the heron and the otter.

I have to acknowledge all of these parts of myself as equal. The ducks and the duck mites. The cyanobacteria. I have to understand where the harm comes from, and how to limit it. I have to listen to the damage that is done to avoid the damage that can be avoided.

*

Cure is a beautiful fiction, even when it is posing as autobiography. For a narrative to end on cure depends on a screen scrolling down that declares 'the end!' just as the cure leans in to kiss the body better. It doesn't mean the end of a life, only of the life in pain, of one part of a partial story. It is nothing but judicious editing, like any happy ending. We don't want to see the sequel, a horror movie in which the pain keeps coming back, an ex you thought had left the country or a monster you thought you had slain. It is there every time you look in the mirror, it is there when you turn out the lights. You throw it out of the airlock into space, but there is always another sequel.

In the afterword to *Sick*, Khakpour reveals the book she wrote is not the book she intended to write, The Book She Sold, which would have had a triumphal end, a cure narrative which was meant to promise 'she got herself better. She made it [. . .] you can do it too.' Instead, she finds she got a different kind of 'miracle book', one that grew in its own patterns, one that moved beyond 'pretty arcs' and 'character development'. This reminded her that, 'Illness will always be with you as long as life is with you.'[101] For some readers, it might sound negative to acknowledge illness will always be present, but for Khakpour it has a transformative, transcendent power. To recognise ongoingness speaks not of cure, but of continuation, and the real beauty in that. It speaks of the miracle of agency.

*

The rusting of the earth was a mass extinction event, a climate catastrophe, but it enabled life as we know it. Whether it was an apocalypse or a revolution depends on your subject position. If you are thinking from the perspective of the anaerobic species who populated the earth then, you might use other names for it – the Oxygen Catastrophe, the Oxygen Crisis. But without it, there would be no fish in the lake, there would be no human swimmer.

I don't know what to think of this, as I think of my own body rusting, the lake slowly greening. As I think of the climate crises our species has generated and all the harms done in the name of progress.

In 2018, Nuskmata linked hope for the future with positive action, saying 'We are not defined by this disaster, we're defined by how we respond to it and what we do, how we activate others, how we lead and share.'[102]

We are only short-term tenants of a world which is beyond our comprehension or our dominion. If we do not recognise its right to life we will kill it without noticing, we will kill it whilst praising its precious beauty, and our own futures with it.

*

Spend time with trees. Swim with ducks. Walk barefoot on bare ground.

Relinquish money. Eat only foods you have foraged yourself. Forgo mechanical transportation. Give up the Internet and washing machines. Crush your mobile phone with a locally significant rock and bury it on a full moon under an oak tree. Light a ceremonial fire and dance round it thrice, widdershins.

Chant *all things will be well* and sound like you mean it.

Nature will keep doing what it does.

Pacing

One of the things I love most about our house is how quickly I can be away from it, away from street furniture and pavements, and on a path in a wood, looking down at a lake, watching a heron stalk a pond. How soon I can be amongst trees and off tarmac. I can be lying on a plushy carpet of mosses that would swallow your foot to your ankle bones, that would soften any fall. How close I am at any time to the lake, how I can feel it breathing, even on days when I cannot be in it.

I love our little house, with a door on each side of it, for escape into daylight whatever the season. Its wide stairs and sturdy banister. Its toilets on both floors that I can reach in only a few paces. Its rooms, only a few paces wide. Ten minutes' walk from the beach at the lake shore. Five minutes uphill into woods.

Even on bad days, I try to go out. To pace up the hill. I do this with a broken toe. With a chest infection. It is so close that even when I am lying on the sofa unable to stand I think I could stretch out my extra-long arm and touch the tree that hangs over the pond, or the one where the owl sits on winter afternoons.

I do not measure achievement in terms of how far I have gone or what distance I have covered. I set the rate of speed against my pulse. I move at a particular gait, depending on injury. There is always some injury. A good performance is a goldcrest in the hedge, a pair of roe deer sleeping the sun off in the dell, or, if I sit very restfully, a red squirrel sitting very patiently too, both of us invisible to the hikers striding by.

*

Pacing

When you live with pain and fatigue, no movement is without consideration or consequence. That which is automatic and unthought for the healthy is a constant process of thinking and rethinking.

Was there a time I moved without thinking? Without pain or the knowledge of pain?

Without the knowledge of falling?

*

Pacing is a side effect of chronicity. A co-morbidity. It requires an intimate oversight of the parallel timelines that spin out from each decision, each action or reaction.

There is the universe in which you manage to bathe and wash your hair today, or the universe in which you manage to do two hours of meaningful work. There is the universe in which you try to do both, and fall on the stairs, your hair still wet, too shaky from the ordeal of cleaning yourself to manage to cling to the illusion that the world is solid and you will not slip through it. Something gives in a leg or an ankle, and from that emerges the universe in which the day ends with a trip to A&E. You run through the potentials that spool out from the choice of *which A&E*. The big one with better services which is farther away, or the little one which is closer and will be quicker.

You use past data to extrapolate the futures. The big one forgot you last time you were there, after they decided you weren't crushing the blood supply to your brain – they left you in a side room without food or water from 8 p.m. to 1 a.m. until a shift change brought you back into play. The little one tends to send you on to the big one anyway, if it thinks you're beyond it. The little one is closer but not necessarily kinder. The little one likes a bit of casual victim blaming, always assumes your injury is your own fault, always asks *were you drinking* and/or *wearing silly shoes?*

You make a decision based on which one you can guess will drain you the least. Which one will do the least damage.

This is pacing in action.

Sometimes you choose not to go at all, and hope that will create another timeline in which the problem is not that serious, in which you can spend the night in your own bed, in which you do not need to explain.

It is hard to know, even after a lifetime of this, whether the injury wants rest or movement. Pacing or peace.

One night, I choose rest. Another, a stretch in a sauna. Another, hospital. Another, to stay home but set an alarm to ring the doctor at the start of the morning surgery. Another, to carry on and hope by deciding it is not serious it will be not serious. It is hit and miss. There is always a different way to get it wrong.

*

When I see the word *pace* written down I also always read *peace*, some part dug deep remembering Latin I didn't think I'd learnt, or just a dyslexic illusion? Without looking it up, I couldn't have told you that *pace* is the ablative of *pax*. That *pace* is to go with peace. Pacing is making peace. But I felt it in the word, I saw it, meaning in misreading.

The English word *peace* replaced the Old English *frið*, which meant not only a peace, as in, a cessation of disorder, and peace, as in tranquility, but also happiness. We used to have a peace which was a happiness. We swapped happiness for quiet. Happiness for agreement. Happiness for silence.

*

One January day I walk out in test mode. I bought myself new snow boots in the sales with Christmas money. I am always trying to find a way to keep my feet warmer, to stave off the chilblains, the frozen bloodlessness of numb cold, the pain. But the first time I wear them they cut through the tearable skin on the back of my right ankle. My paddle-shaped feet are not designed for shoes – wide at the toes, narrow at the heel – if they fit at one end they fail at the other. Everything rubs somewhere. The skin around the creases of my heel joint is thickened with the scars of decades, but no stronger for it.

The first time I wear the boots I only make it a few metres up the old road in the slush before I feel the skin open inside my sock.

The next day, I try again. I dress without washing for the second day in a row: this is how I get outside on days like this, when the fatigue is a heavy downward and backward drag, and winter a rock strapped to my back.

I put blister plasters on my heel, better socks. I walk a little further. My hips hurt. My knees and ankles crack in the cold. This is pacing, moving into one pain to avoid accidentally stumbling into another.

But this is not the kind of pacing they mean in CBT classes or pain management classes when they say they are teaching you pacing, and ask you to fill in a timetable of your activities for a week, and mark them in traffic light colours: green for low energy use or pain triggering, amber for middling, red for worst.

I struggle with this from the start. How do I map out a typical week? A typical day? I don't know what typical means. In my working life each week might look entirely different, as though, to some eyes, they don't belong to the same person's life, and as for energy use or pain? The same thing one day is not the same thing the next, or next month, or next year. You never do the same activity twice.

They ask you to avoid the reds, build more greens into your week. They ask you to slow down, to *pace yourself.*

Make peace, I hear.

Make peace with your slowness.

For years I flail against the whole concept. What they mean is to slow down my slow life even more. They think slowing down is a cure. I find it both hilarious and hateful.

I try to say 'if I stop halfway through a task, I will never finish it'. I try to say 'the only way I do anything is to keep going, despite'. I try to say 'green as a concept didn't exist in the ancient world, it was blue, only blue', by which I mean to say that I don't know what a green activity would be or look like, that a green activity is implausible in the chronic life, that you might as well call it a unicorn activity, that there is no green. But none of this fits the timetable.

*

After exercise of any kind, I get muscle cramps. Sometimes they are worse than other times. Sometimes rubbing magnesium oil into my muscles can help, sometimes not.

At their worst, these cramps and spasms have pulled so hard on my spine and my neck that I've been unable to stand for more than 56 seconds for weeks on end with my head unsupported. At 56 seconds, the growing pain in my head becomes a star exploding, and I lose myself. I lose speech, I lose reason. Everything melts into a tarry bog of pain. I am drowned in it, and far too far under to be able to tell anyone.

I know it is 56 seconds, as you would if it happened every time you tried to stand up. You would make the countdown too.

One spring I lay on my left side on the sofa, the only position I could tolerate, for three weeks, too emptied by pain to weep, too wary of moving to sob, eyes leaking slightly onto the cushion continually.

Pacing

I could get to the toilet within the seconds. I could pour a glass of water.

To get to bed I propped up my head in my hands and counted down.

When my muscle spasms made their magnitude known I was teaching full-time in an institution that I came to believe would have preferred its staff not to inhabit human bodies with all their frailties. There was no contingency for sickness. No understanding of accommodation. I'd never worked somewhere where I was so terrified of the consequences of illness, so absolutely certain in my bones that weakness would not be tolerated. I gave a lecture holding my head up with my hands propped under my chin, because that was the only way to stem the pain enough to speak for fifty minutes, and I knew I had to speak for that fifty minutes or there would be consequences I couldn't quite formulate.

To speak for that fifty minutes I had to take two buses to take a train, then another bus to campus, all the time propping my head up with my hands, all the time trying to breathe away from the pain, to keep hold of the thin thread of myself within the fast river of the pain.

That fifty minutes cost me the next three weeks. Three weeks of lying on my side.

Each day on the sofa, on my left side, leaking into the pillow.

What made the spasms so bad at that particular time? I had been pushing for a long time. I was overloaded at work.

I'd been struggling all year with classes scheduled back-to-back at opposite ends of a campus with a hill so steep in the middle that classes were once called off in the snow because it was too dangerous to get between rooms. Over time I had learnt the hidden ways to travel the hill without pushing my body beyond its limits, following a network of corridors and lifts through various almost connected buildings, each lift with a warning poster on it telling you to climb the stairs for your health. But it took time. I asked for classes all in one building, or at least all on one level. I asked for classes with gaps between. I was told it was impossible to make such changes.

My mentor told me my colleagues thought badly of me for not pulling my weight. I nodded, chastised; cried the long way home. Every day I hauled myself and my course materials down back corridors and into service lifts, my heart palpitating, joints slipping. I was back at school, circling the labyrinthine stairwells of the tenantless houses on crutches, haunting its connecting passages weighed down by bags of Lever Arch files and dog-eared textbooks. Even the library had a monumental staircase before you reached a single book. I asked about disabled access and was shown to a wheelchair lift, but only once I'd ascended the initial staircase. I was too ashamed, and too exhausted, to ask more.

When the spasm took hold, I had been hunched over the laptop for days, mired in online marking. Something clunked in my neck mid-mark. It was a Wednesday afternoon, and I was at home in Grasmere instead of in Glasgow, where I would normally have been. The ancient gas fire – the only heating in the studio flat I rented for term time – had been erratic since I moved in, and was now broken entirely. I couldn't face another night of lying awake shivering, too cold to sleep, too cold to move, frightened to put the fan heater on in case it blew the electric again. I couldn't work in a space that cold. I couldn't think in a space that cold.

I was three months into venesections and my body was not happy about it. It had gone into lockdown, survival mode. I was struggling to walk after falling on the hill between classes during the first dizzy month. Each footstep was agony, and being upright was increasingly precarious. I was moving between classes and places and carrying too much with me.

I was swaying down corridors, bouncing from wall to wall, in continual pre-syncope as soon as I stood. But I kept going, because I didn't think I had an option not to.

The day after my neck clunked, the pain in my head and neck was so bad I couldn't stand, and I realised I had no option but to go to A&E. I spent an evening and half a night in A&E, threatened with a spinal tap. I had an MRI in case the pain was the veins in my neck being crushed – *venous insufficiency* – then was left in a side room and forgotten about when the shifts changed, after the scans showed nothing obviously serious. Though, of course, no one had told me that until the shifts changed again after midnight. The doctor who came on shift then knew EDS, recognised the problem, knew what to do to help.

On the train home after the lecture I held my head up throughout, the lecture that cost me three weeks of immobilised pain, I began to drift. I couldn't keep my chin up. I was sinking into the pain. It was up to my mouth now, taking my words.

Two men, travelling together, were sitting opposite me. They tried to chat over the tea trolley and I tried apologising for not being able to talk – my head – pain – sorry – etc. One of them asked more. Through the sludge of pain I eked out more explanation. At some point I mentioned a connective tissue disorder, and that's when his interest began to make sense. His son had a hereditary connective tissue disorder, but they only found out after he had had an aortic dissection, after it had killed him. The man, his father, now campaigned for awareness, particularly to make sure teenagers have access to heart health checks. I had a sense they were like paramedics, keeping me talking to save me from going under.

After that day, I swore to myself I would never allow myself to be placed in that position again. I would not risk my future on pushing through something I should not have to push through. I would not allow myself to be pushed.

That day changed my life, my attitude to asking for accommodation. I would no longer take 'we can't do that' for an answer. I would no longer damage myself for other people's benefit.

When I feel the muscle spasms coming on, especially in my neck, a combination of muscle relaxants and anti-inflammatories can stop it developing into the grip that stops everything. Sometimes it takes a day or two and a few rounds of medication to stop. Sometimes I can sleep or stretch it off without taking anything. Sitting in a sauna and stretching gently can help. A hot bath is soothing but not enough to stop it. Massage helps make it more comfortable, although it does not make it go away. Maybe regular massage would do more to help, but it is not offered on the NHS, and who can afford to pay for a massage every time they move their body or pick up an object or carry a bag for more than a few moments?

Instead, I try to avoid triggers. Some I cannot account for, like subluxations in the night. Others, I can limit: shivering with cold, carrying anything but the lightest items on my back or shoulders. The way I sit, the way I sleep. I have shifted the way I move through the world to limit the damage. This is pacing.

*

Pacing is giving up on trying to live on land, and sinking myself in the hand-me-down bath moored in the corner of what once would have been the third bedroom of our little cottage.

Lowering myself into the bath one day I find a new deep red bruise on my left thigh. As big as a golf ball? No, bigger. Almost a tennis ball. I have no memory of bumping into anything, although I do it a lot.

Pacing

Another day, another winter, my knee rises out of the bubbles as an enormous bruise. It's the shape of my knee-cap, almost heart-shaped, or like a horror film mask. I know how this one happened. I knelt on the thin rental carpet in the hallway for a few moments – less than a minute – the night before. When I stood up, there was pain, but no sign of any trauma. But now this bruise. A dark red-brown like old blood, or rust, and tender to touch, which includes the touch of my tissues every time I move the joint. My body is full of surprises, even now. It offers up new, unimaginable strangeness from its unfathomable ravines on a daily basis. It is always throwing me off balance, literally, metaphorically. This also is pacing, going back and forth, never getting anywhere, but finding something different each time you turn back along the same stretch. It is not terrible, or delightful. It is somewhere between them, and both.

*

On the pain rehab course I am sent on to learn to manage my EDS, we learn pacing in practice, and it makes sense to me for the first time. It's not the rigid thing that had been presented to me before. They tell us it changes all the time, day to day, hour to hour. We have single sessions with the occupational therapists, and I begin to understand. Pacing is recognising that in April 2015 I can only sit in a neutral posture in a chair for 1 minute and 27 seconds before my neck starts to hurt. That 1 minute and 27 seconds is my 'base point' at that moment, and that as soon as I reach that point, and I'm aware of the pain, and the pain growing, I should move.

This is new.

Pacing is not stopping, but moving. Pacing is changing.

They teach us to stop an activity and change *before the pain grows*. This is revolutionary. At first I think *how*, when pain is always already pushing down on you, or waiting to unfurl itself over you. But I start to see what they mean. Pacing is about not pushing through.

Pushing Through is the opposite of Pacing. Pushing Through is sticking your hands over your ears and singing *lalala* when the noise of the pain ramps up. It is trying not to listen.

I had thought it was impossible to live not pushing through, impossible to do anything at all.

I learn to pay attention to my pain in a different way.

They also tell us we will get it wrong. That pacing is not an exact science. There is no fixed measure of how long you can do any one thing, how long you can sit, walk, type, eat, before stopping, changing. It is a continual adjustment. It is about attention to your pain levels. This is revolutionary.

Pacing in practice might not be stopping before the pain if the pain is always there, but all of us who live with pain know the rise of it from mutter to scream, from single cicada to screeching swarm. Pacing means stopping sometime between noticing the first insect land and the sky blackening.

*

To pace is to quieten, to call a truce. A freedom from the disorder of the body. Temporary. We reconcile. We give permission to rest, to lay down arms, figuratively or literally.

But it is also unrest, it is also unquiet. It is peaceless movement. It is the continual effort to remember to change. To keep changing. To remain alert to the body's disorders, to alter accordingly.

*

Pacing

In *Illness as Metaphor* Susan Sontag wrote of the dangers of using the language of fight and battle to talk about illness.

Like many people who live with illness and disability, I reject the language of battle, of fight. When people die they don't lay down arms; they don't succumb to a battle with, they don't lose the fight to.

The language of battle makes it harder to be honest about illness. It taps into inspiration porn, a term coined by Stella Young, in which the sick or disabled person is positioned as both brave and pitiable. They are brave just brushing their teeth, taking a bus. More than forty years after Sontag published her essay, the language she railed against is more ubiquitous than ever. It spills out of TV adverts, out of charity campaigns. Every sick person is either a brave warrior or a fallen soldier, and if they don't or won't fit this mould, they become a scrounger or a faker. In July 2020, Boris Johnson tells us 'we must carry on waging this long, hard fight against coronavirus' as though the virus is an invading army. If we are at war with Covid-19, we can only lose. No military force can beat a virus. No personal strength can either. A pandemic won't respect your borders or your armies. It doesn't care how many nukes you have stashed away. You can't drop a bomb on it. You can't incarcerate its soldiers. You can't change its mind.

And yet, and yet, illness does sometimes feel like a long battle, doesn't it? Ridiculous in its ongoingness. Ludicrous how you keep going when there is nothing left in you to keep going with. Sometimes the only way to face the day is as a performance of a great victory, to cry 'once more unto the fray' and launch into it, knowing there will be losses. Like the scene from *Monty Python and the Holy Grail* in which King Arthur fights the Black Knight, and the Black Knight will not stop, even as he is spurting blood from the open wounds where his arms used to join his shoulders.

Sometimes the body in pain is repeating *none shall pass!* whilst also cutting itself down, bit by bit, into pieces, and making the tired old jokes at its own expense. Sometimes this is how the body in pain continues.

In continual pain you long for nothing more than a truce with your body, with the world that makes it difficult for you to move through without causing more pain.

You are not asking for cure, just for a little bit of calm, a window of happiness, a brief spell without struggle, without hurt.

*

Pacing is a strategy.

Not the kind of pacing they teach in pain management, the one which means *do less, slow down, rest*, but pacing as continual movement, pacing as counter-manoeuvre. Pacing as repetition, as chronic.

Pacing as a full-body fidget. Fidget as strategy.

The autonomic nurse taught me that fidgeting is a coping mechanism to counteract blood-pooling. The blood sinks down in the elastic blood vessels, overstretched with the blood's weight under gravity. Blood sinks to the bottom of the body and the body cannot move it back up. Capillary action fails because it relies on elasticity, on narrowness, not stretch. We stretch too much. Gravity drags. Blood falls. But movement of the body can move the blood. The muscles squeeze the capillaries as they contract to move the limbs, the blood moves. It is a trick. The nurse taught me *gravity is your enemy*. The nurse taught me *never stand still: keep moving*. Rock back and forth, up and down. Walk on the spot. Keep moving. Pace.

*

Pacing

I was an undergraduate when I first read Flann O'Brien's novel *The Third Policeman*. I fell in love with it deeply, partly because of how it understood the body as permeable, as leaching into the things around it, how a man and a bicycle could become one another, but also because of how it understood repetition. O'Brien writes: 'Hell goes round and round. In shape it is circular, and by nature it is interminable, repetitive, and nearly unbearable.'[103] At the time this was how I felt about life in my body, about trying to negotiate my body through the medical system, about seeking help, helplessly, hopelessly, about ending up back at the beginning, or a different beginning time after time. About the feeling you are learning something with each turn around, but it might as well be nothing, because it doesn't help get you further on. Nothing helps.

Now I can see the worth in the slow journey, the spiral so tight it feels like a circle. But it's not a circle. We come back to the same point but we are never the same, the point is never the same because we have changed.

There were times I thought I was stuck in someone else's hell. Now I understand it as a labyrinth. Not a trap, but a meditation. As chronicity. A spiral that returns us to the same place but also moves us further from it. And I know how to pace as I move through it.

*

To pace is to go over and over again. To repeat. To restep. To retread. Pacing is chronic. Or do I mean dyschronic? It passes time, moving without moving, but it also stops time, folds time up in place – the same space trod and retrod – the time ticking on but not progressing, like the action of walking that only leads back into itself and not forward or away.

A walking that is not for travelling. A walking that is for motion without progress.

*

William Wordsworth wrote by pacing. I'm quoting myself now, words I've said over and over in seminar rooms, in conference rooms. He paced along the turf path that forms part of my daily walk. He paced the public roads muttering fragments of poems to himself.

At Rydal Mount, the home of his success years, he landscaped a terrace into the garden precisely so that he could pace up and down its length to compose his words, his thoughts, to turn the line of his thoughts into poetry. It was these terraces that allowed his sister Dorothy to access the garden in the years when she used a wheelchair. This is pacing as access, and not just for ourselves.

*

Pacing is De Quincey travelling the labyrinthine streets of London every night, the labyrinthine paths of Lakeland. Both of them at once in his dreams. The labyrinth ties one to the other. This is pacing through crip time, through crip space.

*

We are encouraged to dismiss the pain. We are told the pain is real, but an empty message, misinformation in the nervous system. That chronic pain is neurones firing in response to nothing. That the pain doesn't mean anything: it is not giving a message like it is for normal people, people who don't have chronic pain. That there is no injury to find or fix. There is just a damaged system that misfires continually. That that is why we should send chronic pain patients to CBT, to teach them to understand that their pain is a blank envelope, an empty inbox. To teach them to think past their pain. Every time, I want to shout, *life is a series of injuries and micro-injuries. This pain is vital information. Don't teach us to ignore it. Don't ignore it.*

I can tell you exactly where my chronic, ongoing, currently uncurable pain comes from. It is from bodily difference. It is from a trillion tiny, continuous micro-aggressions of the body. It is from the chronic inflammation of the connective tissue in my ribcage, it is from nerve damage around old injuries, from displacement of joints and bones and damage to ligaments, it is from muscle cramps and spasms, it is from dislocations and subluxations, the way my kneecaps grind every time I bend my leg because they sit too far on the edge. It is from the weakness in my structure that makes keeping myself upright, sitting straight, lifting my head, excruciatingly hard work. It is from iron-toxicity in my organs and the cells that constitute my organs. I know I have differences in the way I receive the world – differences that make me hypersensitive to noise, smell, light, touch – but that is not the source of my continual pain.

But we are taught to ignore our experience. I have been told the pain in my hips one day is not because of the micro-injury caused by wading through flood water the night before. It has no because. It has no meaning. But my hips don't lie and I must not lie about or to them. They are screaming out for me to listen to them, and if I don't, we will all regret it. If pain is an empty message, why adjust behaviour to account for it?

I walk through pain to avoid more pain and I stop walking through pain to avoid more pain. Both of these are pacing. We can only have peace if we stop to listen. Pacing is happiness.

*

Are you coming to terms with difference, with illness, or making peace with yourself, your self in sickness, if you reach that stage they call acceptance?

Is acceptance a kind of pacing?

It goes back and forth. It goes nowhere. It retreads the same ground until it wears it to furrows.

Acceptance, like any peace, is not a moment of accord but the continual reliving of that moment. The carrying forward, and back again, of that accord. The process of making peace over and over again.

*

Constant pain changes the relationship of the person to place and to moments in time. Overwhelming pain can take us away from the present, and stop us from enjoying being in a place, and moving in place. But it can also make us more present, more aware. I walk slowly and quietly and stop a lot, and the compensation is that I see and hear things other people don't. I walk less, and swim more. I walk less, I pace more.

When your life is broken down into a series of painful repetitive movements, you have to find joy in small things. Life is made of small things and many of them are painful. The ones which are not are thrown into exquisite relief. Often for me these are interactions with other living creatures, reminders that life is various and continuous, despite my pain. An iridescent feather tucked into the lawn. A greenfinch at the window.

I look at the ground as I walk so I don't fall and so I notice the ground, its beauty, all the things that live there. Tiny mushrooms, newts crossing the road, yellow cinquefoil, all the multitudes of moss. I stop to rest, and in resting I hear red squirrels chittering in the trees above me, their tails bright against the bark as they run and leap. I hear a family of black-cap fledglings in a hedge, a curlew's burbling call. I notice textures and details, neon lichen on a boulder or a drystone wall, pixie cups like a drowned hoard spilled by a fairy ship-wreck, verdigrised and barnacled by centuries underwater, the red tips of its new growth like corals. On a sunny winter morning each tiny goblet holds an orb of frost melt, a reflective planet. I see the heron watching from behind a screen of foliage. The deer always watching from behind a screen of foliage, whatever the season. The long-tailed tits moving in relay between high sunlit branches. The tawny owl blending itself into oak.

*

Eli Clare writes about the rewards that come from moving slowly, differently, through the world. Like me, his relationship to gravity is 'ambivalent': he will 'slip, totter, descend stairs one slow step at a time'. He has to pace himself, and it has rewards:

> On steep stretches I drop down onto my butt and slide along using both my hands and feet, for a moment becoming a four-legged animal. Only then do I see the swirl marks that glaciers left in the granite, tiny orange newts climbing among the tree roots, otherworldly fungi growing on rotten logs. My shaky balance gives me this intimacy with the mountain.[104]

Kathleen Jamie called readers to attend to 'a wildness which is smaller, darker, more complex and interesting, not a place to stride over but a force requiring constant negotiation', asking us to 'marvel at the wildness of the processes of our own bodies, the wildness of disease'.[105] There are wildnesses of disease it is easier to marvel at if you are standing above them, looking down, a wanderer beyond the fog of illness. If you live in the wildness of disease, you have no choice but to attend to its fascinating ecologies.

There is so much to see if you move slowly and carefully through the world. If you pay attention not just to the wildness of your own body but to the wildness it reveals in the world.

*

I keep thinking that to understand this I have to go back, back to where I've already been, and further, back to where something took root.

I decide I need to go to Creswell Crags, and it makes me nervous to think about it. W and I take a detour on a trip down to Nottingham. We cut across the moors and drop down into Derbyshire. It is Hallowe'en, 2018. A bright, cold day. I have a feeling that if I don't get there this week, before they switch to reduced winter hours, I'll never get there. By the time we arrive the sun has already left the gorge, and the sky is turning. Our time is running down. We have to be in Nottingham by six, to go trick or treating with my nephews. They are the same age now as I would have been on that trip to Creswell Crags so many decades earlier. Later, trailing around the cobwebbed houses of Lady Bay, as their pumpkin bags become heavy with sweets and they begin to slow down, lose focus, my brother pushing ahead and calling back, eager to get to a friend's house with a party, I imagine them on the path in the caves, history a dark gap on either side of them. Most of the time, they are far ahead of us, and we are the ones trailing behind.

At the caves I am surprised and not surprised by a shiny new visitor centre. We are distracted by the shop at the entrance. I am more than half tempted by a fluffy sabre-toothed tiger.

I could say it was for research I try on W, making it dance in a toothy, goofy way.

There isn't time for a tour. We get coffees at the cafe and walk towards the gorge. There are pheasants everywhere, their calls prehistoric enough. A few other visitors on foot, and a miniature horse trap pass us on the bridleway. The caves look soft in the pinking light. There are jackdaws roosting in them and in the trees on the ridge, moving between cracks in the stone and the foliage in noisy waves. There are ducks on the water in the centre, that separates one county from the other. We take a lot of pictures. I peer into every cave, through the barred gates at their mouths which are just like the barred gates in the dungeons under school. They are all dressed up for Hallowe'en with plastic pumpkins, LED candles and skeletons.

It is unsatisfactory in its normalcy. If anything, they look sad. I can't work out which cave it was that scared me. I need to go back. To go back again. To be afraid again, or at least see what I was afraid of. I used the excuse of not doing too much – of pacing myself – to avoid it. But it is no good. Some darknesses have to be outpaced.

*

It is hard to retrace your steps when the steps are so painful.

I thought if I went back over all that had happened I could find something, something I had lost or missed the first time. That I could make a pattern out of random motion, or a meaning from the movement.

I thought if I paced back through time, I could make sense of things that seemed nothing but chaos when I walked through them for the first time. I thought I could find truth on the side of the path. That I could go into the dark, into the doubted memories, and dig out something new. Turn to the old cave walls and find a different story.

Perhaps I could find out what happened or why. Who was responsible for every break in the chain that could have diagnosed me sooner. The particular ways in which systems failed me. The particular ways in which the patient was actually right. I thought verifying my experience would mean something.

But I already knew what it meant. I knew how my body reacted and how I remembered it and how I still remember it. I knew what I felt. I was there.

We are taught that, to learn to live the Chronic Life well, we must learn acceptance, but what if acceptance is another trick, a lie like The Nature Cure, designed to silence us when we ask questions? To shame us?

Sometimes I think I catch it in the corner of my eye, acceptance, and recognise it as a member of the same family as the kind of CBT-speak that tells us we make ourselves more ill when we think about it too much, when we talk about it too much. When we invest too much in our sick selves.

I have learnt again now what I knew instinctively twenty years ago, that I have to listen to her, my sick self, or we will both get sicker.

*

In early 2019, Creswell Crags hits the news. The largest collection of witch marks in one site in the UK had been discovered on its walls. Hundreds of letters and figures etched into the rocks' surfaces hundreds of years before. It's not that no one knew the markings were there, but that no one had looked closely enough to realise they were not tourist graffiti but something much older. Cavers from Subterranea Britannica on a tour of the site recognised the marks for what they are – charms intended to ward off evil, to keep evil underground. To keep the past, past.

They are termed apotropaic marks, from the Greek *apotrepein*, meaning 'to turn away'. They ask what is down there to turn away, to go back down, to not rise up and walk out into the present.

They include carvings of the letters PM, standing for *Pace Maria*, calling forth the Virgin Mary's powers of protection. The latin *pace* – peace – containing as always the English pace. Alongside these there are shapes meant to catch and contain evil: boxes, lines, mazes, labyrinths. These trap evil inside their walls, keep evil confused, pacing back and forth unable to find the place it snuck in.

What did they know or guess of, those long dead people who made marks against the longer dead? What did they intuit of what was there, waiting to come up? And was the dread they felt the same dread I felt, or did it come from the same strange shiver of recognition?

John Charlesworth, the heritage facilitator at the caves, was surprised they had walked past the carvings every day and not recognised them as important. The press release quotes him:

> These witch marks were in plain sight all the time! After 17 years at Creswell Crags it makes me wonder what else it has to surprise us.

After all this time, I find I have something in common with the caves. They have shown their history, displayed their truth openly, and it has been dismissed, discounted as meaningless, as something to either ignore or be ashamed of. Now they know it is something marvellous, and they are surprised, amazed to find what was in front of them all the time. It took people from outside, with a different set of knowledge, a different set of preconceptions, to understand the cave's etched skin as communicating important stories, not as babbling nonsense. It is not at all surprising to find the caves too have been misdiagnosed for so long.

*

I take myself to Rathlin Island too. I think if I see the place they found those ancient bodies with their haemochromatosis genes, I will understand something better. I don't know what, exactly, but I'm certain I have to go there.

Rathlin lies six miles from Ballycastle Harbour on the Antrim coast, an uneven chevron, an arrow pointing towards the Mull of Kintyre, only fifteen miles east. It is the most northerly inhabited island off the island of Ireland, its broader arm facing Islay and Gigha. It is an island with a long history of human habitation, going back to the Stone Age, when axe heads were made there with rare porcellanite. It is also an island with a long history of contested sovereignty, of refuge and bloodshed. St Columba or Colmcille is said to have stayed on Rathlin when he left Ireland in 563, before he settled on Iona. In 795 it was the site of the first Norse raid in Ireland. In 1575 English troops massacred hundreds of MacDonnell families sheltering on Rathlin, and in 1642 Covenanter soldiers of Clan Campbell slaughtered MacDonnell men and boys whilst the women watched from a hill named afterwards Cnoc na Screidlinne, the hill of the screaming. Now it is best known for its wildlife, for seabirds and golden hares, a variant of Irish hare unique to Rathlin.

I plan my trip for months, but by the time I get the funding I need, I have too many limits on my time, and I can only fit a few nights in. Also, it's October. Off-season for islands. No puffins, no summer migrants of any kind, avian or human.

Pacing

On the boat over from the mainland, my host rings me to give me instructions on how to get to the B&B I have booked into. She wants to know why I'm visiting at this strange time of year, has guessed it's something to do with the haemochromatosis. I explain a little about what I'm doing, this book, that I have no particular aims, but that I just want to be there, to stand on rock that these ancient carriers of my mutation would have stood on. She tells me a little about how they were found. She tells me of a chieftain carried away from the island in a crisp box. His remains bundled up into recycling. She calls it a shame, but I say there's something beautiful in that, isn't there? Something about continuation. About how no matter how important we are in our lives, in death we are all bones in a crisp box. She sounds unconvinced.

She hopes to come over to Rathlin whilst I'm there and introduce me to some people who might talk to me about the excavation, or about their experience of haemochromatosis. But it is late October. The weather is against us; the sea too stormy to risk her crossing then getting stuck. My first morning on the island I have breakfast in the house made by a young woman who is working for my hosts whilst she finishes her PhD, along with the only other overnighting tourists on the island, an English couple. We chat a bit as we eat. I tell them the bare bones of what I'm doing. They look at each other in some surprise. He has haemochromatosis too. They didn't know about the island's connection with it. They came for the seabirds. Three offcomers on the island and two of them have haemochromatosis.

The storm is meant to worsen that day. They don't know if their planned ferry will be running, but when it is, all three of them leave. I am left alone in the house.

The B&B is next to the pub the bodies were found in the grounds of, so I sleep next to the burial site of men I now

267

think of as my distant relatives. There is nothing to see of the excavation site now. It has vanished under the car park that stirred it up. But I like knowing they were there, just next door, for thousands of years. No one locks their doors on the island. One afternoon I find a man has let himself in to deliver a bag of bacon and eggs to me from my hosts on the mainland. I like to think my dead antecedents, my mutant family, could walk in too, stop in for a drink and tell me what it was like for them.

I walk a lot on the island. More than I have walked since I broke my toe, a year before. My foot has never been right since – the nerve at the junction of the toe I broke has swollen into a neuroma as wide as my toe. It is like a button for pain. Every step pushes it. The more it is pushed, the higher the frequency of the pain.

But on Rathlin I am able to step into it differently. Maybe it is nothing more than adrenalin – the excitement of being there counteracting the signals from the damaged nerve. On the day I am left there alone, I walk to the East Lighthouse in the rain – the shortest transect of the island, across its hinge. I hope to see seals when I reach the other shore, to see golden hares on the way. It is a genetic mutation that gives the hares their distinctive apricot coats and blue eyes. I am sure this gives us a connection, one genetic mutant to another. Blue eye to blue eye. Our coats haemochromatosis bronze. All I meet are a group of shy cows and some horses, only the odd dropping suggesting some hares have been by.

When I get to the lighthouse, the cliff path is too steep and the wind too high to risk my bad balance to it, and I am left peering down a gully to the sea, trying to distinguish seals from rocks between the spray.

I know a cave called Bruce's Cave hunkers below the lighthouse in the cliffs. Legend has it Robert the Bruce and his warriors lie sleeping in the sea cave, ready to rise up when

Scotland needs them, just as Dunmail is said to sleep under the raise at the north of Grasmere, dozing until our desperation stirs him to action. My mum's aunts were known to claim relation to the Bruce once a few drinks were taken, as I suspect many families from Annandale would. It's about as likely as our long arms descending from Rob Roy, but it links family with the island in my mind, it links the island's history to family history, the history of its places to ours.

Bruce lay fallow here over the winter of 1306 to 1307 with an army of three hundred men, sheltering not in the cave but in a castle, after his defeat at Dalrigh. His winter in Rathlin is recorded in John Barbour's epic poem 'The Brus', published in 1377. Sir Walter Scott introduces a spider into the cave, in his series of Scottish myths and legends, *Tales of a Grandfather*, published between 1828 and 1830. Scott's Bruce watches a spider try six times to swing a strand of web from one side of the cave to another, and fail. The six attempts seem to mirror his six battles for sovereignty. On the seventh attempt, the spider fastens its thread, and so Bruce resolves to fight once more, at what will become the Battle of Bannockburn. It is said to be the origin of the proverb 'if at first you don't succeed, try and try again', a favourite saying of my mum and her mum before her. I used to think it meant you had to keep pushing, keep battling even as it hurt you, if you meant ever to get to where you wanted, to achieve what you hoped for.

I squint down from the lighthouse as though that could tell me anything, but all I can see is rain and breakwater, seals or rocks.

Now I think maybe it means it is alright to fail, alright to rest, alright to go to ground for seven years before you rise, swords blazing, to claim what is yours. Alright to work to spider time, crip time, cave time. Alright to see all progress you think you have made, painstakingly, swept aside, and to start again from nothing. That starting again, rebuilding the labyrinth of the web from air and your own body, is the achievement. That the wisdom is in the repetition. That the magic is in the repetition.

There are other caves that claim to be the cave of the Bruce and the spider. One is a cave carved in sandstone, in the village of Kirkpatrick-Fleming, only four miles from my mum's childhood home. Like the sandstone caves under Nottingham, it is a natural cavity that has been carved into, enlarged, sculpted over generations. It is graffitied by eighteenth-century tourists and inscribed by antiquarians now lost to history themselves. Beside the entrance a shield and a five-pointed star are etched into the rock, and above it a promise from one of the estate's owners, Emma Ermengarda Ogilvy –

> within this cave kynge robert bruce
> from foes pursuent soughte a truce,
> lyke my Forbearers who for hym fell,
> i ermengarde doe guard yt well.

My family must have known this cave, its history, its link to the legend, to the king and to the motto of determination and perseverance. Its link to what they thought they knew about themselves.

Rathlin is scattered with sea caves, all with their own histories and mythologies. One is said to tunnel beneath the entire island, a passage connecting east to west. Another is said to have given shelter to the swan children of Lir at the end of their lives. Bruce's cave is only accessible by sea, and only when the sea is calm. An excellent hiding place, if you can get in there yourself.

The next day I walk to Rue Point, to the south lighthouse, where I am told there will definitely be seals. It is raining when I set out, but the sun breaks through, throwing huge double rainbows over the village as I inch away from it, moving slowly, pacing, stopping to take photos and watch sea birds I can't identify. By the time I'm on the single-track road down to Rue Point, the sun is blazing down. I shed layers. I watch for hares; talk to the small, handsome island sheep. I pass ruined settlements that speak of the days when there were over a thousand people living on the island, rather than a hundred. I wonder how many of them carried the same mutations I do, that the Bronze Age men buried under the pub did.

At Rue Point I sit in the lee of a ruined building, grown over with moss and scattered with sheep droppings, and drink tea from my flask. It is only a five-mile round walk, but it is the first time I have walked that far in a long time. I am tired, but I am okay. I am being careful to rest often. I am being careful to set my own pace.

I don't notice the seals are watching me until I move closer to the shore, and a couple slip from the rocks into the water. Even after I have been watching them for five, ten minutes, I cannot unpick the seals on the far rocks from the far rocks, up sun, all mottled grey and white. They are like stars: the longer you look, the more of them you can distinguish.

I watch them for a long time as they play in the water, turning and turning. I know they recognise me as other, not seal. I know I am not one of them, but we are all enjoying the surprise of sun.

I am reminded of a paper I heard at a conference the year of my diagnosis. The speaker talked about different theories of the origin of selkie stories. That selkies might have been a way of remembering Inuit travellers, with their seal skin clothes, or a way to understand genetic disorders – the inheritance of a skin condition from one generation to the next, just as Cally was told in *Seaward*.[106] It made immediate and intuitive sense to me to think of selkies as a narrative mani-festation of a crypto-genetic disorder, or a hidden history of racial and cultural difference.

When Cally is told about the truth of her heritage she is also told about the truth of forgetting, that her 'oldest self is remembering – the part deep down that you cannot control, that comes from your ancestors who are forgotten. Even your mother had forgotten them, and her mother before her – no one had ever told them the truth.'[107]

That is how I feel on the island, watching the seals, held in the warm neighbourliness of long dead family. I feel like I am remembering the oldest self of me. I feel like I am swimming back to myself through time.

*

Chronicity is the gift that keeps giving. Infinite mirrors. The ever unfolding paper chain of diagnosis.

For reasons I may never fully understand, in October 2019 my stomach stops working.

The stomach and guts pump just like a heart does: they work by movement, by the movement of muscles. If those muscles do not contract and relax, moving food through the coiled machine of the gut, the system breaks down.

This is something that can happen with EDS. It is called *gastroparesis* – paralysis of the stomach. I learnt this through community, long before I needed to know it for myself.

When it happens to me, it happens quite suddenly. I eat, and instead of moving through my body, the food sits there in my stomach. That night I feel unwell, my stomach unusually swol-len, but I don't realise what has happened until the next day, when I eat again. My stomach grows and grows, full and fuller. I feel like the wolf in the old tale with its stomach sewn full of rocks as punishment for eating the seven little kids. The pain and nausea are overwhelming. I can't lie down, so I can't sleep. It helps a bit to pace the room. I have become my own colicky baby. I circle and circle our little house, trying with movement of my whole body to simulate movement of my gut.

I know what it is. Because of community, I recognise what is happening. I look up advice.

I eat tiny bowls of mashed potato, mashed sweet potato, drink sips of smoothie.

By the second month I find I can add in bits of feta, portions of lean meat.

The safest food is potatoes. If in fear, potatoes.

I have had poor gut motility for years, maybe for all my life, but not like this, not so completely.

When it does not improve after three months, I go to the GP, full of dismay because I know there is only one option: I will have to go back to gastroenterology in London. There will be more tests. Diagnosis never sleeps.

The doctor agrees: no one locally can help. This is January 2020. I had welcomed the year sitting up in a chair in the lounge, too full and in pain from daring to have a New Year drink that attempting bed became agony.

The New Year was heralded by a lunar eclipse and all my social media timelines were full of it – the wolf moon, blood red – it did not feel like a happy omen. In Grasmere it rained all night. There was no moon to be seen, bloody or clean, though of course it was still there behind the claggy clouds. I felt like something bad was coming then, but I expected a personal trial, not a universal one.

By the time the tests are scheduled Covid-19 has been declared a global pandemic.

At the beginning of June, when I travel south for the first two tests, it is the first time I have left the valley since the first week of March, apart from to go to the doctors four miles away. This is the new circumference of my world.

Taking the train to London felt like travelling to the moon. W went with me. We had to take the first train of the day, leaving home at 5 a.m. to be at the hospital for 9.30 a.m. I had to be fasting, off my meds. I didn't know how I'd manage, how much help I'd need. It was W's first day off work since March. We took a backpack with everything we might possibly need for the day – all food and drinks – so that we didn't have to come into unnecessary contact with anyone. When we got there all the shops and cafes were shut up anyway. The only place open was the small Sainsbury's in the station, and the queue curled away into the distance like something from another reality.

Masks were days away from becoming mandatory on transport. We wore ours nervously all day, our hands in our pockets, trying not to touch our faces, or anything.

In September, I have to go back for one more test. This time it seems safer by car. Measures have come and gone. I have heard people say things I will not forget. I have heard too many people declared expendable. My trust in others has been tried to breaking point. We split the journey at my parents' house so that we can arrive at the hospital by 9 a.m. without driving all through the night. It is the first time we've seen my parents in person all year. We do not hug, but we eat together. We do not yet understand that the virus is airborne, not just spread by droplets or touch. Looking back, that time when we were all isolated from infection is the safest time we have spent together since.

The test is the one I have nightmares about, that wakes me up in a panic for weeks before. The one that makes me afraid of other tests. My natural aversion to the test has been compounded by bad experiences in the past. I prime myself to be firm this time. To ask everyone at every stage for strong sedation. To tell them this is a bad test for me. That I have had bad experiences. I ask everyone, at every stage, for strong sedation. I tell them I have had bad experiences. I try to use a balanced voice. To be firm but polite. I don't cry, or beg. Afterwards I think I should have done.

When I am lying on the trolley in the examination room, placed in position, a cannula in one arm, the endoscopist turns to her assistant and says – over my body, awkwardly arranged at strange angles like the corpse of a minor saint – *don't give her that one. Might as well save that for the next patient.*

I say, no, please, give me all you have. But they just smile, and continue.

Afterwards I am too exhausted from the continual spasming of my throat to complain. I just want to leave. I just want to go home.

The discharge form says *mild sedation given*. It says *procedure went well.*

If you do not ask the right questions . . . if you do not listen when the answers are given . . .

When the results come through they confirm what we already knew: gastroparesis.

Nothing changes. The doctor, the same one who uncovered my haemochromatosis, calls me. She tells me I should avoid any food that needs a knife. She suggests some medication that might help – domperidone – the drug I was told to never ever take again when it gave me Parkinsonian symptoms.

Everything else she suggests I have already been doing for months. Exclude all food that is hard to digest: fibre, fats. Eat small amounts. Walk to let movement and gravity take the place of failed muscle contractions. I keep going, try to listen to my gut.

When I waver, I suffer. In April I drink one gluten-free beer, and sit up all night in agony. In August I eat some slices of tomato, and sit up all night in agony.

I learn to manage it better over time. I learn that fruit and vegetables are my main problem. I learn to appreciate with new depth the many textures and flavours of different varieties of potato. I learn not to eat the crunchy grape as much as I want to. I learn to go for a walk every day even if only for ten minutes, five minutes.

When I get it wrong, and I can't lie down at night, I pace around the house, or wander up the road by moonlight, telling my troubles to the owls.

I learn all over again the lessons of slowness, of smallness, of taking life one step at a time, one bite at a time. Of not expecting too much.

*

I learnt early that my body could not be trusted. Tell it to do one thing and it would do another. Say *walk*, and its feet would stick, hips lock. Say *stand* and it would fall. Say *sleep* and it would flicker into white noise alertness.

It was always complaining. It was always crying out about something or other, as though it were my fault, as though I could change anything.

I saw it as the enemy. I was trying my best but my body wouldn't let me. It kept letting me down. Letting us down.

There were the years it would drop me to my knees midstride, smack on the pavement, as though our strings were cut. Our knees bled and scarred and bled and scarred.

There were the years it would tumble away from itself, a kneecap rolling off like a boulder down a hill.

I tried to feed it, and it sickened.

I tried to be kind to it, and it hurt me.

I tried to make it strong, but it kept on breaking.

My body moves through the world slightly apart from me. We are poorly tethered, like its joints are each to each other. I drag behind or float ahead of it like a shadow, dependent on light to show the distance. This is why we get so confused about spaces. Why we walk into walls, head-butt doorframes and car windows.

Sometimes it forgets what it is doing part way through an activity. It is gripping a kettle and forgets the action for gripping. It is taking a drink and forgets the manoeuvre for swallowing. It is hard to be a body. There are so many operations to consider.

Sometimes I have thought my body is nothing to do with me. I am a passenger, or a stowaway, in its rusty vessel. My body travels through the world, and I travel with it. I have no control over where it goes or how. It travels despite me, not because of me. It does what it wants, but I can do nothing without it, outwith it. I have no independent life. Sometimes I have thought I was my body's prisoner. Sometimes I have thought it was my captive.

In all the wilderness years of my undiagnosis and misdiagnosis I learnt to see my body this way. Feral body. Recalcitrant body. Wilful, obstinate. An unbroken horse from a lifetime movie. A bad dog who will not be taught. Part wolf. Too wild. I thought if I was good enough I could tame it. I thought I could make it good.

Orders mean nothing to it. It has never been anything but its own wild self, a creature of its own.

Now I try to live alongside my body. To live alongside in companionship, in symbiosis, as I try to do with the other co-tenants of this patch of earth: the deer and red squirrels and multitudinous birds I meet on my daily walks, when I talk my body out of the cave of the house to show it the daylight and the woods. I take it out to show it the sky and hope it thanks me for it. If we stay indoors both of us will sicken. I try to treat my body with the same quiet caution I employ when I approach the heron in the tarn, or a deer alert in a dell, ears twitching with sudden knowledge of my presence. I want to be close to it, but I do not want to alarm it.

To be tamed is to be broken. My body has been broken so many times, and never become compliant. My body cannot be domesticated. There is no home beyond it to claim it for. No wildness beyond it to reclaim it from.

In Old English a *deor* was any wild animal, any beast of the woods, four-footed or finned. A living thing, a breathing thing, gasping for life, a cloud of ongoingness pooling in frosty air.

Wild-deerness is skilled vulnerability. In wild-deerness strength is in watchfulness, cunning is in caution. Risk is a predator, the wild itself, the weather, treacherous ground, treacherous skies. Wild-deerness is the ability to vanish your body, to blend the colours and shapes of your corporeality into your locality at will. The wild-deerness ideal is survival.

This is the wilderness I am learning to live with, within and without.

I am learning to step softly on the wild-deerness of myself, to stop when the creature that breathes in me stops, to meet its eye as an equal not an enemy.

I want it to recognise me as kin, as self not other. I want it to not startle. I want to not grasp.

Roe deer have inhabited these islands we call Britain for hundreds of thousands of years, on and off. Forced out by ice ages, allowed back in by land bridges, hunted to near extinction, their territories destroyed. Thriving at the fringes. They keep going. They keep coming back. Wild-deerness is continuation.

To live well with illness I have had to learn to encompass weakness. I have had to learn not to fear it. I have had to learn not to valorise strength or resilience. I am not fierce. I am not mighty. I am small and weak and I break easily. This is not a failure. This is not a personality flaw. I have had to accept my body as prey, and to learn from it.

Even at its mildest the wild deer of my body would not come willingly from the treeline, would not eat from an outstretched hand. It holds generations of wariness in its tremulous pulse. It will observe from a safe distance, safe cover. It knows what it is to hurt.

*

Diagnosis is not an end point, but a beginning. Diagnosis is an initiation. The Chronic Life is what you are pledged to.

Diagnosis is a door opening on the rest of your life, and behind the door there is a corridor, and more doors. There are always more doors. You have to pace yourself for the journey ahead.

For years I was so focused on diagnosis as a key to everything in my own life, that I didn't look at it critically. I hadn't thought about how diagnosis has been used as a weapon, as a tool to segregate, to dehumanise, as a justification for institutionalisation, for forced sterilisation, for doing irrevocable harm. Clare writes about the troubled history of diagnosis, of 'lives reduced to case files'. How diagnosis can 'flatten body-minds onto paper and computer screens, reduced to fit into vaults and servers', how diagnoses 'lay claim to the truth'; how 'they lie'.[108]

During the pandemic diagnosis has been used as a tool to devalue lives. People placed on the shielding list were asked to sign 'Do Not Resuscitate' orders, should they be admitted to hospital with Covid-19. It was later claimed this was a mistake. Of course the government did not mean to suggest that disabled people did not have the same right to treatment as non-disabled people. It would never suggest that.

Yet disabled people have felt abandoned, forgotten, our needs neglected, in so many ways at once.

Data gathered during the first wave in the UK showed that disabled women under sixty-five were 11.3 times more likely to die of Covid-19 than their non-disabled peers.

Daily, on the news, deaths were announced.

N number of people died, but X of them had pre-existing conditions.

Pre-existing conditions became code for already essentially dead. Not really alive. Not worth saving. Nothing to worry yourself about. As though our lives were worth less, worth nothing.

This formulation – *N number of people died, but X of them had pre-existing conditions* – was clearly intended to be comforting, reassuring. It assumed an audience of healthy people without pre-existing conditions, and without people in their lives with pre-existing conditions who they considered to be equally worthy of the chance to live. Whose deaths would be an equal loss.

Through 2020, the language used by the UK government to describe those who need protection shifts from *clinically vulnerable* to *clinically extremely vulnerable* as resources dwindle.

I begin to understand in a new way the fear of medicalisation – of labelling – that I have found so frustrating in some members of my disease community, in some members of my family. I had thought of them as coming from a position of avoidance, of not wanting to be considered disabled, viewing it as a condemnation, of wanting to pass, of a manifestation of the body–mind policing which treats disability as Top Trumps and likes to say you're not disabled *enough*. I read it as stemming from a misunderstanding of treatment versus cure, as a manifestation of ableism. Now I understand it comes from a place of complex fear, not just the fear of losing abled status but of everything that has historically come with diagnosis: fear of losing bodily autonomy, losing a place in society, losing possibility. Losing the right to live.

*

All my life I've been aware of my vulnerability; the particular vulnerability of my body. I've been aware I was more vulnerable than the average person for as long as I can remember, more vulnerable than my peers at playgroup and school, even than my own family, though when I eventually found the reason for my vulnerability, it was all to do with family. Long before we knew the reason and the name, before we could make sense of this vulnerability, it spoke for itself: I was more likely to fall, more likely to hurt myself when I fell, more likely to break a bone, more likely to split skin, more likely to get an infection, more likely to catch an infectious illness, more likely to be more sick with that illness, more likely to fall because I was sick.

I have known, as long as I have known myself, that I have to take extra care of myself. I cannot afford to be casual about risk.

But during the pandemic, my sense of my own vulnerability has completely shifted. Although I have always been aware of my vulnerability – my susceptibility to falling and breaking, to falling ill, to ailing – I don't recall ever describing myself before the pandemic as 'vulnerable'. 'Vulnerable' was a word used euphemistically in social care to group together those more open to abuse or manipulation, or in romance to encompass openness to love and heartbreak, or in self-help to encompass openness to failure and growth.

In the latter contexts, to be vulnerable is a mark of honour, a mark of bravery and creativity, as Amy Poehler has said: 'It's very hard to be vulnerable, but those people who do that are the dreamers, the thinkers and the creators. They are the magic people of the world.'[109]

The Internet is florid with inspirational quotes about how vulnerability is a strength, not a weakness. A quote from a 1996 interview with Alanis Morissette appears on hundreds of motivational posters: 'I found that the more truthful and vulnerable I was, the more empowering it was for me.'[110]

Words from a 2014 interview by FKA twigs are widely quoted online: 'vulnerability is the strongest state to be in'.[111]

It is far easier, of course, to reveal oneself as vulnerable from a position of security. This is as true of matters of the heart as it is with disclosing disability: the more secure our position in society, the less of a risk it is to unveil our tender points.

I understood disability largely via the social model – a product of disabling environments which will not adapt to the needs of a body's impairments.

Nevertheless, I thought of vulnerability as something that resided in the individual – a force that rested in the body or mind and acted on the body or mind. I understood, of course, that other kinds of bodies could also be vulnerable: nations, ecosystems, monetary funds. I thought – or think I thought – of vulnerability as something implicit, folded into the substance of a body, whatever kind of body it may be. Vulnerability as on a level with impairment, not disability.

This of course shows nothing so much as my own lack of insight into vulnerability. We don't become vulnerable in a vacuum.

The pandemic has shifted my understanding of the relationship between my body and the rest of the world so much that I find it hard to remember how it was before.

I have always known I was vulnerable, but I had not before felt *vulnerablised* in the way I have done these last few years. Never before have I felt so much like prey.

*

Pacing

That first spring of the plague, 2020, I find one dropped antler on a path in the woods. It is the path the deer showed me, that lost autumn of the before-times. Inscription of their wild-deerness, their uncivilised knowingness. They remembered what human walkers had forgotten with each passing generation – the ways through the woods, the ways with the woods.

Then there, on the path where I have stepped a hundred times in the echoes of their hooves, a single antler lay shining in the evening sun. It looked like ancient bone, a relic of another era. It looked like porcelain. Two-pronged, smooth at the tips as though worn by water or by touching over centuries, as fingers might an amulet. From the burnished point it crinkles into furrows that deepen towards the root, buckled or bulged into nodules that cluster towards the ruffled coronet. The underside is almost white, glossy. The other, browned and rough.

The deer who shed it must have dropped it there the autumn before. I will have walked over it through rain and frost and snow. Or maybe it was dropped years ago, and the same combination of floods and this strange, long dry spell unburied it as it unburied the Victorian rubbish, pushed it up out of the desiccated mulch. Either way, it happened that it lay in my way, just where I meant to place my foot, in the third week of April, in the fourth week of the first lockdown.

I thought it was a sign. I saw myself walking towards the deer, as they disappeared themselves into the greening birches, and walking away with them. I thought it was the completion of something. *I have made some mistakes at being human,* I wrote. I saw myself becoming the furred face at the window at dusk, drawn down from the woods to look in on my former life. I wondered if anyone I knew would recognise me when I came to them in my new form, or if they would see me only as an oddity, a pest – expendable.

Sometimes I hold the antler to my head and think of my wildness, my wilderness, my deerness. I think of the flush of kinship I feel when I sense the eyes of the deer on me in the woods, when I feel them acknowledge me in the shifting of their muscles, and not run. I think of my own wild body, its refusal of my claims to autonomy. Its refusal of any beast else's authority. And I try to kindle the same fellow feeling in our shared heart.

Body, old body in all your wildness, let us be contented in our shared society, let us live with each other well, in kinship, in kindness. Let us leap as one.

*

There was no great transformation. I am still myself, in all my human particularity. In all my embodied uncertainty, my chronic precarity. Yet I feel the plate of glass between me and my old life, my old ways of living. I am outside, looking in, at a world that is no longer safe for me.

How do we keep going? Keep moving forward when everything seems to push against us?

September 2022. The bracken is dying back little by little and I can cross the common again without too much of a struggle. The wind makes a sea-like sound in the turning leaves of the oaks. Yellow birch leaves, green acorns and bright red rowan berries freckle the path. It is said the Celtic year began in autumn, with summer's close. A beginning, not an end. A start, not a death. In the same way the day began at dusk, at nightfall. We have been marking time all wrong, back to front and upside down. I read that new year fell in November, in the middle of the season called 'back-end' in Cumbria. The Celtic year had two halves – the light half and the dark, Samhain and Beltane where they met. At Samhain the doorways to Faery were revealed and the inhabitants of that other realm came up from their cavy dwellings. Some mortals might go back down with them, into that other place. Some might touch it, briefly, and never be quite of the living again.

These traditions may be partly the invention of Victorian antiquarians, partly misrememberings of something much older, that predates Celtic culture and lived on through it. Some Neolithic passage tombs on these islands are aligned to fill with light as the sun rises on Samhain, as others are at Winter Solstice. I wonder about Ballynahatty Woman, with her haemochromatotic genes, and the passage tomb she was removed from, the henge built around it later. There is little left of the structure now. I wonder what quality of light warmed her bones in her long sleep, what season she was left to face towards.

We begin in the dark. We go into the spring – into the dawn – midway on the journey through the seasons or the day, just as we need it most. Is it convenient for me to be thinking this, here, in the midpoint of my life, as I stand on the common watching the sun's rays spread from behind Silver How on this, the first evening after the autumn equinox, the first night of a new season that will outweigh the day? Maybe. But I need it. I need to think of this as the beginning of something, just as I need to think of the connection my conditions give me to my ancestors not as a curse but a gift. A kind of understanding, or a promise of understanding to come. The light will come back, the trees will blossom and fruit. The bluebells will rise up from their slumber sweeter than ever. The summer birds will return with the light evenings of May. The deer will lose their antlers, grow more antlers. There will be owl babies in the woods and lambs in the fields. There will be slow worms sunning themselves in gaps in the drystone walls and dragonflies skimming food from air. I will survive, as those who carried my genes forward to me did, through the long night, through the bleakest winter.

We will sleep for four months in the dark of the cave house. We will sleep for seven years in the burrow, the barrow, hibernating or petrifying. We are small animals or ancient kings. Someone may carry what is left of us out in the spring in a crisp box, take us to a museum to study us. Or we may wake into a gentler season, ready to return to the surface life, ready to green again.

When I come down through the wood to the old road it is 7 p.m. and almost dark. I am trying not to be afraid of what is coming. I think instead of deer in the bare trees in the low yellow sun of November, of January. I think of the wrens singing from the bracken almost invisible against it, red-brown on red-brown, and the heron's vigil at the icy pond. We will get through. In the last light I see a young roe deer standing on the overgrown duck pond, and a robin races me downhill to the house, hopping along the drystone wall as though to say *it's my time now*.

*

This isn't the end to an illness story you might be expecting. This story has no recovery. There is no ending, happy or sad. There is just ongoingness. There is just chronicity. I live in a state of unsteady equilibrium.

Doing your exercises, trying to get outdoors, taking medications. Trying to get outdoors. Doing your exercises. Trying to avoid getting worse.

Watching the birds on the feeder. Rubbing your cheek on the mossy pelt of an oak tree. Letting water take the weight for an hour.

There are nights you dream you are swimming in a summer ocean. There are nights you dream you are flying over imagined cities.

There are days you feel terrible, and days you feel almost passable. There are seasons you shrink down, sink into deepening dark. But there is always, eventually, a sliver of light.

There is just continuation. In continuation, there is life.

Acknowledgements

I have so much gratitude to so many people who have helped this book at every stage of its development, and helped me keep faith in what I was trying to do. Particular thanks to my fantastic agent, Caro Clarke, and editor, Jo Dingley, for understanding what this book wanted to be and helping it become the best version of itself. To everyone at Sceptre who has been so helpful and supportive through the publication process, especially Holly Knox, and to Sadie Robinson for her excellent copyedits and Vivienne Church for such attentive proofreading. To Chloe Currens for helping rescue the draft at a difficult time. To all the early readers who helped me see what was working and what wasn't, including Sophie Mackintosh for feedback on parts of 'Maintenance', and Patrice Lawrence and Emilie Pine for feedback on parts of 'Genetic'. To Sally Huband for posting me her copy of Eli Clare's *Brilliant Imperfection* and for all her encouragement along the way.

Thanks to Penguin Random House's WriteNow programme for getting me to first draft in 2018 and spurring me on to work out how to tell this story the right way. Having a supportive community in the other WriteNow participants has been invaluable. Thanks to Bea Hemming for seeing potential in my first thousand words and telling me to keep going.

Thanks to Gladstone's Library for my residency in 2018, during which I wrote the first draft of 'Genetic', and to Molly Heal for visiting me there and driving me to the strange little castle in the woods. Thanks to the Society of Authors for a grant that enabled me to visit Rathlin Island. Thanks also to the Vulnerability Studies Network, and particularly Dr Zalfa Feghali for inviting me to talk to the research group about disability, Covid-19 and vulnerability, and funding work which has fed into this book.

Thanks to Manchester Metropolitan University's Centre for Place Writing, for commissioning what would become parts of this book as part of the PLACE 2020 project, published online as 'Commonality' and also included in a slightly shorter version in *North Country: An Anthology of Landscape and Nature*, edited by Karen Lloyd (Manchester: Saraband, 2022). Thanks to Lancaster Litfest for commissioning work on my walks around Lancaster in 2020 as part of the 'Walking Solo' podcast project, which also fed into this book. In places I draw on a commission I did for *Magma 72: The Climate Change Issue* in 2018, in which I was paired with Blaise Martay of the British Trust for Ornithology. I also draw on research into disability and nature writing I began through a commissioned essay for *New Welsh Review*, published as '"Why Is It Always a Poem Is a Walk?": Towards an Ecocrip Poetics' in 2019. Thanks to Emily Blewitt for supporting this work as commissioning editor, and to ASLE 2019, and ALECC 2020 at which I presented updates of that research, funded by part of an Arts Council England DYCP award.

Thanks to those who took a chance on publishing previews of the book as it floundered in limbo. An extract from the chapter 'Maintenance' was published as 'Swimming Against the Nature Cure' in *Ache* magazine issue 3 (April 2020). An extract from the chapter 'Chronic' was published as 'Chronicity' in Sick magazine issue 3 (July 2021).

To all my fellow disabled and chronically ill writers: I have learnt so much from you, you have saved my life a thousand times over. The world needs your stories, told your way.

To everyone who has been by my side through it, through the years: there are too many of you to name. Especial

Acknowledgements

thanks to Emily Hasler, for all the swims, past and future: may a wagtail always watch over you. To Lois Roberts for being your wonderful self and holding my hand through a lot of it. To Eileen Pun – you will always be my sister of the long arms. To Justine Hall and Mary El Shammaa for inadvertently giving me my title, and for understanding what it is to fall down a lot. To Laura Scott for crossing the lava with me. To the Dead Cardinals for keeping me laughing through the depths of the lockdowns. To my family, for always being there to patch me up, and for trusting me to tell some of your stories in telling mine. Finally, to Will, for his steadfast support in all things, and without whom none of this could have been written.

Notes

1. William Wordsworth, 'Home at Grasmere', in *Home at Grasmere: Part First, Book First, of The Recluse*, ed. Beth Darlington (Ithaca, NY: Cornell University Press, 1977), MSB, p. 40.
2. Ibid., p. 44.
3. D. H. Lawrence, 'The Ship of Death', in *Last Poems*, ed. Richard Aldington (London: Martin Secker, 1933), pp. 60–4.
4. Dorothy Wordsworth, 8 February 1802, *The Grasmere and Alfoxden Journals*, ed. Pamela Woof (Oxford: Oxford University Press, 2002), p. 64.
5. Wordsworth, 18 March 1802, *The Grasmere and Alfoxden Journals*, p. 81.
6. Seamus Heaney, writ. and narr., *William Wordsworth Lived Here: Seamus Heaney at Dove Cottage*, dir. David Wilson (BBC, 1974).
7. Thomas De Quincey, *Confessions of an English Opium-Eater* (London: Penguin, 1971), p. 67.
8. De Quincey, *Confessions*, p. 40.
9. Yi-Fu Tuan, *Topophilia: A Study of Environmental Perception, Attitudes, and Values* (New York: Columbia University Press, 1990) (1st edn 1974).
10. Yi-Fu Tuan, 'Sense of Place: What Does it Mean to Be Human?', *American Journal of Theology & Philosophy* 18.1, January 1997, 47–58 (51).
11. Ben Lerner, *10:04* (London: Granta, 2014), p. 3.
12. Ibid., pp. 6–7.
13. Dawn L. Rothe, 'The Failure of the Spectacle: The Voices Within', *Critical Criminology* 24.2, 2016, 279–302.
14. Lerner, *10:04*, p. 14.
15. Thomas Dormandy, *The Worst of Evils: The Fight Against Pain* (New Haven, CT, and London: Yale University Press, 2006), p. 402.
16. Susan Cooper, *Seaward* (London: Puffin, 1985), pp. 11–12.
17. Ibid., p. 168.
18. Virginia Woolf, *On Being Ill* (Ashfield: Paris Press, 2002), p. 12.
19. Susan Sontag, *Illness as Metaphor* (New York: Farrar, Straus and Giroux, 1978), p. 3.
20. Woolf, *On Being Ill*, p. 3.

21. Ibid. (my italics).
22. Ibid., p. xxvii.
23. Ibid.
24. Susanna Clarke, *Jonathan Strange & Mr Norrell* (London: Bloomsbury, 2017), p. 221.
25. Ibid., p. 215.
26. Ibid., p. 199.
27. Ibid., p. 660.
28. Thomas De Quincey, 'Lake Reminiscences, from 1807–1830, By The English Opium-Eater, No.1', in *The Works of Thomas De Quincey*, ed. Grevel Lindop, et al. (London: Pickering & Chatto, 2003), II, ed. Julian North, p. 44.
29. Ibid., p. 45.
30. Ibid., p. 44.
31. De Quincey, *Confessions*, p. 43.
32. Kathleen Jamie, 'Pathologies', in *The New Nature Writing* (London: Granta, 2008).
33. Dorothy Wordsworth to Dora Wordsworth, 1838, *The Letters of William and Dorothy Wordsworth, Vol. 6: The Later Years: Part III: 1835–1839* (Second Revised Edition), ed. Ernest De Selincourt and Alan G. Hill (Oxford: Clarendon Press, 1982), p. 528.
34. Sonya Huber, 'Welcome to the Kingdom of the Sick', in *Pain Woman Takes Your Keys* (Lincoln, NE: University of Nebraska Press, 2017), pp. 18–20.
35. Letty McHugh, *Book of Hours* (Haworth: self-published, 2022), p. 38.
36. Ibid., p. 67.
37. Polly Atkin, author's notebook (2014).
38. Porochista Khakpour, *Sick: A Memoir* (New York: Harper Perennial, 2018), p. 124.
39. Rodney Grahame, 'Hypermobility: An Important But Often Neglected Area Within Rheumatology', *Nature Clinical Practice Rheumatology* 4, 2008, 522–4 (523).
40. Joanne C. Demmler, Mark D. Atkinson, Emma J. Reinhold, et al., 'Diagnosed Prevalence of Ehlers-Danlos Syndrome and Hypermobility Spectrum Disorder in Wales, UK: A National Electronic Cohort Study and Case-control Comparison', *BMJ Open* 9.11, 2019.
41. Marco Castori, 'Ehlers-Danlos Syndrome, Hypermobility Type: An Underdiagnosed Hereditary Connective Tissue Disorder With Mucocutaneous, Articular, and Systemic Manifestations', *ISRN Dermatology*, 2012.

Notes

42. Anna Deborah Richardson, *Memoir of Anna Deborah Richardson: With Extracts from Her Letters,* ed. John Wigham Richardson (Newcastle: J. M. Carr, 1877), p. 273.
43. Ibid., p. 185.
44. Bradley Wertheim, 'The Iron in Our Blood That Keeps and Kills Us', *The Atlantic,* 10 January 2013.
45. *East Midlands Today,* 17 October 2016.
46. 'Scientists Sequence First Ancient Irish Human Genomes', 28 December 2015, *Trinity Colllege Dublin.*
47. Huber, *Pain Woman Takes Your Keys,* p. 18.
48. Alice Wong, 'Disabled Oracles and the Coronavirus', Disability Visibility Project website, 18 March 2020.
49. Abby Norman, *Ask Me About My Uterus: A Quest to Make Doctors Believe in Women's Pain* (New York: Nation Books, 2018), p. 254.
50. Michele Lent Hirsch, *Invisible: How Young Women With Serious Health Issues Navigate Work, Relationships, and the Pressure to Seem Just Fine* (Boston: Beacon Press, 2018), p. 34.
51. Walter Scott, *Rob Roy* (Edinburgh: John Ballantyne & Co., 1818), Volume II, pp. 212–13.
52. David MacRitchie, *Fians, Fairies and Picts* (London: Kegan Paul, Trench, Truebner & Co., 1893), p. 4.
53. William Wordsworth, 'Rob Roy's Grave', in *The Poems of William Wordsworth: Collected Reading Texts from the Cornell Wordsworth Series,* ed. Jared Curtis (Penrith: Humanities Ebooks, 2009), I, p. 652.
54. Kate Davies, *The West Highland Way* (Kate Davies Designs, 2018), p. 68.
55. Albert S. Cook, *Asser's Life of King Alfred: Translated From the Text of Stevenson's Edition* (Boston, MA: Ginn & Co., 1906), p. 17.
56. BBC News website, 7 July 2014.
57. Thomas De Quincey, 'Suspiria De Profundis: Being a Sequel to Confessions of an English Opium-Eater', in *Works,* ed. Grevel Lindop, 15, ed. Frederick Burwick (2003), pp. 126–204, 175.
58. Woolf, *On Being Ill,* p. 37.
59. Harriet Martineau, *Life in the Sick-Room,* ed. Maria H. Frawley (Peterborough, Ont.: Broadview, 2003), p. 44.
60. Ibid., p. 91.
61. *Westmorland Gazette,* 9 August 1890. Accessed through the *British Newspaper Archive.*
62. Wordsworth, 14 June 1802, *The Grasmere and Alfoxden Journals,* p. 109.

63. Wordsworth, 2 June 1802, *The Grasmere and Alfoxden Journals*, p. 104.

64. Thomas De Quincey, 'Sketch of Professor Wilson', *The Works of Thomas De Quincey*, ed. Robert Morrison (London: Pickering & Chatto, 2000), VII.

65. Sarah Manguso, *Ongoingness: The End of a Diary* (London: Picador, 2018), pp. 74, 79.

66. Miranda Hart, Instagram post, 2 May 2020.

67. Clarke, *Jonathan Strange*, p. 631.

68. Huber, *Pain Woman Takes Yours Keys*, pp. 111–12.

69. Claudia Fonseca, Soraya Fleischer and Taniele Rui, 'The Ubiquity of Chronic Illness', *Medical Anthropology*, 35.6, 2016, 588–96.

70. Ellen Samuels, 'Six Ways of Looking at Crip Time', *Disability Studies Quarterly* 37.3, 2017.

71. Thomas Hardy, *Tess of the D'Urbervilles*. One of my A Level texts.

72. Eli Clare, *Brilliant Imperfection: Grappling With Cure* (Durham: Duke University Press, 2017), pp. 14–15.

73. Clare, *Brilliant Imperfection*, p. 15.

74. Kate Davis, Twitter comment, 23 August 2018.

75. Roger Deakin, *Waterlog: A Swimmer's Journey Through Britain* (London: Vintage, 2000), p. 3.

76. Sarah Jaquette Ray, 'Risking Bodies in the Wild: The "Corporeal Unconsious" of American Adventure Culture', in *Disability Studies and the Environmental Humanities Toward an Eco-Crip Theory*, ed. Sarah Jaquette Ray and Jay Sibara (Lincoln, NE: University of Nebraska Press, 2017), p. 29.

77. Kathleen Jamie, 'A Lone Enraptured Male', *LRB*, vol. 30, no. 5, 6 March 2008, pp. 25–7.

78. Ibid.

79. Sarah Jaquette Ray and Jay Sibara, 'Introduction', in *Disability Studies and the Environmental Humanities*, p. 2.

80. Stacy Alaimo, 'Foreword', in *Disability Studies and the Environmental Humanities*, p. ix.

81. Ray, 'Risking Bodies in the Wild', p. 29.

82. Ibid., p. 37.

83. Kate Davies, 'Swimming in Carbeth Loch', *Kate Davies Designs*, 1 July 2018.

84. Wordsworth, 'The Tables Turned', in *The Poems of William Wordsworth*, I, p. 366.

85. Carol Linnitt, 'Jacinda Mack Wants to Get Real About What That Mine Is Actually Going to Do to Your Community', *The Narwhal*, 21 June 2018.

Notes

86. Nuskmata on the Planetary Cost of Luxury, *For The Wild*, 14 June 2018; InTheField: Nuskmata (Jacinda Mack) on the Gold Rush That Never Ended, *For The Wild*, 18 May 2022.

87. Alex Fox, 'Toxic Algae Caused Mysterious Widespread Deaths of 330 Elephants in Botswana', *Smithsonian Magazine*, 23 September 2020.

88. Haijun Wang, Chi Xu, Ying Liu, et al., 'From Unusual Suspect to Serial Killer: Cyanotoxins Boosted by Climate Change May Jeopardize Megafauna', *The Innovation* 2.2, 100092, 28 May 2021.

89. Vivek K. Bajpai, Shruti Shukla, Sung-Min Kang, et al., 'Developments of Cyanobacteria for Nano-Marine Drugs: Relevance of Nanoformulations in Cancer Therapies', *Marine Drugs* 16.6, 179, June 2018; Emily Leclerc, 'Scientists Find Blue-Green Algae Chemical with Cancer Fighting Potential', *Smithsonian Magazine*, 4 March 2021.

90. R. M. M. Abed, S. Dobretsov and K. Sudesh, 'Applications of Cyanobacteria in Biotechnology', *Journal of Applied Microbiology* 106.1, January 2009, 1–12.

91. William Wordsworth, 'The Prelude' (1805), in *The Thirteen-Book Prelude by William Wordsworth, Volume I*, ed. Mark L. Reed (Ithaca, NY: Cornell University Press, 1991), p. 130; William Wordsworth, 'The Excursion', in *The Excursion by William Wordsworth*, ed. Sally Bushell, James A. Butler and Michael C. Jaye (Ithaca, NY: Cornell University Press, 2007), IX, p. 276; William Wordsworth, 'To Joanna', 'Poems on the Naming of Places', in *Lyrical Ballads and Other Poems, 1797–1800 by William Wordsworth*, ed. James Butler and Karen Green (Ithaca, NY: Cornell University Press, 1992), p. 246.

92. Wordsworth, 'The Prelude' (1805), in *The Thirteen-Book Prelude*, p. 134.

93. George Middleton, *Some Old Wells, Trees, and Travel-tracks of Wordsworth's Parish* (Ambleside: St Oswald Press, 1918), p. 7.

94. The Science Museum website.

95. Charles Schieferdecker, *Vinzenz Priessnitz, or, The Wonderful Power of Water in Healing the Diseases of the Human Body* (Philadelphia: Burgess and Zieber, 1843), p. 18.

96. *Westmorland Gazette*, 25 January 1845.

97. *Carlisle Patriot*, 1 August 1845.

98. Elizabeth Battrick, *Guardian of the Lakes: A History of the National Trust in the Lake District from 1946* (Kendal: Westmorland Gazette, 1987), p. 118.

99. Schieferdecker, *Vinzenz Priessnitz*, p. 52.

Notes

100. Harriet Martineau, *A Complete Guide to the English Lakes* (Windermere, London: John Garnett; Whittaker and Co., 1855), p. 50.
101. Khakpour, *Sick*, p. 245.
102. Linnitt, 'Jacinda Mack Wants to Get Real'.
103. Flann O'Brien, *The Third Policeman* (London: HarperCollins, 1993), p. 173.
104. Clare, *Brilliant Imperfection*, p. 88.
105. Jamie, 'A Lone Enraptured Male'.
106. See work by Clair Le Couteur.
107. Cooper, *Seaward*, p. 95.
108. Clare, *Brilliant Imperfection*, pp. 114–15.
109. Brené Brown, *Dare to Lead: Brave Work, Tough Conversations, Whole Hearts* (London: Vermilion, 2018), p. 43.
110. Jon Pareles, 'At Lunch With Alanis Morissette', *New York Times*, 28 February 1996.
111. Ben Beaumont Thomas, 'FKA twigs: "Weird Things Can Be Sexy"', *Guardian*, 9 August 2014.